Bold in Her Breeches

Notes on the contributors

JO STANLEY (MA) would rather eat chocolate in her heated water bed than battle with desperados on stormy decks. A radical cultural worker, she is a socialist feminist who writes fiction and non-fiction, usually about women's work and representation. Her most recent work includes editing *Cultural Sniping, the art of transgression* (a volume of Jo Spence's collected writings, Routledge, 1995). From a working-class Liverpool seafaring family and fond of a rambling life, she currently lives in North London and on the wild Norfolk coast. She is a member of the national steering committee of the Women's History Network.

ANNE CHAMBERS (MA Hist.) lives in Dublin. She is the author of four biographies: *Granuaile, The life and times of Grace O'Malley, 1530–1603*; *As Wicked as a Woman, Eleanor Countess of Desmond*; *Chieftain to Knight*; and most recently *La Sheridan, Adorable Diva*. Involved in creating television documentaries and lecturing on her books, she has recently completed her first historical novel and two film screenplays and is currently designing the Granuaile Heritage Centre in County Mayo. She is a member of PEN, and an executive member of the Irish Writers' Union. Her hobbies are tennis, golf and walking.

DIAN H. MURRAY was born in Sac City, Iowa in 1949. Currently Professor of History and Associate Dean for Undergraduate Studies at the University of Notre Dame, Indiana, she has been researching Chinese history since 1975. Her publications include *Pirates of the South China Coast, 1790–1810* and *The Origins of Tiandihui: the Chinese triads in legend and history*. She is also the author of articles on gay and female pirates of China. Her hobbies include cross-country skiing, kayaking and cooking.

JULIE WHEELWRIGHT is a broadcaster, critic and journalist. She is the author of *The Fatal Lover: Mata Hari and the myth of women in espionage* and the critically acclaimed *Amazons and Military Maids: women who dressed as men in pursuit of life, liberty and happiness*, which was relaunched by Pandora Press in 1994.

Bold in Her Breeches

Women Pirates Across the Ages

Edited by Jo Stanley
with contributions from Anne Chambers,
Dian H. Murray and Julie Wheelwright

An Imprint of HarperCollinsPublishers

Pandora
An Imprint of HarperCollins*Publishers*
77–85 Fulham Palace Road,
Hammersmith, London W6 8JB
1160 Battery Street,
San Francisco, California 94111–1213

First published in hardback by Pandora 1995
Paperback edition 1996
1 3 5 7 9 10 8 6 4 2

A catalogue record for this book is available
from the British Library

ISBN 0 04 440970 2

Typeset by Harper Phototypesetters Limited
Northampton, England
Printed in Great Britain by
Caledonian International Book Manufacturer, Glasgow

For Eve Stanley and Rachel Sweetman – may they swashbuckle humanely

Whether I desire it or not
My vessel slices
Through the black shadows of uncertainty.

ZINAIDA HIPPIUS, 1869–1945

Contents

Acknowledgements		ix
List of illustrations		xii
Preface		xiv

SECTION I: INTRODUCTION 1

Chapter 1. Brigand dominatrices for utopia-seeking
masochists: the idea of women pirates 3

Chapter 2. A cool look at a hot topic 17

Chapter 3. The women among the boys 36

Chapter 4. Uncovering the oceans' Roaring Girls 51

SECTION II: WARRIOR WOMEN IN COMMAND 61

Chapter 5. Artemisia: adviser or Amazon? 63

Chapter 6. Arms and amours: Alfhild 78

Chapter 7. 'The Pirate Queen of Ireland':
Grace O'Malley by Anne Chambers 93

SECTION III: WORKING FOR A LIVING 109

Chapter 8. In the right place at the right time 111

Chapter 9. Criminals, communards or crumpet? 139

Chapter 10. Living beneath the Jolly Roger 162

Chapter 11. Tars, tarts and swashbucklers
by Julie Wheelwright 176

SECTION IV: CHINESE WOMEN PIRATES   201

Chapter 12.   Cheng I Sao in fact and fiction by Dian H. Murray   203
Chapter 13.   Between warrior junk and *A Doll's House*   240

SECTION V: WOMEN AND PIRACY TODAY   251

Chapter 14.   With fax and fast outboards   253

Endnote. Today's eyes on their old breeches   273
Further reading   278
Index   281

Acknowledgements

I want to thank many people for the direct and indirect roles they played in helping me to create this book.

First of all the contributors, who with different degrees of speed and excitement helped make this book challenging and authoritative.

In the category of feminist theorists and historians whose ideas have helped to shape this book are people whom I would also call 'lovely friends and influences'. I thank Catherine Bristow, Rosy Martin, Liz Stanley, Val Walsh and the late Jo Spence for their exciting approach to auto/biography. Jean Tate introduced me to Moll Cutpurse and Robin Hood. Sally Alexander, Joanna Bornat, Norma Clarke, Anna Davin and Cathy Lubelska were important figures in my view of myself as a particular kind of historian. The national steering committee of the Women's History Network always provided encouraging context. The Working Class Educated Women's Group – Helen Lucey, Joan Solomon, Valerie Walkerdine – made me feel that I had valid approaches to the history of women's lives and to any daunting work. Nanna Damsholt at Copenhagen University Centre for Women's Studies was extremely generous in giving me her views on the Danish pirate Alfhild.

Many historians helped me by example and sometimes directly. In the field of maritime history I am glad to have had the company of Sheila Jemima and Donny Hyslop at Southampton City Heritage Oral History Department and Chris Howard Bailey at the Royal Naval Museum Portsmouth. Bob Parker and Caroline Cooper of the

University of North London taught me how to question imagery and encouraged me through my studies of Carmen Jones as a wild figure. For developing my interest in transport history I will always be grateful to Phillip Bagwell, Dave Thompson, Dad and Mr Venn.

One of my larger debts, maybe the biggest, is to the staff at the National Maritime Museum, Greenwich, who made my work possible. These include above all David Cordingly and John Falconer, but also Margarette Lincoln, Sue Miller, the excellent library staff for their helpfulness, the attendants for their jokes during the breaks, and the Friends of the Museum.

The British Council funded a trip to South-East Asia, ostensibly for me to deliver the keynote speech at the world's first conference on women and the sea at Wellington National Maritime Museum. This enabled me to visit some of the areas where pirates operate today. I am grateful to the many maritime experts, feminist historians and local people who talked to me about piracy in Indonesia, the Philippines, the Singapore Straits and Hong Kong. Among the many people worldwide who helped me with this chapter are Mazlan Abdul-Samad, Sani Bakar, Dea Birkett, Eric Ellen and the staff of the International Maritime Bureau, Rosemary Lim, Ken Luck, Tony Paris, Rosalinda Pinado Ofreneo, Celia and Bill Pomeroy, Ken Scadden, Steve Vine and the staff at *GQ*, Hugh Walters, Jan Euden, as well as the staff at Manila Coastguards and the University of the Philippines library.

The people who read the manuscript are always very important, and I was lucky in receiving warm encouragement as well as a high level of expertise from David Cordingly, Anna Davin, Eric Ellen, John Falconer, Bronwen Griffiths, Jan Jordan, Sarah Palmer, Cathy Porter and Dominic Sweetman. I am deeply grateful for all their work.

Producing this collection of pages called a book is a major process. At Pandora, Belinda Budge, Karen Holden, Vicky Wilson, Michele Turney and Lara Burgess were endlessly co-operative – a real pleasure to work with. Maria Habershon's willing and interested support work made producing the manuscript a much less arduous undertaking. Manny Bermejo helped with fast translation; Julie Wheelwright had a facilitating role in the early stages of the book. The Writers' Guild, especially Nick Yap from the Books Committee, was especially helpful on contractual matters. When my computer died, I would have been unable to continue without the generosity of Dinah Murray and

Jeanette Buirski. Tim Sweetman and Jocelyn Cuming did sterling work checking the footnotes.

Images were a vital factor in my understanding of women pirates, as well as in making this book richer. Bronwen Griffiths was enormously helpful on the question of imagery. Actors Sara Mair-Thomas and Helen Atkinson Wood gave me many insights in interviews about acting as pirates; Talkback Productions, Central TV and Psychology News were most helpful in enabling me to see contemporary television images. The British Library was diligent in its research and generous in facilitating many aspects of the picture research. Martin Cole gave friendly and fast practical help.

I thank the following for permission to quote from their books: the author and Allen Lane: The Penguin Press/Viking, for Peter Linebaugh's *The London Hanged*; Penguin Press for Aubrey de Selincourt's Translation of Herodotus' *The Histories*; the author and The Press Syndicate of the University of Cambridge for Marcus Rediker's *Between the Devil and the Deep Blue Sea*; Thames & Hudson for David Mitchell's *Pirates*; Collins & Brown for David Cordingly and John Falconer's *Pirates: fact and fiction*; the author and Edinburgh University Press/Wolfhound Press for John Appleby's chapter in *Women in Early Modern Ireland*.

Books are an emotional process, with long roots. For help in coming to this point I would like to thank Vera Stanley, and Pauline and Claire Stanley – my sisters who like being go-ers. Cathy Porter and the late Viv Afia always tenderly believed in my work. Sarah Jack and Assuntina Cardillo-Zallo provided a bedrock of permission to swash-buckle *and* cry. Dorothy Badrick equipped me with her positive approaches to success and to needs. Without my osteopath Joyce Vetterlein, I would have been immoblised. Most of all, I thank Dominic Sweetman who gave me endless support – practical, emotional and intellectual.

Every one of these people, and many more who sent cuttings, advice and information, enabled this book to be not only feasible but fun.

Jo Stanley
Happisburgh, Norfolk, 1994

List of illustrations

1. Ann Bonny, frontispiece of the 1725 Dutch edition of *The General History of the Robberies and Murders of the Most Notorious Pyrates* by Charles Johnson.

2. Alfhild, captioned 'Alwilda the Female Pirate', engraving from *The Pirates Own Book, or Authentic Narratives of the Lives, Exploits and Executions of the Most Celebrated Sea Robbers* by Charles Ellms, 1844 edition. (By courtesy of the British Library.)

3. 'Grana Uile introduced to Queen Elizabeth', frontispiece to *Antholgia Hibernica*, vol. 11, 1793. (By courtesy of the British Library.)

4. 'Horrid abuse of helpless women in the cabin': passengers on the *Morning Star* facing attack by pirates in 1827, from Ellms, 1844. (By courtesy of the British Library.)

5. Ann Bonny and Mary Read, etching by B. Cole. (By courtesy of the Mansell Collection.)

6. 'Mary Read killing her antagonist', from Ellms, 1844. (By courtesy of the British Library.)

7. 'Gibbs carrying the Dutch Girl on board', frontispiece from Ellms, 1844. (By courtesy of the British Library.)

8. 'The crews of Blackbeard's and Vane's vessels carousing on the coast of Carolina', from Ellms, 1844. (By courtesy of the British Library.)

9. 'Mrs Ching in action', 1836 illustration to a penny pamphlet. (By courtesy of the British Library.)

10. 'Lai Choi San: she was now to be obeyed, and obeyed she was', photograph used in *I Sailed with Chinese Pirates* by Aleko Lilius, Oxford University Press, Hong Kong Ltd, 1992.

11. Cover of Henri Musnik's *Les Femmes pirates: aventures et legendes de la mer*, 1934. (By courtesy of the British Library.)

12. Jean Peters as Ann Bonny, captain of the *Sheba Queen*, in *Anne of the Indies*. (© 1951, Twentieth Century Fox Film Corporation. All rights reserved. BFI Stills, Posters and Designs.)

13. Linda Darnell is taken prisoner in *Blackbeard the Pirate*. (© 1952, RKO Pictures Inc, used by permission of Turner Entertainment Co. All rights reserved. BFI Stills, Posters and Designs.)

14. Tabea Blumenschein in the *Orlando's* prow in *Madame X, an absolute ruler*, 1977. (BFI Stills, Posters and Designs, reproduced by permission of director Ulrike Ottinger.)

15. 'If you thought Bonnie and Clyde were dangerous, wait till you meet Bonney and Read.' Poster from the exhibition 'Pirates, Fact and Fiction', National Maritime Museum, 1992–. (By kind permission of NMM publicity department.)

16. Sara Mair-Thomas as Mary Read faces the press gang in Psychology News' *Pirates*, Discovery Channel and S4C, 1993. (By permission of Huw Walters.)

17. Helen Atkinson Wood as Captain Connie Blackheart takes a shooting break in the television series: *Tales from the Poop Deck*. (By permission of Central TV, with thanks to Talkback Productions.)

Preface

The first thing people say when I announce that I write about women pirates is, 'Oh! Were there any, then?', and they start to smile: fascinated, almost salacious. Yes, there were women pirates, at least ten, depending on how you define a pirate. And there still are. But were they swashbuckling desperadas, lonely outcasts manoeuvring out of the depths of poverty, wild tempestuous beauties in breeches or weary prostitutes lifting their petticoats to make another ducat on a tossing ocean? Free spirits – or pregnant, seasick, syphilitic mothers?

Male writers' stories about women pirates traditionally tell of glamorous ruthlessness, hedonism on tropical islands, heterosexual and lesbian adventures amid the Portugese wine and gunsmoke of pirate sloops awash with gore. In fact, women pirates are part of a large number of women who worked at sea and whose existence is barely recorded. I would like the female pirates in this book to be seen as women who happened to work on a particular sort of ship: pirate vessels. The more I learn, the more I have come to see female pirates as women in a man's world dealing with a situation of privation and conflict. Most women pirates were in it for what they could get, while they could; there were not many other opportunities around. But the mythology – that's the fun.

This book was written in 1992–4 as part of a larger project about women who worked at sea. My interest in the topic began as a result of a significant absence. I discovered that my family knew nothing about the seafaring life of my great aunty May Quinn, a stewardess who served on Elder Dempster ships to West Africa in the early 1950s. As a working-class feminist interested in the ways unprivileged women throughout history have got up and gone, and have been affected in their choice by existing transport and patterns of mobility, I wanted to find out more about my foremothers who had refused to stay at home, who chose to see the world for themselves instead of just listening to stories about it. With my academic background in labour history, and as a former journalist specialising in industrial relations and women's issues, I knew where to look for information. And I found almost nothing.

In those early stages, I had planned to write a play about stewardesses. I worked backwards in time, finding and interviewing twentieth-century women who had worked on the great floating hotels in traditional female servicing roles such as those of stewardess, masseuse, nurse, swimming pool attendant, purserette, shop assistant, hairdresser, stenographer. To back up their accounts, I looked for earlier documentary evidence of women working on ships. I found not only whaling and naval wives but also women who had cross-dressed to survive as seamen, boatswains, privateers, cooks and the much-mythologised cabin boys. In sea-related jobs on land, women ran navigation schools in Caernafon and Thameside Wapping, presided over boarding houses and bars, laboured in ships' chandlers and victuallers and serviced mariners in harbour-front sex industry work.

It was during a break in a day's diligent reading at the National Maritime Museum library that I wandered round the shelves, stretching my aching shoulders, and found pirate books. I immediately thought, 'Could there have been *women* pirates?' For weeks I had dwelt disenchantedly with fragments about apparently upright matrons who chaperoned women migrants to Canada and the US, attacking their lice, guarding their hymens, leading their hymn-singing, doling out cotton for therapeutic blouse-making. Suddenly here was an occupation after my own rebellious heart: women who had strode the decks powerfully as fighters, not as timorous paying passengers or pseudo-slaves; women who had actively sought a shipboard life, and one that did not run on scheduled routes.

But opening some of the books that included women pirates was shocking. I had never seen such ridiculous information about working women – it was worse than Hollywood fantasies about nuns or tabloid tales of princesses and madams. As I started to prod and think, I found literature about women cross-dressers in history and about women in pirate movies. But the outrageous and implausible stories I read about women pirates bore no relation to accounts about other seafaring women. I could not believe that women on pirate ships were so very different – and so began my search for the possible subjective realities of women pirates that lay behind the glamorised myths.

In talking to people about my discoveries, I slowly realised what a rivetting book it could make. It was one that publishers were much more interested in than any sober account of the mass of ordinary women working at sea (the ones I actually identify with). Everyone wants to know about transgressive rovers.

Many people asked me if I was writing this book because I want to be a pirate. I do not. I love the fantasy of steering a huge rusting container ship across oceans and lying on yachts in the Caribbean, but I also like to treat people generously, not abuse them. I have the impression that I would not like most of these women pirates; they might steal my best bath oil and laugh at my poems. I also believe that people should be free to travel without fear of molestation: why else would I go on 'Women Reclaim the Night' demonstrations or support the Women's Transport Charter Campaign? As I think human beings should not have to risk death in the course of their work, how could I hold a brief for people – whatever their sex – who attack employees? I mistrust glamorised jobs – from stripper to managing director – and I suspect the mythology that has grown up around women pirates too. But I am driven by two interests.

Firstly, I have always wanted to know more about the woman subject who is transformed into a popular-culture glamour queen or sex idol. My MA thesis was on the 1950s movie *Carmen Jones*, its heroine an ordinary woman who like some female pirates epitomised wild sexual freedom – in men's eyes. I wanted to understand the gap between what such women may have felt like themselves and what men did and do to them in cultural products – whether sexualised racist Twentieth Century Fox movies or Defoe-esque novels of atrocities, defamation and adventure.

As far as women pirates are concerned, I wanted to know about the woman who liked to be made love to as well as she who took the initiative. I wanted to know how the palms of her hands felt when she held a sword handle rather than washed the brine out of her canvas trousers. I want to know if she panicked before battles. Was she revolted by her companions – the physically half-destroyed, greedy men who expected her to be sexually available, brave, unsentimental, inhuman? Indeed, were they so? What economic systems was she part of: was prostitution or theft ashore the only other way she might have earned a living? What was it like to come back to the constraints of female life on land when you had been a plunderer at sea? Can pirates have children and love them? This book has had to make guesses much of the time, but finding good grounds on which to speculate has been a joy that has constantly shifted my views.

The second of my interests was that I wanted to say, urgently, that I – and other women – exist and should be part of recorded history. This desire has become focused on women who have worked on ships – like my stewardessing great aunty May – because this domain has been claimed to be male and is an important metaphor and symbol. Most formal histories of seafaring deny women's presence, yet we have been there, from rowing tiny coracles to having babies and passing the powder (gun, not talcum) in the Battle of Trafalgar, to mopping up movie stars' seasick on 1930s cruise liners. We were and are at sea, as we were and are on land. This book is a way of retrospectively claiming my/our place in every area of the universe – for future record.

What I and the other contributors to this book try to do is to debunk pirate myths. We look at the women behind the lurid tales, as well as trying to understand why the tales were told and how they were received. I hope that this book, with its detective work and unearthings, will offer a picture of what might really have gone on behind the titillating illusion, that the reader will experience a gasp of recognition and a peaceful sense of 'Ah, so *that* is how we have been duped! At last I see the connections!'

Bold in Her Breeches is part of a growing international move to carry out historical research and writing that is aware of the structuring effects of class, gender and race. I am proud to be part of the international progressive feminist history movement and to contribute this book to our body of work.

I hope you too enjoy this delving beyond received knowledge. It could be thrilling – in unexpected, satisfying and provocative ways.

Section I:

Introduction

1 Brigand dominatrices for utopia-seeking masochists: the idea of women pirates

His spike-heeled fantasies/
my lust . . .
for seedlings, bread and brine.
Our need: for that near fearless place –
continent not isle –
and charts whose certain flowing ink
will never wash awry.

Pirates – especially women pirates – are on the one hand real seafarers and on the other figures who stand for pirates. In the 1951 Twentieth Century Fox movie *Anne of the Indies* (see plate 12) they are women who confront men. In biographical novels such as Frank Shay's 1930s version of the life of Mary Read, *Pirate Wench*,[1] they are sexy, feisty brawlers little different from the women pirates who appear in more 'factual' non-fiction accounts such as those by inter-war writer Philip Gosse. With weapons at the ready, they terrify in posters and illustrations or love passionately, as in Steve Gooch's 1978 play *The Women Pirates Ann Bonney and Mary Read*.

The idea of pirates of both sexes in western eighteenth-, nineteenth- and twentieth-century imagery is of figures who are larger than life, the stuff adventures are made of. They transgress for us, and when they are brought to justice, the hangman's rope is never slipped around their necks. They live on the sea, traditionally a place of otherness where all kinds of terrors lurk for people at the mercy of the elements. Above all, they are hedonistic to a greater extent than we are. As Charles Ellms wrote in 1837 (though with a moralising after-statement), a pirate's

> hours of relaxation are passed in wild and extravagant frolics amongst the lofty forests of palms and spicy groves of the Torrid Zone, and amidst the aromatic and beautiful flowering vegetable productions of that region. He has fruits delicious to the taste, and as companions, the unsophisticated daughters of Africa and the Indies.[2]

Reading this in the late twentieth century, perhaps as angry and sophisticated mothers of Africa and the Indies, many of us might retort that the pirates lazing on this metaphorical golden isle were able to do so because it was stuffed with exploitable resources and unpaid labourers. The illusion of a tropical paradise with money growing on trees has its roots for British readers in a mixture of Robert Louis Stevenson's *Treasure Island* and J.M. Barrie's *Peter Pan*, advertisements for Captain Morgan's rum, Gilbert and Sullivan's operetta *The Pirates of Penzance* – and a refusal to see the reality of a terrorising trade. Historian A.L. Morton – writing about Utopias such as Cokaygne and Atlantis – describes the setting of Utopian fantasies as 'a classless society . . . [where] abundance is possible without the burden of unending and soul-destroying toil.'[3] As in the US folk song: 'they sleep all day [and] . . . they hung the Turk that invented work, in the Big Rock-Candy Mountains.'[4]

In this magic land, simply to believe in fairies, as *Peter Pan* audiences are urged to do, can rescue people from any danger. There is no such thing as an unvanquishable Captain Hook or misery over class divisions. Gender and race discrimination are absent, as is hardship. The jolly rogue who staggers to his next puncheon of rum cannot be a desperate social exile with severe alcohol addiction and a damaged liver. Long John Silver with his wooden leg, and every archetypal eye-patched ruffian, are only indulging in a fancy-dress charade, not human beings with occupational injuries who never receive compensation. They are not shown struggling to get up gangways or coping with home-improvised prostheses. And pirates never grow old.

Their palm-fringed isle is full of wooden casks spilling over with glittering Spanish doubloons, pieces of eight and shining ducats. No one asks about the human cost of acquiring this plunder or discusses how it can be divided without abuse of power. The role of the national élites in containing or encouraging the pirate trade is never mentioned: this island is not part of a world where imperialistic forces battle for land, power, gold and cheap labour. On the golden island to which the buccaneers triumphantly return (with no need to heat up their own dinner), no one finds the gaudy parrots who repeat 'Pieces of eight' irritating. No one remarks that perched on a shoulder, a parrot looks like a witch's familiar. And no one notices that there are no women among this gang of treasure-seekers.

When these terrorisers of the maritime world occasionally deign to go to sea, it is on sloops decorated with gold, their blood-stained decks piled high with diamonds, Madeira and bananas. In a world of cannon smoke and gangplanks, they fire successful broadsides between taking pinches of snuff from a jewelled box and grabbing their willing molls' derrières.

The pirate in twentieth-century western thinking stands for someone exciting who profitably and confidently operates outside society. He is not a pillar, or even the obedient servant, of any community – he pillages communities rather than contributes to them, disregarding their laws and setting up his own. Fantasy piracy is committed on the high seas, out of sight of land and under the jurisdiction of no nation. Anything is possible because nothing requires permission: no one controls the pirate's morality.

Like a highwayman or a Great Train Robber, the pirate daringly appropriates the fabulous booty more law-abiding fools only dream of. *We* fill out pools coupons or strive for promotion; *he* just grabs his fortune from any passing vessel. Unlike housebreakers or meter-fiddlers, the larger-than-life pirate figure is admired and celebrated as a media personality or a pantomime baddie. A free spirit who roams the world's sea lanes at will, he cannot be imprisoned and cares little whether some profitable prey will cross his bows. And he robs for fun, out of high spirits rather than abject need. He does not connive meanly; he swoops grandly.

The preoccupation in these fantasies is with bloodthirsty pirate leaders' deeds accomplished with ease rather than with the daily life of the mass of workers on pirate ships. This legendary sort of piracy has a similar eroticised thrill about conquering as that of Westerns, but to find it exciting we have to make ourselves blind to the brutality and sexist and racist attitudes that accompanied it. We have to ignore the viciousness the pirates showed towards captives from other ships, to people ashore whose services they needed and to each other.

Of course, this idealised western picture of piracy is one I am setting up in order to knock down, especially the notion of women's absence and the glamorised image of the few women present in this melodramatic scenario. The best-known women pirates today are Ann Bonny (sometimes called Anne Bonney) and Mary Read, who worked in the Caribbean around 1720. But the popular image we have of women on pirate vessels is an unrealistic composite which reflects little of their lives. In the amalgam of contemporary myths, *women* pirates are even more exciting than those ungendered – but actually male – things, 'pirates'. They owe much to female archetypes from Lilith to the leather-clad Mrs Peel in the cult television series *The Avengers*; like an *idea* of Mrs Thatcher with a cutlass, or Tina Turner gone into the transport business, women pirates are beautiful, unbeatable, thrilling. These roaring girls, Moll Cutpurse's seaborne sisters, like to be on top – 'bestriding' might be their characteristic action – and maraud fiercely where maidens should step sweetly. In their flashing eyes is a lust for danger; they would never have a second of premenstrual wimpishness. A bejewelled dagger is clutched between their glittering white teeth; they stride the decks in thigh-high leather boots with stiletto heels and black fishnet tights; they swashbuckle through Caribbean ports in dashing red bandanas and gold hoop earrings. In their strategically torn frilly shirts (with no grubby lines on their collars) and bold breeches, they are desirable to themselves and to all spectators. The figure of a woman pirate is *not* deferential, there primarily for men, hindered by motherhood, stingy, nurturing, slow-witted or ever at a loss.

Women pirates are social outrages – and the embodiment of women's terrifying power. The woman pirate figure is sexually desirable because of her wickedness – a devil; she is bound to come to a bad end – because all *femmes fatales* do; and she offers a breath of fresh air in ideas about women and power.

Sexy Devils

Tanith Lee, in writing about devil women, sums up the fascination of the sexy-because-wicked heroine. 'It was and is the *glamour* of the wicked lady that endeared her to me . . . the villainess, with her dashing accoutrements of sin, she turns the head. An equation evolves: bad is beautiful.'[5] On that other myth-filled frontier, the Wild West, the 'prairie madonna' may have been forced to wield her blunderbuss to defend her babes and her honour, but the bad-and-sexy 'notorious women of the West – the bandittas, desperadas, and wild women: prostitutes, dance hall girls, and faro dealers' such as Calamity Jane and Belle Star 'the Bandit Queen' go down in mythology as having taken to lawlessness simply for the pleasure of pulling out their sharpshooters, riding hard, terrifying and equalling men.[6]

Just as Victorians saw the pub as an 'amorous furnace'[7] in which the barmaid acted as accessory and focus, so the woman on the pirate ship, surrounded by virile desperadoes, is automatically imbued with sexual allure. Seductive glamour, in this scenario, is a necessary qualification for jobs such as acting that have a (delightful) badness attributed to them. The pub or pirate ship is a wicked place partly *because* it has a tarty woman in it; an honest job description for a metaphorical – not real – woman pirate or barmaid would have to include the provisos 'must be sexy' and 'must be prepared to bring decent men to a bad end – fast'.

The mythological desperada on the high seas is an expression of men's fear of women as castrators as well as of their desire for a woman's approving regard as they commit violent acts themselves. Women pirates are a vestige of the pagan godesses and matriarchal fantasies that had to be stamped out for men's safety. Some armchair spectators may enjoy piracy as a way of castrating others by proxy: to be a 'pirate' is to fell phallic masts and rob ships' owners of what gives them potency, pride and a sense of manhood. The fact that pirates do this in the company of brothers lends them even more kudos. Pirates in mythology are the most virile of males, unscared of any force (they even sail willingly in that terrifying womb full of fluid, the sea), their 'weapons' always at the ready. And women pirates, as companions and replicas of this butch and wicked bravery, offer complex pleasures to female spectators who psychically cross-dress as well as to men.

These sexy demons also appeal to spectators as 'phallic women'. The term, from 1980s feminist psychoanalytic film theory, offers a way of understanding the gap between female and male views of women pirates. The argument is that male viewers desire women who imply that they have a penis. This pretence is achieved either by the women putting on a dildo or by presenting their whole body as though it were a phallus. Because women pirates in mythology have unsheathed swords and are often dressed in tight garments which give an erect, boyish impression, they can be seen as a particularly exciting penis which the man would like to have for himself, the presence of what he has always wanted and thought women should have/be. The male spectator may well want to abase himself for not having this phallus, at the same time as feeling thrilled at its visible existence, especially in a high-adrenalin situation like a righteous and winnable battle on the high seas.

Men's desire for sex with a dominatrice and masochistic interest in bondage movies can be part of this pattern. Freud believed that men have a deep need for their mother not to be castrated (that is, to have genitals like theirs). When they realise the mother does not have a penis, they panic that they too might be castrated. Then instead of maturely acknowledging the difference, they make a fetishised aspect of womanhood stand for a phallus – for instance stiletto-heeled shoes, which often play a strong part in fantasies where men place themselves in a humiliating position.

The phallic figure of a pirate woman can therefore stand as someone who has the proven potential to degrade the male onlooker.[8] Alternatively, the man in such fantasies is the heroic buccaneer with the power to terrorise any lily-livered landlubber who comes his way, with the woman as his flatteringly fit companion, extra tool or even his admired superior. By playing Satan or Dracula to this female hero, says Tanith Lee, 'a man may find the image of an anti-hero liberates him from certain gender ghettos – *false* courtesies, imposed roles – while becoming ensnared by the dangerous *femme fatale*, be she Countess Bathory or Morgan le Fey. There is nothing inherently wrong in any of that – except where it loses the true nature of the game or experiment, and begins to cloud visions of . . . the lived-in world.'[9]

Femmes fatales come to bad ends

One of the main ways phallic women are represented in film is as *femmes fatales*. But Marina Warner has shown that mythology has for centuries featured a number of female types whom men see as 'agents of fatality' through the desire they inspire rather than experience: Pandora, Eve, Helen of Troy.[10] While woman pirates might in fact have been steadfast, chaste workers with the potential to create a harmonious domestic environment, they are cast in popular mythology as destroyers whose progress must be halted. The degree of their destructiveness varies greatly from version to version, depending more on the need of the story-teller than the reality of the woman herself.

The opposite to muses, women pirates as *femme fatales* are not inspiring, sweet, melancholy or principled. They seem to have no emotion beyond a lust for power, they are protagonists to whom words such as duplicitous, ruthless and heartless are applied. More positively, their traits include being able to think on their feet, to do unusual work effectively and respond creatively to problems. Feminist film lecturer Jackie Stacey sees the *femmes fatales* of 1940s *film noirs* as the successors to 1920s vamps. Constructed by Hollywood males fearful of the new woman and 'as a legitimation of masculine desires to maintain control over women's increasingly independent sexuality', they appeared in movies such as *The Lady from Shanghai*, *Rebecca* and *The Woman in the Window* as:

> Wicked, scheming, creative, sexually potent and deadly to the male . . . Since the power of the *femme fatale* comes at the expense of men, nothing less than her destruction can control the threat she poses to the patriarchal order . . . whether she is murdered (as in *Double Indemnity*), rendered symbolically powerless (as in *Sunset Boulevard*) . . . or unconvincingly married off (as in *Gilda*), the *femme fatale's* punishment is necessary for narrative closure.[11]

Using this perspective, women pirates *had* to be destroyed by males as a punishment for challenging the power of the father (by being phallic, destructive and operating in men's terrain). This is also the reason why women have to resurrect them – because power is much more complex than that.

Ideas about power

The empowering pleasure of the woman pirate for female and male spectators lies in the fact that she may be seen symbolically as a female who appropriates a lifestyle that is not hers by tradition – a daring, mobile, male, sea-roving life. And she takes it in order to gain the metaphorical and literal plunder she desires: power, wealth, excitement. Piracy symbolises the freedom from having to graft obediently for the means to survive. German playwright Bertholt Brecht's heroine Pirate Jenny, a lowly kitchen-maid, dreams of potent pirates who arrive on an eight-masted ship to capture the city. When they ask her who should be spared, she answers 'no one'. Women pirates go further than Jenny – instead of waiting for men to arrive and offer them options, they take power and choose for themselves.

Actor Sara Mair-Thomas, who played the part of Mary Read in a recent S4C television series on pirates, saw Read as 'feeling all the time that freedom is more important than anything else, including money – and what the lack of it does to you. Each new ship on the horizon is another do-or-die adventure . . . I got a sense that for Mary [Read] and Ann [Bonny] it was like the film *Thelma & Louise*: once they'd gone so far, they'd rather go out in a blaze of glory than go back.'[12]

Mair-Thomas discovered that her sense of her own power was affected by trying on male pirate clothes – wearing oversized leather three-quarter-length trousers with ribbons falling out of her hair, wind in her face and weapons strapped across her chest, 'everything that was happening physically was reinforcing that sense of being bold in your life . . . there were lots of layers and as more layers went on, it felt more free. The jacket was always off your shoulder.' And when playing against men: 'It felt like the fun was matching them. You've got a secret that no one else knows, it emboldens you.'[13]

In some ways, the woman pirate figure denies the female/male split by taking on both roles. The fact that men as well as women enjoy the idea of these maritime Amazons, and have done for centuries, suggests a complex interest in women's power and how it can be exercised.

Through female pirates, women can be assertive protagonists, experiencing what Jung defined as their 'masculine principle' or *animus*. And men can consider whether their own denigrated 'female' side, or *anima*, is not in fact more courageous, independent and worthy of respect than they might usually think.[14]

The woman pirate in myth refuses to be a passive object. But in reality, of course, women pirates were subjects – people who existed for themselves as well as for others. As women under men's control – on ships as in society – they were powerless as well as powerful, secondary as well as primary, object as well as subject.

Women and the sea

Until the late nineteenth century, non-Naval lowly seafarers in general were seen as a bizarre sub-species, almost like beasts. The sea on which they worked also stood as a foreign, unknowable area where unusual things happened and unusual creatures existed, from ghostly vessels such as the *Marie Celeste* or extraordinary storms to mermaids and sirens. Piracy is perhaps the most colourful, the least natural and the most often discussed of such wonders.

The notion of sea-people as 'outsiders' gained in intensity thanks to the traditional (nominal) exclusion of women. The world of the seafarer is both a world unfit for ladies and one where women's presence leads to disaster. Women on ships bring bad luck, they are 'the devil's ballast'; in Shakespeare's *Pericles* even the queen is urged by the crew that she 'must overboard. The sea works high, the wind is loud, and will not lie' until she is jettisoned. Yet the sea also stands for women's huge and unknowable force: 'The Sea is Woman, the Sea is Wonder/ her other name is Fate!' wrote Edward Markham.[15]

In the sea poetry I scoured in preparing this book, women tended to write about the sea as something they gazed upon and dreamed about, a sphere where only men could go. As early as the eleventh century, an anonymous woman ashore wrote: 'I sing of myself, a sorrowful woman . . . First my friend went far from home/ over the waves; I was awake at dawn,/ I wondered where he was, day and night.'[16] By contrast, verse by men portrays the sea as an element they work on and use functionally (as well as fear). The age-old lyrical longing for 'a tall ship and a star to steer her by' is classically expressed by John Masefield: 'I must down to the seas again, to the vagrant gypsy life/ To the gull's way and the whale's way, where the wind's like a whetted knife/ And all I ask is a merry yarn from a laughing fellow rover'.[17]

For Masefield, this is not a hopeless longing: as a man, he could indeed go down to the sea, again and again; a laughing fellow rover might indeed tell him tales rather than rape him. Women, by contrast, have been largely dispossessed of their ability to act on their sea fever. Seamen's ballads present Poll or Susie as going to sea only to follow their male lover, Jolly Jack Tar,[18] while legends depict women as mysterious, inhuman, wrecking sirens, drawing good-hearted sailors on to dangerous rocks.[19] Eighteenth-century cartoonists from publisher Thomas Tegg's stable show women being rowed out to ships or catching sailor lads ashore – as depraved and thieving prostitutes. Nautical dictionaries are full of sexist references which imply that women are incompetent, dangerous, immoral, dirty. While such images are not true reflections of what happened in reality, they limited women's expectations of what they might do. 'Oh, I would rule that tossing ship/ And hold helm firm and guide her true', wrote Annette von Droste-Hulshoff in the late eighteenth century. But most women do not go to sea; like her, 'Instead I sit here – delicate/ Polite, precise, well-mannered child./ Dreams shake my loosened hair – the wind/ Lone listener to my spirit wild.'[20]

This legacy means that the women who did listen to their 'spirit wild' and go to sea by any means, let alone as pirates, were special and daring in the nineteenth- and twentieth-century western imagination. After all, it is only in the last two decades of this century that we have seen women naval officers and lone yachtswomen taking to the world's oceans as conquerors not interlopers, legitimate sailors not ousted nuisances.

Wild bandits

The piracy of eighteenth-, nineteenth- and twentieth-century popular legends stars bold young men who refuse to be confined by society's laws. They epitomise physicality, as well as the power and freedom that can be attained through the violent suppression of others. And yet they also stand for justice: heroic rebels who act out the need of the poor and weak to redress wrongs. These noble, invulnerable avengers appear in popular pirate literature – including the misogynistic works of pirate writer Philip Gosse – as deserving acclaim and accomplices in their evasion of official justice in the name of natural justice. An expression of outlaw daring, almost the height of masculinity, they stand as examples of what the weak would and should do if they could: fight, purloin, resist and never say die.

The sexiness and lust for Robin Hood-style justice that pirates represent make them a criminalised version of space travellers who aim 'to boldly go where no man has gone before'. But they go not as *Startrek* heroes policing the galaxies or as naval crusaders for the glory of the empire. They have some, but not all, the approval patriots confer on foot soldiers. What does this suggest about the societies they belong to?

Like any people operating on the periphery, bandits shed light on the denied desires of those who set themselves up as respectable. They are symbols of unusual daring and transgression, and in the case of women pirates this transgression is doubly spectacular. It is no accident that bandits operate outside the sites of normality and domesticity. Brigands lurk far from cities in the mountains, by wild creeks, plundering major trade routes but not legitimately riding those highways themselves. Similarly pirates lurk on distant islands, preying on major shipping routes. They are beyond the reach of the authorities and part of a world of similar outsiders; they do not mix with upright citizens. Like male mini-cab drivers today, they are outlaws with their own rules.

Myths about pirates, like myths about bandits and brigands, belong to a certain sort of peoples' – rather than official – remembering, believes bandit historian Eric Hobsbawm. Like the Robin Hood myths that have existed for at least 600 years:

> They are part of a history which is not so much a record of events and those who shaped them, as of symbols of the theoretically controllable and actually uncontrollable factors which determine the world of the poor: of just kings and men who bring justice to the people. That is why the bandit-legend still has power to move us . . . what remains when we strip away the local and social framework of brigandage [is] a permanent emotion and a

permanent role. There is freedom, heroism and the realm of justice ... The bandit is brave, both in action and as victim. He dies defiantly and well ... In a society in which men live by subservience, as ancilliaries to machines or moving parts of human machinery, the bandit lives and dies with a straight back ... We long for justice and rebel against the social order that denies it to us. We want to have things, even if only in story form. That is perhaps why all sagas exist – for everyone. A universal need.[21]

For this reason, Hobsbawn explains, bandit myths have a far wider appeal than in the place where the banditry occurred. 'Germany has a literary category *Rauberromantik* (robber romanticism) and a huge number of *Rauberromane* (bandit novels) not designed for reading by bandits or peasants.' So too pirate myths are not written for pirates but for – and by – those in increasingly urbanised countries where people need 'a sometimes imaginary heroic past, and to provide a concrete locus for nostalgia, a symbol of ancient or lost virtue, a spiritual Indian territory.'[22]

Roland Barthes saw myths as a ceaseless striving, a perennial demand that people should recognise themselves in an image both timeless yet time-specific, which was created at a certain moment but then exists forever. Myths about desperadas on the high seas illustrate an eternal image of powerful women as vengeful witch-godesses. But do such figures in fact belong only to the early eighteenth century, when 'the world was turned upside down' and male powerholders were threatened by resistant women? While the myth of male bandits offers a picture of timeless redressers of wrongs, the water clouds when women are included, the picture losing something of its clarity when the fine principles of freedom, heroism and justice are mixed with objectifying sex and sado-masochism.

The question of how and why myths of women pirates are permitted and perpetuated is a difficult one. One answer is that some men need to create highly coloured stories of women at sea because they find it difficult to believe that women can be ordinarily competent and ordinarily incompetent: simply seafarers. Better to invent someone who can be placed in the realm of extraordinary wonder than to acknowledge the existence of a realistic and worrying possibility.

But are women pirates heroines of liberation? Today some feminist fiction writers – for instance Erica Jong and Fiona Cooper – present female pirates as heroic transgressors of traditional boundaries. They fit into fiction genres that include sci-fi, exploration and Hilary Bailey's *Hannie Richards or the intrepid adventures of a restless wife* and non-fiction genres that encompass biographies of Victorian lady travellers, lesbian guidebooks to European cities and anthologies on women of achievement.

And indeed women pirates do move around the world, refuse docile roles, act with daring. Like early aviatrices or women despatch riders in the First World War, they are doing work women are thought never to have done before. They are women who have escaped the complex structure of subordination and repression; at the extreme edge of their work is a revenge not normally available to women. And for some oppressed groups, asserting any power is a triumph, as Hobsbawm found: 'Killing and torture is the most primitive and personal assertion of ultimate power, and the weaker the rebel feels himself [sic] to be at bottom, the greater, we may suppose, is the temptation to assert it.'[23]

But what of real women seafarers? What price did they pay emotionally, intellectually and physically for refusing docility and confinement on land? How did they gain access to the knowledge that they could behave differently from other women and how did they deal with the painful role of outcast bandit? Above all, how do stories of piracy change if we add flesh-and-blood women and delete the violent glamour?

Notes

1. Frank Shay, *Pirate Wench*, Ives Washburn, 1934.
2. Charles Ellms, *The Pirates Own Book, or Authentic Narratives of the Lives, Exploits and Executions of the Most Celebrated Sea Robbers*, Sanborn & Carter, 1837, p. 5.
3. A. L. Morton, *The English Utopia and Seven Seas*, Lawrence & Wishart, 1969, p. 43.
4. *ibid*, p. 38.
5. Tanith Lee, *Women as Demons*, The Women's Press, 1989, p. x.
6. Teresa Jordan, *Cowgirls: women of the American West*, University of

Nebraska Press, 1992, p. xxvii.

7. Peter Bailey, 'Parasexuality and Glamour: the Victorian barmaid as cultural prototype', *Gender and History*, 2:2, Summer, 1990.

8. Annette Kuhn with Susannah Radstone (eds), *Woman's Companion to International Film*, Virago, 1990, pp. 313–4.

9. Lee, *op cit*, p. x.

10 Marina Warner, *Monuments and Maidens: the allegory of the female form*, Picador, 1987, p. 222.

11. Jackie Stacey, *'Femmes Fatales'* in Kuhn, *op cit*, pp. 153–4.

12. Interview by JS with Sara Mair-Thomas, for this book, November 1993.

13. *ibid*.

14. Alan Bullock and Oliver Stallybrass, *Fontana Dictionary of Modern Thought*, Fontana/Collins, 1977, p. 24.

15. 'Virgulus', 1905, cited in *Oxford Book of Quotations*, Oxford University Press, p. 565.

16. Carol Cosman, Joan Keefe and Kathleen Weaver (eds), *The Penguin Book of Women Poets*, Penguin, 1981, p. 62.

17. John Masefield, 'Sea Fever', in Kevin Crossley-Holland (ed), *Oxford Book of Travel Verse*, Oxford University Press, 1986, p. 21.

18. For a discussion of these ballads see Dianne Dugaw's *Warrior Women and Popular Balladry, 1650–1850*, Cambridge University Press, 1989, and her article '"Rambling Female Sailors": the rise and fall of the seafaring heroine', *International Journal of Maritime History*, IV, no. 1, June 1992, pp. 179–94.

19. For less sexist explanation of such legends see Barbara G. Walker, *The Women's Encyclopedia of Myths and Secrets*, Harper, San Francisco, 1983.

20. Cosman, *op cit*, p. 162.

21. Eric Hobsbawm, *Bandits*, Pelican, 1972, pp. 113–15.

22. *ibid*, p. 112.

23. *ibid*, p. 56.

2 *A cool look at a hot topic*

I stitch a bare-bones balance sheet
atop your superseded chart.
And on its face I place
– in plainest canvas not damask –
maps of theft by water, death by toil.
And hoist this stiff encrusted flag
above still-rotting crops of grain.

The women pirates in this book range from Queen Artemisia commanding her vessel in the Persian Gulf in 480 BC to the West Africans who robbed a ship's laundry in Bonny in 1983. By exploring this varied history across centuries and continents, we can see what the specific experience and milieux of piracy might have been like both for the women we know about and for those who are not recorded but may have been present.

In the vast panorama that is the history of piracy, visible women are few. This is partly because all the available accounts are by writers who were not looking for women but at other factors. The stories I have collected here are best read with the question 'Were there more?' always in mind.

The word 'pirate' comes from the Greek *peiran*, to attack. Without all the fuss and glamour of inverted commas and capital letters that signify 'A Pirate's' mythological status, The Shorter Oxford

Dictionary defines a pirate simply as 'one who robs and plunders on the sea etc; a sea robber . . . one who roves about in quest of plunder; one who robs with violence, a marauder, despoiler.'[1] But this definition ignores basic contextual truths such as the fact that piracy is frequently (but far from always) against foreigners (and so has links with war); that it is enhanced by a thrilling image; and that it is often not committed randomly by individuals but is part of a complex structure of trade and territorial power. Piracy and privateering (licensed piracy) would not have developed how and where they did had it not been for English and French rivalry over the Spanish crown; if European traders had not plundered native cultures; if Muslims and Christians had not been antagonistic; and above all, if economic development had been conducted in egalitarian and mutually respectful ways instead of exploitatively, as is usual.

Today, maritime law experts in different countries have developed more complex and contested definitions of piracy.[2] But broadly speaking, pirates are individuals who take goods from a ship or take a whole ship while it is on 'the high seas', that is, sea that does not belong to any country. They do this for their own personal gain, unlike navies which make such attacks for the supposed benefit of the country that employs them. Robbery in coastal waters is not strictly speaking piracy because only that coastal state, and no one else, has the right to apprehend the pirates.

And what is the definition of a *woman* pirate? Were there really 'no women pirates, except the odd few' or 'no women pirates at all, just pirates' molls and prostitutes'? In researching women dockers in Liverpool, Eileen Kelly found that women had been defined out. Dockers usually said, 'No, there weren't any women on the docks.' When confronted with evidence of women's presence, the men replied, 'Well, yes, but they were only canteen workers', or 'Yes, but they only shifted cargo for a little while in the First World War', or 'Yes, but they're only cleaners'.[3]

This 'Yes, but she wasn't a proper one' ploy has been indentified by feminist novelist Joanna Russ as one of the ways men write women out of occupational groups. Russ was looking at the way women writers are dismissed by such comments as, 'She wrote it but she only wrote one of it/but it isn't really art/but she shouldn't have/but she's an anomaly.'[4] If a pirate ship's cook was female, would she be counted as a pirate as a male cook would be? If a pirate's sister was on board during an engagement (fight) with another vessel, would she be counted in as his brother or nephew would? The most likely answer is that she would be dismissed as 'not really a proper pirate' because of her sex.

In *Does Khaki Become You?*, Cynthia Enloe found that women in the US military were defined as support staff rather than frontline workers because it was economically useful to do so. She found that, 'The military relies on a particular idea of sexuality to mould women and men into the kind of organisation it needs . . . designing and redesigning usual divisions of labour. Debates in the media and legislatures over just what constitutes "combat" and the "front" – as versus "support" and the "rear" – are nothing less than arguments over how to make use of women's labour without violating popular notions of femininity, masculinity and the social order itself.'[5]

Women pirates may not always have been or be on the front line as it is traditionally defined, but women were and are involved in piracy. After the Battle of Evesham in 1265, 'Followers of the defeated Simon de Montfort took their families to sea and subsisted by piracy until royal policy changed from prosecution and dispossession to clemency.'[6] Did the women not cook and clean and look after children on ship as they had at home? Did not they live off the proceeds of piracy? Were not they enlisted to fight if necessary? In China, too, scores, possibly hundreds of women in the nineteenth century sailed as wives (and mothers) on their husbands'(or sons') pirate ships, taking part in the action. French passenger Fanny Loviot, captured by Chinese pirates in 1858, witnessed, 'The women assist in working the ships, and are chiefly employed in lading and unlading the merchandise.'[7] Ann Bonny and Mary Read willingly took part in the fighting, as chapter 11 shows.

In many periods, plundering at sea was taken for granted: if any stigma was attached, it was only to those who plundered from ships of their own country. When seafarers were far from land and supplies ran out, plundering another vessel was a logical means of survival; if nearer land, they might plunder a seaside village for food.

One cause of piracy is greed and delight in forcible appropriation of others' goods. Another factor is that wealth and power are not available to all and those who have them frequently abuse them at the expense of those who do not. People in physical need of food and decent living conditions often steal those things if they cannot get them legitimately, especially in revenge if they have been abused. This then becomes 'crime'.

Like banditry, piracy is and was greatest at times of social upheaval, which are also times when the conditions for explosions of cruelty are most favourable, argues Eric Hobsbawm in *Bandits*.[8] But as Hobsbawm points out, banditry (and piracy) are not revolutionary activities: instead people are seeking solutions to their situation through individual evasions of unsatisfactory social conditions, dealing with the symptoms of crisis rather than challenging social standards that allow that crisis to continue.[9]

Piracy also exists because it is allowed to exist as long as it furthers national interests or those of corrupt local officials. Hong Kong-based pirate sociologist Jon Vagg recently found that, 'The main exceptions to this statement were those where the pirates became warlords in control of their own states, as was the case in North Africa in the 1500s, and Malaysia and China until the last century.'[10]

When is a pirate really a pirate?

Piracy is often in the eye of the beholder. Though a hero to the English, privateer Francis Drake was seen by the Spanish as a scoundrel; US hero John Paul Jones was called a pirate by the British. The label 'pirate' has often been applied in a hypocritical way, with those in power being blind to their own transgressions. Alexander the Great asked a pirate what right he had to infest the seas. 'The same right as you have to infest the world,' the pirate replied. Noam Chomsky is one of many commentators to make the point that the way pirates are treated is political and partisan. States and multi-national corporations commit all kinds of robberies – including the under-development of those countries in which piracy is most rife. But the actions of organisations and nations are usually made to seem natural and defensible; they are not scapegoated.

Pirates may be particularly vulnerable to political outlawing because they are not only proven miscreants but itinerant groups of workers, operating outside the main social structures. From travelling stonemasons and troupes of actors to New Age travellers today, roving bands exist for particular ends: usually to survive economically away from urban and formal constraints. Because they are a casual work-force, their labour is undervalued. Periodically such groups are labelled as 'criminal', 'anti-social' or 'deviant', whether or not they have offended against the law, as pirates certainly did. Often this categori-sation includes a stated concern for the moral survival of women and children in the gangs. This denigration is partly to do with any ruler's fear of groups that look difficult to control. The group is then portrayed as wild, in need of discipline, and threatening to decent people. Ultimately, it can be subject to pogroms and outlawed.

Societies create outlaws as a means of dispensing with people whose services they no longer require. Prosperous national economies have been founded on organised piracy: ancient Crete benefited greatly from it. A similar covert use of 'crime' was made by London bishops, who from the eleventh century profited from brothels.[11] Piracy has been differently viewed in different periods: 'The ancient Greeks and Carthaginians had no qualms about . . . piracy being proper conduct. [English] Merchants of the Middle Ages felt much the same way.'[12]

The history of piracy

Pirate writer Philip Gosse proposes a simple – if offensive – illustration of how piracy began: 'In the far dim ages . . . when some naked savage paddling himself across a tropical river, met with another adventurer on a better tree trunk or carrying a bigger bunch of bananas.'[13] Take out the racism, sexism and individualism and it is possible to see some truth in this scenario. Acts of piracy are committed by those who are prepared to fight for what they want, who are deprived of access to the goodies in life and see opportunities to seize them.

As civilization developed, those needy or greedy individuals on tree trunks imagined by Gosse became gangs. Stems of bananas became crates of jewels or mercury medicines. Tree trunks became American schooners and Muslim galleys.

But piracy is also systematic and political. Pirates are not always free operators but part of international power struggles for profits that include trading rights. As men have been the main people involved in travelling, economic pursuits and warfare, piracy has largely been a male world, in which women had support roles except for leaders such as Granuaile, the 'pirate queen of Ireland' (see Chapter 7). But in different cultures and periods, women and children sailed aboard pirate ships, especially as relatives of the captain.

Nor was piracy such a distant operation. M. J. Peterson explains that

> Though popular images from the eighteenth century picture pirate attacks as one ship overhauling another on the high seas, most piracy has been a coastal operation. This makes sense. It is far easier for pirates to find victims if they operate in straits or other narrow areas of sea, and to get away after committing their crime if they do not venture too far from base.[14]

Today, most peoples' vision of piracy is of eighteenth-century European fleets of square riggers with 20 cannons blazing. It is easy to forget that most embryonic pirates probably began by rowing a stolen fishing boat out to a merchant craft which they took over, adapted, and used gradually to build up a fleet of stolen vessels.

As Peterson points out, 'unless pirates had very powerful sponsors ashore they were not able to equip themselves by visiting the local shipyard'[15] and so had to steal both ships and stores. They chose the fastest vessels, which they would lighten by removing most of the fore and after castle and equip with extra gunports and cannons. Merchant ships usually carried few cannons because they wanted to profit from every possible square inch of cargo space and because they sailed with too small a crew to handle many guns. A crew of 19 aboard a 280-ton three-masted square rigger in the late seventeenth century might manage three cannons, whereas a pirate vessel of the same size could hold a crew of 75 and as many guns as they could cope with.[16]

Piracy, said to be the third oldest profession (after prostitution and medicine or agriculture – or law, or religion, or hunting), has been conducted for at least 5,000 years. The history of piracy is the history of the uneven development of the nations of the world and their trading patterns rather than simply of thousands of individual instances of maritime mugging. A battle for power and profit, piracy focuses on maritime commerce. A pirate works where the best booty can be seized most easily. In different periods from the days of ancient Greece and Rome, 'Red Sea Arabs, Malays, Chinese warlords' followers, Dutch Sea Beggars, Danes and Vikings, people of Kent and Cornwall' and a range of privateers, corsairs, pirates, buccaneers and sea rovers have made large- and small-scale raids on almost anything (lucrative) that moved. The earliest site of piracy was the Persian Gulf in 5000 BC, where the fishing people of the Oman Gulf, first in ships with oars and later with sails, ferried Indian merchandise, as David Mitchell describes:

> By the ninth century BC they were trading with Canton and had established trading posts in Java, Sumatra and Siam, not without a good deal of piratical force and fraud. Cargoes of frankincense, spices (including myrrh for embalming), silks, jewels, gold and silver ware, ivory, teak and copper were re-shipped at Omani ports and carried up the Euphrates to Babylon.[17]

The pirates attacked in the area later called the Pirate Coast, the 150 miles between the Qatar peninsular in the west and Oman in the east, on the north coast of what is now the United Arab Emirates. The whole Persian Gulf area, including the narrow Straits of Hormuz,

> With its narrow twisting creeks, sandbanks and jagged coral reefs . . . a barren forbidding region, scorching hot in summer, in winter whipped by sandstorms and lashed by gales when the *shamaal* howls from the north. Using swift manoeuvrable shallow-drafted craft and knowing all the uncharted hazards, pirates were in a position of almost unassailable strength.[18]

I use this early example in detail because it demonstrates three key facts: that piracy depends on rich targets, favourable working circumstances and appropriate vessels. Pirates have always worked primarily where profitable goods were transported on major routes by merchants, but they also needed the maximum opportunities for escape after an attack. In the case of the eighteenth-century Anglo-Americans, 'Theaters of operation . . . shifted . . . according to the policing designs of the Royal Navy. Pirates favoured the Caribbean's small, unsettled cays and shallow waters, which proved hard to negotiate for men-of-war that offered chase.'[19] They also needed somewhere to moor and careen their hulls: because pirate ships rely on speed, the crew of ships in tropical waters careened the barnacles, seaweed and wood-boring worm off the hull three times a year, by comparison to merchant vessels which were careened only once a year or less and were therefore much slower.[20]

In the heyday of piracy, Anglo-American pirates found ideal condtions at Port Royal in Jamaica; Tortuga (Turtle Island) off the west coast of Hispaniola; Madagascar; and Nassau in the Bahamas. Dutch pirates used the colonies of Curaçao, Saba and St Eustatius; French filibusters (free-booters) used the Virgin Islands.[21] At these piratical stations coastal women came into contact with the pirates, victualling, healing and sexually serving them, as described in chapter 8, as well as learning about life aboard pirate vessels and sometimes setting sail with the men. Almost all the women pirates in this book are from coastal areas where pirates landed.

The oldest continuous history of piracy has been in the Mediterranean, where the existence of the great civilisations of Egypt, Rome and Greece led to political and economic competition and lavish consumption. As the Roman Empire declined c. 500 AD and fewer valuable goods were transported by sea, piracy declined too. It did not fully restart until the Vikings, with leaders such as Eric Bloodaxe and Bjorn Ironside, plundered the Baltic, North Sea and Atlantic between the eighth and tenth centuries. They were preceded by Danish woman pirate Alfhild, who sailed c. 400 AD, and succeeded by Sigrid the Superb in 1000 AD, as described in Chapter 6.

By the time of Sigrid the Superb, pirates were also sailing the ocean beyond the Cape of Good Hope off the tip of South Africa. Marco Polo reported the dangers of piracy in the Indian Ocean around 1290, when hundreds of craft with the pirates' wives and children aboard cruised the sea from Gujarat and Malabar. In fleets of between 20 and 30 ships sailing six miles apart, they divided up the sea and snapped up all the shipping in their net.[22] The most vicious of these were the Gujarati rovers, who made captured merchants swallow an emetic called *Tamarindi* mixed with sea water so that they would vomit up any concealed pearls and gems. When explorer Vasco de Gama rounded the Cape of Good Hope in 1497, the sea route to the east was opened up. For a century afterwards, Portuguese traders dominated the eastern seas, until the Dutch and English broke that monopoly and founded their own trading companies, including the Dutch and British East India Companies.

As David Cordingly and John Falconer point out, 'Operating under the protection of government charters, these "merchant adventurers" claimed a freedom of action in their pursuit of trade that would be unthinkable today.'[23] There appears to have been little difference between trading voyages and privateering (licensed piracy) attacks: from the shores of the Red Sea to Sulawesi in South-East Asia, native pirates attacked European traders, just as those traders stole from local merchant vessels in the name of religion. Islamic people were seen as fair game for Europeans, and a situation of attack and counter-attack developed, in which local traders fought to protect trading networks that had existed for centuries before the Europeans came.

Further north, Japanese piracy reached its height in the early sixteenth century. This was led by warlords who controlled fleets and armies and sailed as far south-west as the Strait of Malacca. Banned from Portuguese Indian ports because of their violence, they carried out attacks on the coast of China from the sixteenth to the nineteenth centuries. Piracy was just one of these warlords' many weapons in their fight for political and imperial power, as David Cordingly and John Falconer describe.[24] They point out that:

> The word 'pirate' with all its moral implications, was insufficient to describe the complex political and economic situation of the Eastern Archipelago. The development and composition of small native states with swiftly changing tribal allegiances had no counterpart in European political systems; and the arrival of European merchants and colonialists profoundly altered and ultimately destroyed a fragile and intricate web of inter-island commerce.[25]

For centuries, outside commerce with the Eastern Archipelago had been in the hands of the Chinese, whose junks full of 'spices, rattans, camphor, edible birds' nests, sharks' fins and pearls' came south during the north-east monsoon and returned with the south-west monsoon. In the sixteenth century they were displaced by Portuguese then Dutch traders, whom they attacked in retaliation for the destructive monopolies they created.

Further south-west, along the north coast of Africa, piracy was highly institutionalised and operated on a national scale from the late Middle Ages to the early eighteenth century in the struggle of Christians and Moors, and the fight to control Mediterranean trade. The sixteenth-century Moors led by Aruj and Khair-ed-Din and the Barbarossa (Red Beard) brothers spearheaded the resistance to the Spanish invasion and became legendary figures. When the North African Moslems (part of the Ottoman Empire) were weakened after losing the 1571 Battle of Lepanto to the Christians, they relied on mercenaries, the Barbary corsairs, for naval warfare. 'Corsair' was the name given to pirates sailing in the Mediterranean but as they acted as arms of the state, they were more like privateers. On one side were corsairs based in the Barbary Coast (Berber) states of Tunis, Tripoli and Algiers, a mixture of pirates and privateers; on the other were European traders trying to muscle in on the Levant trade. M. J. Peterson found complex power plays at work in this war over trade and domination:

> because rulers on both sides of the Christian-Moslem divide employed or encouraged them . . . [The] Christian ones operated first out of Rhodes and then out of Malta under the protection of the Knights of St John . . . All governments concerned treated Mediterranean corsairs as state agents. When Maltese activities near Levantine shores seemed likely to disrupt growing European trade because local rulers threatened to retaliate against merchant ships for corsair attacks on Levantine vessels, Popes and Kings of France combined to force the Grand Master of the Knights of St John to prohibit corsair operations in the Eastern Mediterranean.[26]

So piracy there was structural and widespread. Tunisian and Algerian corsairs operated as far afield as the English Channel. Rip-roaring, hard-drinking English and Dutch pirates in Barbary and Morocco, who committed many cultural sins including 'sleeping with the wives of Moors', were temporarily tolerated by the Moslems until their seafaring skills had been acquired by local people. They brought not only their abilities as pilots but also the Northern European style of round ship, which enabled the corsairs to break out of the

Mediterranean and into the Atlantic, whose rough waters were unsuitable for (unstable) galleys.

The booty these Barbary corsairs sought was not jewels but people: 'white slaves'. Around 8,000 women, men and children were carried off to the Barbary Coast and sold into slavery. 'In 1617 an entire fishing convoy returning from the Newfoundland Banks to Dorset was captured by Barbary men-of-war, and in 1631 the corsairs raided Baltimore in Southern Ireland, taking over 100 slaves.'[27] The slavery caused immense diplomatic problems, and according to David Delison Hebb, the English were 'far more often the victims of piracy' than 'a nation of pirates'.[28] The only way to evade brutal treatment once incarcerated in the *bagno* (slave barracks) was to 'turn Turk': to become a Moslem.

While this complicated scenario of attack and counter-attack, trade and religion was unfolding in Asia and Africa, in South America buccaneers were operating on the 'Spanish Main'. The glamorous name for the north-east coast of South America, this came to refer in the late seventeenth and early eighteenth centuries to the Caribbean Sea; instead of being 'the main land', the Spanish Main became 'the main sea'.[29]

Although today the words 'buccaneer' and 'privateer' are used interchangeably, they were once specific. *Boucan* comes from the French for barbecue, used in seventeenth-century Hispaniola (now Haiti and the Dominican Republic) for the place where men living rough on pigs and cattle, often French colonists, dried and salted their meat. These land-based 'savage, filthy and fierce men . . . ate and slept on the ground . . . their bolster the trunk of tree, and their roof the hot sparkling heavens of the Antilles', according to seventeenth-century buccaneer-scientist William Dampier.[30] When the Spanish rulers destroyed their cattle in order to get rid of them, these self-styled 'Brethren of the Coast' joined the runaway slaves, deserters and others who preyed on passing ships, especially hated Spanish ones,[31] contributing to the eventual end of Spanish power in the Caribbean. By the end of the seventeenth century, the word 'buccaneer' was applied to all privateers and pirates operating in the Caribbean.[32]

Women are seldom referred to in accounts of buccaneers, for instance in the main source, Exquemelin,[33] except as victims of men who whored, diced, drank and allegedly could get through 3,000 dollars a day. More sober accounts suggest that women were irrelevant: 'each Buccaneer had his partner, they travelled together, protected each other in combat, and when one of them died the other inherited his belongings. It was a companionship like marriage . . .'[34]

Domestic piracy

Unlike this piracy on the high seas, largely against foreigners, a different sort operated around Britain's coasts: 'The same person might well be trader, fisherman, pirate and naval employee by turns.'[35] Grace O'Malley and the O'Malley and O'Flaherty families illustrate this versatility, as Anne Chambers shows in Chapter 7. Devon and Kent seafarers worked the English Channel; Fife and Berwickshire seafarers worked the Firth of Forth. Sea brigandage – whether licensed or unlicensed – was widespread and unextraordinary. 'If every person directly or indirectly involved in piracy had suffered the penalty demanded by law, the south coast of England would have been virtually depopulated and the Spanish Armada would have met with little opposition', claims David Mitchell.[36] Limited gains – fish, wine, wool – were sought by too many pirates in too small an arena. In the face of poor pickings, one pirate turned to human plunder and kidnapped merchants, holding them for ransom in a Lundy Island dungeon. Later records show that coastal women, as well as men, eased slim earnings by taking part in the shoreside plundering of vessels, smuggling and wrecking, as described in chapter 8.

Privateering

From the thirteenth to the nineteenth centuries, Europe waged war through privateers: people authorised by commission – 'Letters of Marque' – from a government to attack the merchant vessels of hostile nations. Regular fleets attacked the enemy's troops, coastal towns and naval vessels, while the privateers attacked its commerce. The government received part of the proceeds and did not have to finance privateers as it would a regular navy. In England in 1243, Henry III granted privateering licences to Adam Robernolt and William le Sauvage, '"To annoy our enemies at sea and by land wherever they were so able, so that they share with us half of all their gain." (Similar licences were issued by Church officials and rulers in the Mediterranean, against Moslem shipping).'[37] Two women privateers are recorded: Flora Burn and the unnamed commander of a French privateer (see Chapter 9).

By the early 1300s merchant associations, leagues and companies were conducting transport businesses with government charters. 'The piracy indulged in by such merchant groups was part of the legacy of conduct from the ancient world where the right to hinder economic rivals at sea was never questioned.'[38] Privateers' commissions, issued at times of war against specific national enemies, were signed by the English sovereign until the reign of Queen Anne (1702). After that point they were issued by the Lord High Admiral, and later by governors of colonies. Such a commission meant that privateers were sanctioned to engage the merchant ships of a hostile country – in effect, to carry out naval actions. In the fifteenth century there was more scope for corruption and commissions were sometimes issued blank. By the seventeenth century, the system of 'Letters of Marque' was well established and internationally recognised.

Sir Francis Drake is the classic example of the English privateer. Queen Elizabeth I (reigned 1558–1603) is said to have taken no notice of advice to build up her fleet, preferring to encourage privateering. When Drake sailed off in 1585 to plunder Vigo in Spain, the Cape Verde islands and Spanish cities in the Caribbean, this 'typical privateer's adventure at the time . . . was financed by a joint stock company, with London merchants and Elizabeth I both contributing money.'[39]

It was a profitable period. The Spanish domination of the Mexican Aztec Empire and Inca peoples in Peru meant that gold and silver in vast quantities were being shipped to Spain. Drake was preceded by the French Jean Florin, who captured treasures that Spanish *conquistador* Hernán Cortés had taken from the Aztecs: 'three huge cases of gold ingots, 500 pounds of gold dust, 680 pounds of Aztec pearls, coffers of emeralds, and other precious stones, Aztec helmets, shields and feathered cloaks, and a miscellaneous collection of exotic animals and birds.'[40] The English-Spanish alliance ended with the death in 1558 of Mary I of England, who was married to Philip II of Spain. The power and wealth of Spain, Europe's leading force, grew still greater with more silver mines and the defeat of the Turks at Lepanto in 1571. Philip II, who ruled repressively through the Spanish Inquisition and in 1588 dared to try to invade England with the Spanish Armada, was the focus of great hostility.

English and French privateers targeted not only Spanish treasure galleons as they sailed for home, but the tiny harbours with gold-stacked dirty lanes where the vessels loaded up: Cartagena, Nombre de Dios and Portobello. Another focus of attack were the trains of mules bearing tons of gold and thousands of pesos of silver on their trek from Peru and Ecuador to the Caribbean coast near Panama. A mule train attacked by Drake in the 1570s was said to have been worth enough to build and equip 30 Elizabethan warships.[41]

David Cordingly and John Falconer describe the sequence of events:

The privateers were followed by the buccaneers who usually, but not always, operated with the official approval of the French or English Governments. And the buccaneers were followed by pirates – highwaymen of the sea operating for their own gain. But as far as the Spanish were concerned, they were all pirates.[42]

A century later, in the Caribbean, much piracy still stemmed from government policy.

The English tolerated Buccaneers based at Jamaica as long as they concentrated their energies on Spanish vessels. This was simply a continuation of Queen Elizabeth I's policy of carrying on undeclared war with Spain by tolerating and sometimes helping finance the activities of the 'Sea Dogs'.[43]

Piracy's Golden Age, the period between 1650 and 1730, earned its name because so much piracy occurred. This included the routine and less dangerous 'Pirate Round' of 1690–1700, when captains such as Thomas Tew and John Avery worked between the North American colonies, including Carolina and the Guinea coast. They plundered Arab and Moghul shipping in the Red Sea, using Madagascar as their base, and sold off booty from silver to parcels of elephants' teeth in the Americas. Financiers and governors took a cut of up to 50 per cent.[44]

The most intensive period of piracy followed the Spanish War of Succession (1701–14), when England, the Netherlands and many German states fought France, Spain, Bavaria, Portugal and Savoy over French and Spanish royal power. Once the war was ended, men – and women, including Mary Read – from disbanded armies would take almost any work in order to survive. Piracy was one – often unfreely chosen – job option when the trading halted by the war resumed and inhabitants of the colonies avidly attempted to stock up on what had been unavailable in wartime – lace, brocade, silk stockings and wine. Merchants were happy to ship out their requirements, and many of their crew were to turn pirate under duress, after being attacked.

Powerful citizens on the North American coast benefited from the actions of their hired hands at sea. A lady connected with shareholders of shipping enterprises dealing with pirates might well relish her petticoats woven from (stolen) cotton and gowns of (stolen) brocade. Her morning beverage might be (stolen) cocoa, her evening tipple (stolen) Madeira or Portuguese wine. Her maid could tie her hair with ribbon dyed by (stolen) indigo and dream of the (stolen) silver in the storeroom. And her cook could spice her winter meat with (stolen) cardamom and her summer apple pie with (stolen) cloves.

Early eighteenth-century pirates profited from the American colonial resistance to English domination – expressed in the opposition to the tax on tea, for instance, and the 1773 Boston Tea Party – which culminated in the American War of Independence (1775–83). Colonial governors had not the ability to suppress piracy, but in any case a number of them actively supported and benefited from privateering. People in America provided markets for the booty of pirates such as Thomas Tew, who was publicly fêted by Governor Fletcher of New York, his wife and daughters glittering in diamonds and silks by his side.[45] 'Pirates sold large volumes of goods at prices undercutting merchants who complied with Britain's Navigation Act, which required goods from the East to America to be shipped via Britain.'[46]

Piracy was temporarily a viable job. From 1714 to 1720 there was extensive piracy in the Caribbean, off the coast of Carolina and Virginia, in the Gulf of Guinea and the Indian Ocean. Veterans who had sailed with notorious English captains such as Blackbeard and Bartholomew Roberts mixed with relative newcomers including Ann Bonny and Mary Read. These women were among the many who, in choosing this life, gambled with the possibility of it ending with a hangman's noose around their neck as more and more pirates were rounded up and tried by specially established Courts of Admiralty in Jamaica.

An end to the trade

How did piracy, or at least this Golden Age, come to an end? In many instances, governments shifted from tolerance or indifference to active suppression as legitimate trade was disrupted. When the Moghul emperor, in his annoyance with piracy declared an embargo on all European trade in 1698, the British Admiralty was impelled to send a naval squadron to Madagascar.[47] M. J. Peterson summarises these trends:

> British attention focused on the Caribbean in the 1680s and 1720s because pirates had succeeded in virtually stopping trade. Singapore began its anti-piracy activity in the 1820s because the Chuliaks of the Coromandel Coast refused to sail southward of Penang. This meant that at least 60 fewer ships a year were coming to Singapore, a real dent in the port's revenues . . . Nineteenth century efforts to abolish the slave trade between Africa and the Americas, and then slavery itself in all parts of the world, also contributed to the suppression of piracy. Abolition meant cutting off the market for captives, always a major pirate commodity. Second, suppressing the slave trade led several maritime powers to establish more regular naval patrols in the southern Atlantic, the Indian Ocean and the Caribbean. This made piracy in those areas more hazardous by increasing the likelihood of being caught.[48]

European imperialistic powers carried on with a different version of what might be seen as mass plunder for another two centuries. To defend capitalism's growing trade, countries such as England further developed their navies (state-sanctioned seaborne warriors) throughout the eighteenth century, attacking piracy, which began to wane. The deaths of scores of the thousands of Anglo-American pirates were made exemplary. They were hanged in chains from gallows on prominent headlands, as a warning to passing ships and seafarers, and in England were strung up on the foreshore. Men's corpses (no women were hanged for piracy) were staked to the ground at Execution Dock, Wapping, where they were washed over by three Thames tides before being removed; some were grieved over by lovers and mothers. Other pirates hung up their boots in privileged white style, with several 'wives' in foreign countries. John Plantain, the self-styled 'King of Ranter Bay' lived in 1722 in a stockaded fortress in Madagascar with 'many wives whom he kept in state of great subjection . . . They were dressed in richest silks and some of them had diamond necklaces.'[49] Maria Cobham ended up a pillar of the Le Havre community, as Chapter 11 describes.

The Anglo-Dutch bombardment of Algiers in 1816 and then the French occupation of Algeria brought piracy in the Mediterranean to an end – a useful public-relations plug for colonial occupancy. By 1800, piracy in the west had virtually halted. The last pirate was hanged in England in 1840, in America in 1862. Britain, France and Russia agreed at the 1856 Paris conference to abolish privateering and the United States and most other countries followed suit.

Chinese piracy continued on a massive scale in the nineteenth century. Cheng I Sao's career captaining her dead husband's fleet of 700 junks in the South China seas is discussed by Dian H. Murray in Chapter 12. After 1900 China had two minor women pirates: widows Lo Hon-cho in 1922 and Lai Choi San in the 1930s (see Chapter 13).

Today piracy in the South China seas and off the west coast of Africa, is viewed by commercial and political leaders as a major problem for trade, menacing the safe passage of freight and affecting international relations. There is still high-level collusion and corruption in the maritime crime business. And seafarers' unions and green organisations insist that piracy must be stopped on humanitarian and ecological grounds, warning of disastrous oil spillages if tankers go aground because their crews have been tied up by pirates.

Fast, opportunistic and daring, piracy today involves robbing a vessel of the safe's contents, portable computers, Walkmans, video-players and credit cards – not the hogsheads of molasses and gold moidores of legend. Some heists are tiny, and the booty just saucepans or other domestic items. The vessels that are taken over wholesale have decks the length of two football pitches, and their cargoes come in containers big enough to house desperate families in less developed countries.

Any women pirates who exist today are yet to be adequately recorded, let alone turned into mythological 'pirate queens' like Artemisia and Granuaile. The limited number of women associated with the 1990s piracy of faxes and fast outboard motors are in lowly roles. In two of the three cases revealed in Chapter 14, women pirates are at the bottom of the pile in poverty-stricken societies where prostitution is a more usual way for entrepreneurial women to survive.

Notes

1. *The Shorter Oxford Dictionary*, 1983.
2. See P. W. Birnie, 'Piracy, Past, Present and Future' in *Piracy at Sea*, edited by Eric Ellen, ICC Publishing SA/International Maritime Bureau, Paris, 1989.
3. See *Women on the Docks* by Liverpool Second Chance to Learn Women's History Group, Harrison Jones School, Liverpool, 1987. Also 'Waterfront Women Remembered', my interview with Eileen Kelly in *Morning Star*, 17 February 1987.
4. Joanna Russ, *How to Suppress Women's Writing*, The Women's Press, 1984, front cover.
5. Cynthia Enloe, *Does Khaki Become You?*, Pluto Press, 1983, p. 7.
6. M. J. Peterson, 'An Historical Perspective on the Incidence of Piracy' in Ellen, *op cit*, p. 41, using as source T. B. Costain, *The Magnificent Century*, Doubleday, 1951, pp. 320–21.
7. Fanny Loviot, translated by A. B. Edwards, *A Lady's Captivity among Chinese Pirates*, 1858, stored at the British Library under 10057 a19 26, pp. 78, 111.
8. Eric Hobsbawm, *Bandits*, Pelican, 1972, p. 58.
9. *ibid*, p. 17.
10. Jon Vagg, 'Rough Seas: contemporary piracy in South-East Asia', paper to the International Congress of Asian and North African Studies, Hong Kong, 1993, p. 3.
11. E. J. Burford, *Bawds and Lodgings: a history of the bankside brothels c.100–1675*, Peter Owen, 1976, pp. 41–2.
12. Ralph T. Ward, *Pirates in History*, York Press, 1974, p. 108.
13. Philip Gosse, *The Pirates' Who's Who*, Dulau, 1924, p. 11.
14. Peterson, *op cit*, p. 43.
15. *ibid*, p. 42.

16. *ibid*, p. 44–5.
17. David Mitchell, *Pirates*, Thames & Hudson, 1976.
18. *ibid*, p. 24.
19. See the discussion of piracy in this period in the chapter 'The Seaman as Pirate, Plunder and Social Banditry at Sea' in Marcus Rediker, *Between the Devil and the Deep Blue Sea: merchant seamen, pirates and the Anglo-American maritime world 1700–1750*, Cambridge University Press, 1987, p. 257.
20. Peterson, *op cit*, p. 44.
21. Gosse, *op cit*, p. 19.
22. David Cordingly and John Falconer, *Pirates: fact and fiction*, Collins & Brown, 1992, p. 68. This book, Rediker's and Peterson's chapters and David Mitchell's *Pirates* are clear summaries of the history of piracy and invaluable further reading for this chapter.
23. *ibid*, p. 69.
24. *ibid*, p. 104.
25. *ibid*, p. 113.
26. Peterson, *op cit*, p. 52.
27. Cordingly and Falconer, *op cit*, p. 64.
28. David Delison Hebb, *Piracy and the English Government 1616–1642*, Scolar Press, 1994.
29. Peter Kemp (ed), *The Oxford Companion to Ships and the Sea*, Oxford University Press, 1992, p. 820.
30. See Gosse, *op cit*, p. 120.
31. See Cordingly and Falconer, *op cit*, p. 32–3.
32. *ibid*, p. 10.
33. A. O. Exquemelin, *The Buccaneers of America* (1678), The Folio Society, 1969.
34. Cordingly and Falconer, *op cit*, p. 32.
35. Mitchell, *op cit*, p. 11.
36. *ibid*, p. 12.
37. Ward, *op cit*, p. 102.
38. *ibid*, p. 108.
39. *ibid*, p. 144.
40. Cordingly and Falconer, *op cit*, p. 16.
41. *ibid*, p. 15.
42. *ibid*, p. 17.
43. Peterson, *op cit*, p. 52.
44. Mitchell, *op cit*, p. 102.
45. *ibid*, p. 104.
46. Vagg, *op cit*, p. 3.
47. Peterson, *op cit*, p. 49.
48. *ibid*, pp. 49–50.
49. Mitchell, *op cit*, p. 192, citing Clement Downing's voyage journal.

3 *The women among the boys*

In waters scarlet with slaves' blood,
brown with cloves, flecked in gold,
I sail bandana'd.
Around me?
Corsair boys and buccaneers.
And in me?
A certainty of battle
cries.

Amid the huge sweeping history of plundering at sea, involving thousands and thousands of sea brigands, are ten women. Their existence suggests that many more – overlooked and unrecorded – sailed the world's oceans. And hundreds of thousands more must have been deeply involved in the pirate world as lovers, wives, mothers, sex-industry workers, informants, fences, suppliers, nurses, cooks and seamstresses – because pirates did not exist in isolation, but in the world.

Ann Bonny and Mary Read are the most famous women sea-rovers in Britain, not least because they worked in the early eighteenth century, the period of piracy that is best recorded. At least one other woman pirate is known to have been active in that period: Maria Cobham. As this was a high point in women's mobility, especially disguised as soldiers and sailors, it is inevitable that many more women than just Mary, Ann and Maria sailed the oceans. But there are far more stories of women pirates in plays and books than known women pirates, a similar situation to that found by Julie Wheelwright in looking at cross-dressed women soldiers and sailors: 'The long years of war in the eighteenth century . . . produced more than 100 female warriors who surface in more than 1,000 variations of Anglo-American ballads.' [1]

Apart from Mary Read and Ann Bonny, the women pirates most people are aware of are the pirate queens: Artemisia in 480 BC, the sixteenth-century Irish princess Granuaile and Cheng I Sao, who sailed in the early nineteenth century. Only a few have heard of the fifth-century Danish pirate Alfhild or the 1920s and 1930s pirates Lo Hon-Cho and Lai Choi San.

There were perhaps several hundred women pirates during the thousands of years of piracy, with only a few pirate queens thanks to women's limited access to power. Cheng I Sao and Granuaile were pirate leaders because of family wealth and connections; Cheng I Sao commanded while clad metaphorically in her dead husband's cloak and breeches. Given the familiar pattern even today of men mutinying against women's rule, there must be instances of widows failing to maintain their status as pirate captain (though I have found no records of this). There must also have been women who reached high status through merit rather than by virtue of their husband's or father's rank (records of their lives, too, are yet to be discovered).

At the other end of the social scale are the more lowly women who worked on pirate ships – women who might otherwise have been serving wenches or prostitutes, market traders or milkmaids. Some, such as Mary Read, were official crew members; others, such as Ann Bonny, were aboard informally for personal reasons. Mary Read was one of a number of working women masquerading as men in order to get a job at sea. Usually, a woman could not be a sailor in her own right (unless she was a woman of privilege: class and clout won out over gender every time). Records of female transvestites in the period from 1550 to 1830 confirm that women worked on ships in traditionally male roles such as deck hand, boatswain and carpenter. [2]

Many pirates started off as seafarers and then changed ships. The transition from working on merchant vessels to privateers to pirate vessels could be seen as akin to the gradual move a woman might make from doing housework at home, to becoming a home help, to becoming an office cleaner – taking whatever opportunity she could to earn money in an increasingly alienated way, further from home. Mary Read is an example of a woman who slipped from working on privateers to the more outlawed world of the pirate vessel, but I suspect that if she reflected on her position the difficult issue was not so much the difference between being a woman on an ordinary ship and an outlawed women pirate as the transition from being a land-based woman to a woman seafarer. In stepping on board she breached the discouraging wall of hostility towards women at sea. For such working women, being on a pirate ship was a way to make a necessary living; they had no other wealth, unlike Granuaile for instance.

Accounts of general seafaring history indicate that there may have been women on ships who worked openly as females. My guess here is that ships unable to get a male crew together fast enough might have allowed women to sail, either openly or perhaps turning a blind eye to some implausible breeches. Men may have made this acceptable to themselves by setting women up as 'not proper pirates' – as adjuncts rather than workers in their own right: 'she is only helping him out; she is not really doing his job.'

By contrast to these openly female or 'out' women mariners, the 'out' women providers of services would have had the status of semi-independent traders, conducting their business (sex, most likely) within the main business of the ship, protected by an officer as a sponsor or type of pimp. It is a system that was later formalised as shop-keepers or barbers operated on a concessionary basis on passenger ships, paying a fee for being allowed to profit from the needs of the people the ship carried. A historian of nineteenth-century maritime life found that some captains of merchant vessels who wanted to retain their (scarce) male crew arranged to have sexually available women on hand – paid – to keep the crew happy.' Such women may also have operated on pirate vessels in earlier times.

But the bulk of women pirates in the early eighteenth century were probably there because of their connection with male pirate leaders, working on their father's, husband's or lover's ship – as was Maria Cobham. This was certainly the usual reason for women's presence on non-pirate vessels. Mrs Crofts in Jane Austen's 1818 novel *Persuasion* always sailed with her beloved Royal Naval husband and 'gloried in being a sailor's wife'. She claimed 'women may be as comfortable on board as in the best house in England. I know nothing superior to the acommodations of a man-of-war.'[4] In pirate accounts such as Captain Charles Johnson's history,[5] local women in the tropics were sometimes found on ship, seemingly as pirates' servants, especially when the ship was at anchor. This presence as men's sexual companions is a variation on the way pirate queens such as Cheng I Sao came into piracy – solely because of their connection with a husband or lover.

Popular mythology suggests that pirate captains' lovers traipsed round the decks in frilly frocks behaving boldly or bountifully as the second-in-command or even 'the real boss' (see plate 13). But Maria Cobham, as Captain Cobham's wife, was reported to have made rules about how the crew should behave and to have intervened in her husband's decisions; other, less mythologised women may have been beloved or abused stooges. In Hollywood terms, their role was more likely to have been that of a gangster's dumb moll than a multi-skilled co-director of his international enterprise.

Counting women in

When Ann Bonny and Mary Read were sailing, the estimated number of Anglo-American pirates ranged from 1,000 to 5,000. (At this time the total population of Liverpool was only 6,000 and the white population of the West Indies just 38,000. England and Wales had a population of 5.5 million – half the population of London today and nearly three times that of Jamaica now.) The number of pirates was less than one-tenth of the total number of common British seamen, which was 50,000 in 1688.[6] (The word 'seaman' in records actually means seafarers; even today women in the Merchant Navy are called seamen and most statistics assume all seafarers are male.) I propose that perhaps half of one per cent of these pirates could have been cross-dressed women, perhaps 50 to a few hundred.

An average of approximately 79 pirates worked on each ship in this period.[7] Given all the incidences of exceptionalised women's presence that can be unearthed, it may be that some crews included as many as two females at times (after all, Mary Read and Ann Bonny were coincidentally on the same ship). In at least two other cases, there was a known woman working on privateers: Flora Burn was one of the 35-member crew of the *Revenge* and another woman was captain of a crew of a hundred.[8] While recorded instances suggest that a surprising number of women may have been on ships, some pirates had a code of practice that forbade women to sail and may have forbidden their captain – or anyone else – to bring women aboard (unless they were shared out). So there may have been fewer 'out' women on pirate ships than on naval and merchant vessels.

Why be a woman pirate?

Seafaring in all its different locations, cultures and periods has varied enormously: ships, food, crew, clothes, methods of fighting, frequency and type of encounter with targets, booty, opportunities ashore, reactions of people back home. But some general points can be made.

At best, a woman pirate's job satisfactions included adventure, wealth, an open-air life and the opportunity to see different places. The role offered a working-class woman extraordinary mobility, with the chance of doing well financially on some voyages and ending up if not with gold doubloons and trunks full of rubies, then at least with a length of saleable calico or tropical hardwood. The pleasures included the sweet taste of avenged wrongs (the Robin Hood motive) and the better food than naval ships; the self-regulation aboard as well as the fun – be it dancing or sonnet-writing. But I suspect that the problems of being a woman in a world of men who were deeply hostile to all that women stood for usually outweighed the joys.

Lesbians in the sixteenth, seventeenth and eighteenth centuries may have gained some limited freedom by passing as men on pirate and other ships. Historians of tranvestism Rudolf Dekker and Lotte van de Pol found, 'Sexual desire and love was thought of as something that could only be experienced with a male. We can therefore assume that most women who fell in love with other women could not place or identify those feelings. Therefore, it is logical that those women would think: if I covet a woman, I must be a man.'[9] If women cross-dressed and acted as men, it enabled them to love women at a time of long-standing European inability to conceive of lesbianism. A pirate vessel may not have been the best place for a 'Flatt' [10] to find her true love, but eighteenth-century Anglo-American pirate ships were known as places where people of all backgrounds were welcome – unlike naval ships. The relatively 'no questions asked' nature of pirate life could have meant that a pirate ship was a more likely place of employment for a cross-dressed woman than any other vessel.

Were these 'counterfeit men' changing their visible sexual identity as a way of challenging their destiny as women? Julie Wheelwright, in looking at cross-dressed woman soldiers, said that they 'appear largely unconcerned about changing the society that produced the inequity which they felt most keenly in their own lives . . . they traded roles rather than forged new ones.' [11] This suggests that women pirates who passed as men, as did Mary Read, were not early feminists seeking an existence that affirmed better values, but simply took men's places (perhaps uncritically) in dissatisfaction with their own. Although it was an attempt at a type of self-liberation, it was one with a limited perspective.

Some women may have been on pirate ships because they liked the company of male pirates, just as 1970s' ship girls relished seamen's companionship (see Chapter 8). In the light of B. R. Burg's suggestions that there was extensive homosexual sex among seventeenth-century pirates working in the Caribbean, [12] we might imagine pirate sloops appealing to fag hags. Though highly unlikely, this is a useful antidote to the usual view of gender relations aboard sloops as a simple scenario of butch men ravaging femme women. Much more complex relationships may yet be revealed, although neither Burg nor Rictor Norton, who investigated working-class homosexual subculture in seventeenth- and eighteenth-century Britain, discuss women's friendships with the 'Mollies' on land – blacksmiths, milkmen, waiters and chimney sweeps – or at sea. [13]

Who were women pirates?

There is no such typical, timeless thing as a 'woman pirate' any more than there is such a thing as a 'woman outlaw', 'woman warrior' or even a 'seafarer'. There are simply women in different periods and countries whose temporary livelihood was piracy. Those who commanded seafarers to rob and sailed with the mariners while they did so, as did Granuaile, were women used to leadership, negotiation and strategic daring on a grand scale. Others probably ranged from economic migrants to refugees from constricting homes; from women searching to ease misgivings about their sexuality to footloose itinerants unable to settle. They may have been hoydens hungry for violence or obedient workers who carried out instructions. The job could also have appealed to women who identified more with men than with women, for a variety of reasons. And it surely attracted women for the same reason as it attracted men – as a source of fast money and a way of escaping difficulties on land.

Women seafarers in the seventeenth, eighteenth and nineteenth centuries were mostly working-class women who would have been expected to stay on land and keep house. Just as women healers and wise women refused to accept their male-alloted roles, so women seafarers expressed their discontent with domestic labour by leaving the milieu deemed appropriate for them and moving into a more public sphere. Feminist sociological studies show that women who break out of old patterns require courage, impetus, an ability to be hard when appropriate, curiosity, a huge need for change and shrewdness to see and act upon opportunities. Women seafarers were probably choosing a way of living never before experienced by any woman in their family, forging a new mould and perhaps unconsciously demonstrating the need for a change in women's social position.

Some women may have had knowledge or experience that made them hungry for a larger world. Obviously pirates did not write home urging their relatives to take up the trade. But being in a coastal community would have given women access to seafarers and stories of seafaring. The idea that women could be sea-rovers was enshrined in popular ballads and dramas of the eighteenth century which celebrated the feats of cross-dressed women (even if some did come to terrible ends) and there is some evidence that these led more women on land to don breeches.[14] But by depicting women sailors, soldiers and outlaws as bold, brave, unusual and ultimately happy to marry, the ideology such works built up denied that other parts of the female population were struggling for less fettered lives.

To be 'born with the sea in your blood' implies a knowledge or orientation passed on through families, usually to men. Women too may have experienced a longing for the sea, when the same blood flowed in their veins, the same stories flowed into their ears and the same nearby ocean assailed their nostrils. Desire must have been created by proximity to possibilities coupled with an interest in new experiences and perhaps a sense that there was nothing to lose. Piracy may have seemed a natural step to women already outlawed by working at sea or as dockside prostitutes. Or it might have appeared better and more profitable than anything else available. In some cases it appears to have been an activity people fell into as the result of a train of accidents, as Mary Read's life demonstrates.

Piracy was probably not an occupation young girls dreamed of in the way that young women in the 1960s saw being an air hostess as the height of excitement. Nor was it that piracy appealed to angry viragos who lusted to commit brutalities and improve their street credibility, as male SM fantasy might have it. It was probably not something women felt they had a vocation for, like working in a convent healing the sick. It was just an option that presented itself. Male pirates, and Mary Read herself, told courts they were only pirates reluctantly and would rather go straight[15] in much the same way as studies of prostitutes show that some women take up the work out of necessity and will continue only until they earn enough to retire.

If there is a common factor among women pirates in different periods and cultures, it is probably that piracy seemed the best available option in their situation. It is likely that they were women with little sense that they could change their destiny; not because of any failure of imagination but because they were products of their period. The possibility of wearing trousers – of a new way of behaving as a woman – acted as a psychic green light, however little it was consciously recognised as such.

Wearing the breeches

Accounts of women pirates in different periods – Alfhild, Ann Bonny and Mary Read, as well as Lai Choi San – say they wore trousers.

These accounts should not be taken at face value – it may be that story-tellers had to make women sound like men or almost men to accommodate the idea that they could be pirates at all. But on the other hand, wearing trousers did make practical sense. The reason most women donned breeches was to travel safely, to avoid molestation and to get into situations where only men were supposed to be. Wearing trousers allowed women pirates the freedom to climb, work with ropes, go up and down ladders. Anything that dragged in puddles on open decks would have been a nuisance and could have taken days to dry. It was easier to afford, launder, patch or replace breeches than boned bodices and several layers of skirt. Women may also have worn these clothes for the reasons people wear any work uniform: they thought they had no choice; the clothes indicated admission to corporate identity; such clothing was all that was available after months at sea; breeches were proven to be practical and utilitarian. And trousers were also protection against wandering hands and sexual harassment.

A number of stories about cross-dressed women seafarers indicate that male colleagues suspected or even knew they were female (though these could have been face-saving claims made with hindsight). So a woman pirate discovered to be female might have continued to wear breeches for practical reasons or in order to be allowed to continue with the privilege of working in a nominally all-male workplace. While I believe women wore trousers primarily on practical grounds, there may have been less conscious reasons as well. For instance, some lesbians may have worn breeches as part of living out a masculine identity. Breeches could also be taken as a statement that women were seizing power, laying claim to the privileges of the more powerful group: like power-dressing, they may have been both a conscious and unconscious way of appropriating the trappings of authority. Breeches – in illustrations if not in reality – also indicate that the women pirates are part of an oppositional gang removed from land values, in much the same way as young women gangs such as the Slick Chicks and Black Widows in the US of the 1940s wore zoot suits to indicate their place in an aggressive, rebellious movement.[16]

Conversely, by wearing trousers women pirates may have been capitulating to men and reassuring themselves of their acceptance by men. As Elizabeth Wilson points out in *Adorned in Dreams*, today:

. . . while the trousers for women might symbolize a myth in Western societies that women have achieved emancipation, it can hardly be interpreted as unproblematic of their status. If it were interpreted in this literal way it would lead us to think . . . that in so far as women have made progress in the public sphere of paid work, this has been on male terms and within the parameter of masculine values.[17]

Women pirates in breeches would not necessarily have been an indication that progress was being made, but simply a sign of women's continued confinement.

Interpreting the breeches

When the title of this book, *Bold in Her Breeches*, first occurred to me it seemed immediately right. Cross-dressing is a significant part of the mythology of women pirates, with its implication of a woman who is stepping out of her usual station, taking power. As *The Shorter Oxford Dictionary* notes, 'To wear the breeches: to be master, said of a wife.'[18] The phrase is used derogatively against both the woman (too butch) and the man who allowed it (too soft). And as used by some men, there is also an implicit, sexualised, masochistic admiration.

Breeches – as coverings for absent phalli – have been fetishised by western culture as a way of dealing with women who take on unwomanly roles. Ninety per cent of illustrations of women pirates play on their masculine attire, a play which is especially apparent in the movie *Anne of the Indies* (made just after the Second World War when more western women wore trousers than at any previous time). Illustrators and writers of pirate tales, the majority of readers until the late nineteenth century and Hollywood film-makers have mostly been male. Presenting women pirates in swashbuckling breeches is an expression of the narcissistic assumption that men are the prototype and women the adaptation, the pirate-ess, the mini-version of 'proper' male pirates.

Fashion analyst Anne Hollander has argued that in the twentieth century the female leg symbolises movement.[19] While some illustrations of women pirates show immobile legs swathed in voluminous drapery (see plate 1), many popular nineteenth- and twentieth-century images show their legs trousered and active – fighting, walking, lunging, standing threateningly – to a degree unusual among male portrayals of women. The fact that breeches are short, cut off at the knee, and that the lower leg is either naked or encased in a tight-fitting boot that reveals its shape indicates movement more dramatically than, say, bell-bottoms or leggings. Western men have long fetishised fragments of women's bodies such as legs or breasts. The nude leg hints that eighteenth- and nineteenth-century men saw women pirates as having an animal sexual availability, especially outrageous and exciting in the Victorian period when even piano legs had to be swathed for fear they would incite lustful thoughts.

Women who take up public space have been seen in many cultures as sexually available. Such a woman is not chastely in her own home with her own man; her eyes are not cast down and her mouth is not closed in a compliant smile. To wear the trousers in public is a daring transcendence of woman's traditional role as well as an indication that the woman in question is not maidenly but available for sex (whether or not she is hypocritically chastised for that). Marjorie Garber's *Vested Interests: crossing dressing and cultural anxiety*[20] sheds light on what cross-dressing means for women from folk singer k.d. lang to explorer Isabel Eberhardt, from Shakespeare's Rosalind/Ganymede to French novelist Colette. However much the woman might be cross-dressing for sexual safety, the outside world sets her up as all the more sexually desirable and accessible. Elizabeth Wilson points out that:

> For centuries western women's legs had been concealed, trousers and pantaloons worn only by actresses, acrobats and women of dubious morality . . . until the 1900s only working women, and then usually only those engaged on the coarsest labour, and entertainers, wore trousers and showed their legs, and when they did so their morality was impugned.

Wilson adds that roaming field gangs of women agricultural workers, sometimes wearing trousers, were seen by the Medical Officer of the Privy Council in 1864 as 'looking wonderfully strong but tainted with a customary immorality and heedless of the fatal result which their love of this busy and independent life is bringing on their unfortunate offspring who are pining at home.' [21]

The mere fact of wearing breeches places a woman pirate in reality or fiction in the position of a sexualised outlaw. Breeches reinforce the idea that only 'strange' women can work at sea and that if you want to work on ship, the price you pay is loss of feminine identity. If wayward members of society are so visibly proved to be strange or abnormal it renders the centre more safe.

How did women pirates feel?

One of the exciting aspects of writing women's history is to imagine how women who have been called unusual, wayward or not quite human might have felt. How can we guess what women pirates were conscious or unconscious of being? How can we understand the women as individuals and as products of a particular world? One answer is to speculate on the basis of what we know of women in male work situations today, as described in occupational sociology books and newspaper reports.

On the positive side, women pirates may have felt bold, free and full of excitement at their ability to meet unfamiliar challenges, sentiments echoed by some women admitted into the armed services during the Second World War. Those less powerful than the pirate queens may have felt the same determination to fight against male hostility shown in fire stations, the composing rooms of the print trade and police departments today. Sometimes they might have been defeated: even high-ranking women today have been unable to face the prospect of more years of harassment and have left their jobs.[22] A young New Zealand woman working on fishing trawlers described at a recent 'Woman and the Sea' conference her anger at being sabotaged for not co-operating sexually with male colleagues, at twice being dumped in foreign ports and at having to change jobs nine times because of the intolerable daily injustices. Other women seafarers have been able to persevere because they have had women around them to support them and share their moans.[23] A woman pirate alienated by the restrictive conventions of shore life may have hoped for and found a more compatible existence on pirate ships; her sense of whether or not it was an improvement would be determined by how badly she had been treated elsewhere.

Surveys of women at work show that they want to be respected and not made into the butt of lewd remarks, gropings or rapes. But because pirates and seamen were used to warfare and to sometimes mutually exploitative relationships with women, violence and abuse were far from exceptional. Pirates' captives of both sexes were tortured. When captives were women, especially black women, men's violence was sexualised. Exquemelin[24] tells many tales of gang rapes by buccaneers. Violence by pirates was influenced by xenophobia too, and black women – captives and colleagues – must have been even more threatened. A woman pirate might have felt constantly under threat of male violence and have had to indicate by every means possible, especially tough body language, that she was not to be abused. Competent work skills could have earned her respect and some safety as well as a way into future jobs.

Seafarers were frequently beset by boredom, especially when ships lay becalmed. And people often say that a day at sea is twice as long as a day on land, so a pirate may have appreciated high-adrenalin engagements when they arose. Studies on the psychology of confrontation show that such encounters can arouse fear, excitement and an exalting sense of power, though post-combat trauma can bring depression, terror and guilt. If women pirates were involved in extensive fighting, their later reactions may have been similar to the rage, despair and sense of futility experienced by soldiers returning from the Vietnam, Falklands and Gulf wars.[25] The nightmares never stop and human relationships are impossibly scarred. And women pirates today may well feel like and stage themselves as under-privileged citizens driven to work in the alternative economy, like Philippines mail-order wives or Piccadilly Circus rent boys.

Of course, we will never know how women pirates feel and felt since this has never been described by the women themselves or by people in search of authenticity rather than sensationalism. But we can put ourselves into these sea-brigands' sailcloth breeches and imagine.

Notes

1. Julie Wheelwright, *Amazons and Military Maids: women who dressed as men in pursuit of life, liberty and happiness*, Pandora Press, 1989, P. 8 and note 26.

2. Rudolf M. Dekker and Lotte C. van de Pol, *The Tradition of Female Transvestism in Early Modern Europe*, MacMillan, 1989 and Wheelwright, *ibid*.

3. Discussion with maritime historian SF, London, August 1993.

4. Jane Austen, *Persuasion*, Secker, 1930. See in particular pp. 75–7, 100–01, 184–5.

5. Captain Charles Johnson, *A General History of the Robberies and Murders of the Most Notorious Pyrates*, (1724), published as Daniel Defoe, *A General History of the Pyrates*, Manuel Schonhorn (ed), Dent, 1972.

6. B. R. Burg, *Sodomy and the Pirate Tradition: English sea rovers in the 17th century Caribbean*, New York University Press, 1984, p. 55.

7. Marcus Rediker, *Between the Devil and the Deep Blue Sea: merchant seamen, pirates and the Anglo-American maritime world 1700–1750*, Cambridge University Press, 1987, p. 256, footnote 4.

8. See Chapter 9 for more details of Flora Burn and the woman privateer captain. Burn's reference comes from John Franklin Jameson, *Privateering and Piracy of the Colonial Period*, MacMillan, 1923, p. 394, citing the journal of the sloop *Revenge*, 5 June to 5 October 1741.

9. Dekker and van de Pol, *op cit*, p. 57.

10. 'Flatt' as eighteenth-century slang for a lesbian is a reference to playing cards (flatts) and to the idea of the game of rubbing together two flat (i.e., non-projecting) genitals. 'Flatfuck' was a colloquial term for lesbian activity by the nineteenth century. See Rictor Norton, *Mother Clap's Molly House: the gay subculture in England 1700–1830*, Gay Men's Press, 1993, p. 233.

11. Wheelwright, *op cit*, p. 12.

12. Burg, *op cit*.

13. Norton, *op cit*.

14. See Wheelwright and Dekker and van de Pol, *op cit*, for a fuller discussion of this.

15. See records of admiralty trials of pirates in the Public Record Office, Kew, numbers Co 137/14, x C18 757.

16. Elizabeth Wilson, *Adorned in Dreams: fashion and modernity*, Virago, 1985, p. 198.

17. *ibid*, p. 165.

18. *The Shorter Oxford Dictionary*, p. 235.

19. Anne Hollander, *Seeing Through Clothes*, Avon Books, 1975.

20. Marjorie Garber, *Vested Interests: cross dressing and cultural anxiety*, Penguin, 1992.

21. Wilson, *op cit*, p. 162 and p. 260, footnote 9, citing Dr H. J. Hunter's 'Report on rural housing', P. P. 1864 (3416) XXVIII, 6th Report of the Medical Officer of the Privy Council, Apps. 13–14, p. 456.

22. For a useful discussion on this see, for example, Cynthia Cockburn, *Brothers: male dominance and technological change*, Pluto Press, 1983.

23. Informal interviews and formal (unpublished) presentations at the 'Women and the Sea' conference, Wellington Maritime Museum, New Zealand, December 1993.

24. A. O. Exquemelin, *The Buccaneers of America*, (1678), The Folio Society, 1969.

25. See first-person accounts in Reese Williams (ed), *Unwinding the Vietnam War: from war into peace*, The Real Comet Press, 1987.

4 Uncovering the oceans' Roaring Girls

I'll trample myths' padlocks
though my feet are on brine.
I'll sing of my sea-skills
in no fairground jig-time.

I'll tell of my voyage
as mulled praise and warning.
I'll show you my moidores
and my heart's deforming.

Most chapters in this book explain the process of finding out about women's piracy and describe how a historian has picked her way through the projections, censorings and lurid myths. I am used to doing life-history work hand-in-hand with the women who are its focus, whose formal narratives I can challenge and with whom I can work directly to find varied and solid ways of telling their stories. So writing this book has seemed like trying to build a sturdy house on a few grains of sand. Not only are women's own words absent, but the records that are available spring from ways of thinking that disempower women rather than creating a picture that respects their realities. This entire book is based on mens' few – very few – words, which are often dismissive, romanticising or semi-pornographic. Above all, they turn the ten known women pirates into exceptional figures rather than symptomatic people.

Feminist historians today, for example Joan Scott, argue that deeply structuring ideas around gender crucially affects the ways knowledge is produced:

> Gender is the social organisation of sexual difference. But this does not mean that gender reflects or implements fixed and natural physical differences between women and men; rather gender is the knowledge that establishes meanings for bodily differences . . . Sexual difference is not . . . the originary cause from which social organisation ultimately can be derived. It is instead variable social organisation that must itself be explained.[1]

Deidre Beddoe, a feminist historian working at grass-roots level, protests that recorded history has been 'the history of the monarchy, the aristocracy and the ruling elite . . . the history of men and male affairs . . . wars, diplomacy, politics and commerce.'[2] Gender relations affect the ways pirate women's history is written, seen and understood.

Because this book is also about differences of social status, as between pirate queens such as Granuaile and lowly labourers such as Mary Read, we need to consider the class basis of historical records. Just as privileged (white) men have either failed to notice women, have judged them as not worth mentioning or have described them only in certain ways, so the history of women pirates reflects the hidden power structures in the societies from which the writers come.

Records of the pirate queens have been discovered in general histories. Alfhild was buried amid the mix of mythology and 'fact' in a history of Denmark; Artemisia was just one warrior-leader in the early history of Greece. Many women are present only in a phrase or half-sentence, and certainly not indexed.

Women pirates were basically seafarers, so to understand their experiences we also need to understand those of their non-piratical but travelling sisters on land and at sea. But women at sea are regarded as 'not really there' or written down as sea*men*; women are especially absent from histories of organisations such as armies and navies because they were not supposed to be there. Feminist researchers have discovered them through fragments, for example autobiographies where mariners mention proudly that they were born at sea – undeniable proof of their mothers' presence. Camp followers, nurses (such as Mary Seacole), wives, healers, prostitutes, cooks and sutlers, who provided wayside cooked food, have been uncovered and their existence has transformed our knowledge. It is not just a matter of adding on a few women but of re-ordering the whole picture of men *en masse* working on the move.

The rawest information on seafaring women in the last 500 years comes in the form of a few newspaper reports of the unmasking of cross-dressed women – the point at which they came under scrutiny from a judging (male) world.[3] Not all cross-dressed women were literally or metaphorically stripped of their male disguise, and many whose masquerade remained undiscovered must have existed. Only two women pirates faced the bench, unless we count Stephanie Sterns, the 1970s yachtjacker (see Chapter 14). The main 'official' source of information about Ann Bonny and Mary Read is the printed report of the trial where as members of Rackham's crew rather than as women their piracy was described by witnesses and judged by a jury. That document can be found amid correspondence and ephemera about Britain's plantations in the Caribbean,[4] part of the formal records of English control of distant disorder.

Captain Charles Johnson's hugely rich account of seventeenth- and eighteenth-century pirate history, *A General History of the Pyrates* (first published in 1724),[5] is as central an early text as the bible to Christians or *The Second Sex* to modern European feminism. Johnson (who was initially thought to be Daniel Defoe) includes far more on women than other writers: Bonny and Read's story runs for 15 pages of the 695-page account edited by Manuel Schonhorn. Several men wrote accounts of their travels as buccaneers, particularly William Dampier, Basil Ringrose and Alexander Exquemelin,[6] but women are neglible to these and certainly not present as active pirates. I made an index of the 40 or so one- or two-line references to women in Exquemelin and found no female pirates but the following telling categories: wives of pirates, wives of buccaneers, wives of turtle-fishers, wives of Indians, wives of Spanish settlers, women prisoners (the biggest category), nuns and women slaves.

After Johnson's time came popularisers who presented pirates in specific ways. Nineteenth-century British romantic writers encouraged a home-grown interest beyond the days of Anglo-American piracy. Byron wrote about the minor Greek and Turkish corsairs in his 1814 poem 'The Corsair', which added a Robin Hood tinge to pirate myths, shaping ideas of pirate chiefs as despotic, the victims and enemies of society. Christian Socialist Charles Kingsley in his poem 'The Last Buccaneer' idealised pirate life as a harmonious collective where poor folk brutalised by cruel England 'made laws so fair and free' and chose their own 'valiant captains'. Kingsley's novel *Westward Ho* portrayed Elizabethan sailors as crusaders for Protestantism and plunderers for patriotism. Such accounts were masculine in tone and did not feature women as protagonists.

Ellms in the nineteenth century and Philip Gosse, A. Hyatt Verrill and Joseph Gollumb in the early twentieth were among the main authors of more factual accounts which presented pirates as excitingly criminal. This balance is being righted now by a new generation of historians.[7] Today's research is more scholarly: a 1993 summer school in Amsterdam ran a programme on 'The Life and Deeds of Pirates in Past and Present Times' with international historians talking on topics from 'The Utopian Dimensions of Piracy' to 'The Political Economy of Piracy in Sixteenth and Seventeenth Century East Asia'.[8]

No autobiographies, diaries or letters of women pirates are known to exist, perhaps unsurprisingly since the tradition of autobiographical writing is quite a modern development. Historian Christopher Lloyd found only a handful of accounts by early ordinary seamen.[9] Also, historian of seventeenth-century popular literature Margaret Spufford has noted that from the sixteenth to nineteenth centuries girls were generally not taught to write.[10] Between 1580 and 1700, although 75 per cent of the women who could make marks could read, only 11 per cent of all English women could sign their name. This was also true of 15 per cent of labourers (in contrast to 65 per cent of yeomen).

Eighteenth-century Hannah Snell (not a pirate) created perhaps the nearest thing to a cross-dressed seafaring woman's autobiography. After 'swallowing the anchor' in the 1740s she played on stage in men's clothes and later took a public house in the Thameside area of Wapping. 'On one side of the sign was painted the figure of a jolly British tar and on the other the valiant marine, underneath which was inscribed "The Widow in Masquerade or the Female Warrior".'[11] The roles expressed in that double-sided signboard and its caption (which she presumably commissioned herself, with a weather eye on marketing) reveal much about her split self-identities.

Self-representation is a complex process of negotiation, as Liz Stanley theorises in *The auto/biographical I: the theory and practice of feminist auto/biography*.[12] One of the ways feminist historians deal with the absence of working-class women from records is by asking them to speak about their own experiences, as in Elizabeth Roberts' interviews with Lancashire weavers, maids and shop assistants about their lives before the Second World War.[13] Dealing with a parallel exclusion of black people from recorded history, American Alex Healey visited Gambia and found the Kinte clan tradition-bearer or *griot* who could relate three centuries of his family's 'lost' history.[14] Interviewing the person who experienced the life in question is the only form of historical research that enables sources to be challenged and permits discussion about ways to represent what has happened. Oral historians differ about how many generations back memory can go (some say as many as 14). But today we would have to go back at least ten generations to hear about buccaneering eighteenth-century pirate foremothers, and as Margaret Spufford points out: 'By 1700 . . . the circulation of . . . printed ballads, chapbooks and plays . . . already made an indelible mark on the oral tradition,'[15] which affected the ways people told their life-stories.

In looking at the kinds of records and stories of women pirates that exist, we can make use of the distinction made by historian of the eighteenth-century criminal world Peter Linebaugh between the proletarian and the *picaro*. Fundamentally, Mary Read and other lowly pirates had only their labour to sell:

> Like the *picaro*, the proletarian has nothing: neither a mess of potage today nor the land and tools to work with that he or she may fill his or her bowl with tomorrow . . . [but] while the *picaro*'s stance towards the world is active and resourceful – qualities promoted by the literary forms that arise from the individuality of the protagonist, the proletarian as individual is left passive and dumb by the historical records, more like a drone or a brute.[16]

The charm of many pirate stories is that they describe people like the *picaro* who take action to change their circumstances – loudly and spectacularly. Scandalous roaring girls, such as cross-dressed pickpocket Moll Cutpurse, conform to this type.

Linebaugh defines the *picaro* as someone born poor who learned to survive by roguery.

In England the dramatists of the early seventeenth century welcomed such figures on the stage with hilarity and bloody-mindedness . . . it reached an apogee in the publication of *Moll Flanders* in 1722. By that time, the *picaro* had become a social type, the 'sharper' or 'blade'.[17]

Accounts of seventeenth-century women's piracy reflect this view of a certain sort of character and worker: Mary Read, for instance, hardly comes across in these records as proletarian, the lowest of the low.

One possible reason for this transformation of the pirate into a dashing figure is that in order to minimise fears of disorder, pirates were cast as individual and untypical rather than a frightening resistant collective force threatening society. Linebaugh has described the *picaresque* story as:

a prose narrative with an episodic structure, [an] individualist attention to the protagonists, [a] structural resolution by accident, fate or fortune. [As such, it was] ill-suited to showing the collective power of the proletarian in the face of its many enemies or through the course of its history.[18]

But however gleefully writers and readers might have concocted and consumed accounts of pirates as *picaresque* individuals the waves of piracy trials showed that rogues could not necessarily escape social justice. The stories of Ann Bonny, Mary Read and Maria Cobham have *picaresque* endings in that the first two evaded the noose by claiming to be pregnant while Cobham finished up a lady by dint of entrepreneurial individualism. But the tales' closures are flat by some feminist standards: the women do not carry on sailing the seven seas or committing ever-greater feats of daring in triumphant gangs.

The accounts of pirate trials were written with particular audiences and principles in mind: pirates had to be presented as proletarian, that is, low and unable to win. Trial reports conveyed the message that social problems can be righted through discipline and that others should not go down the reprobate's slippery road. 'Criminals' have to be portrayed in a way that deprives them of their validity, so the trial report of Read and Bonny contains no information about their daily lives or details that would reveal their humanity. Instead, the pirates (female and male) in these admiralty court reports are written up as voiceless dogs. By comparison, Johnson tried to provide biographical information that made pirates into understandable characters – perhaps not least because of his antipathy to the élite ashore.

The distinction between the proletarian reality and *picaresque* image of pirates overlaps with the polarised sexist stereotypes developing in seventeenth-century popular literature: madonnas or whores, good or bad. The issues raised by the English Revolution (1640–60) had led to increased interest in debate and printed material. As Margaret Spufford points out, the sales of 'ephemera, ballads, almanacs and chapbooks . . . were all booming by the 1660s'[19] and there was a familiar slot in this popular literature for a figure such as a woman pirate, one that emphasised her active sexuality and final come-uppance. Ann Bonny as consort of Captain Rackham could be inserted into the much-embellished shoes of Jane Shore the mistress of Edward IV, or the Fair Rosamund in *Henry II*. 'Stories of royal mistresses were popular . . . the chapbooks were simply excuses for a good story of adultery, high life, rich living and repentance . . . reinforced with a moral at the end.'[20] As well as being romantic lovers, women pirates could be presented as larger-than-life, a chapbook tradition exemplified by Mother Bunch, the gigantic ale wife who solved her morning flatulence 'with one blaste of her Taile, she blew down Charing Cross, with St Paul's aspiring steeple.'[21] This Rabelaisian image is echoed in the apocryphally cruel daring attributed to Read and Bonny.

The idea of women pirates as a particular kind of rogue heroine is likely to have been passed down a long line. And whether embellished tales were told warningly to adolescent girls in dame schools or lasciviously in low dives, they may well have been inscribed in print as a kind of 'truth'. Oral stories were often the source of broadsheets (single sheets of saleable 'news' or polemic) and Margaret Spufford has discovered that 'At least 80 per cent of folk songs gathered in the major collections . . . early this century were derived from printed broadsides.'[23] While no archive today seems to contain any broadsheets about women pirates, they are the stuff the medium was made of: exciting criminal individuals. So it is possible that the idea of women pirates as *picaresque* heroines came from seafarers' (and others') oral testimony and was passed on via long-lost broadsheets into long-lost songs and plays performed by pedlars and players from Plymouth up to Scotland's farthest islands. Who knows whether landlocked shepherdesses and swine maidens sat in the shade of an oak singing the latest ballads about these desperadas on the high seas?

One reason we have little information about women pirates' lives once they left the sea may be that pirates had to be seen to come to a just end, as in many of Gosse's potted biographies of Anglo-American pirates in *The Pirates' Who's Who*. The convention suggests that story-creators were influenced not only by fairy tales and medieval romances but by witchcraft trials and Old Testament stories of divine retribution. A simple structural analysis shows that many pirate stories conform to the pattern of fairy tales: lack (of money, power, freedom) followed by the intervention of an outside agent (fairy godmother, magic beans, or being invited to be a pirate by one of the best captains) followed by compensation for lack (thrills, power, travel, money, reconciliation with God) and then some kind of moral accommodation. Audience demand for life stories with fairytale structures – and economic pressure on printers to supply them – must have had an impact on what writers wrote, however much they consciously sought accuracy.

Twentieth-century critic Jack Zipes argues that fairy tales had a political function, quelling dissent and making social injustice seem natural.[23] Stories of women pirates contain a simple warning, along with the pleasures: 'Go off with wild pirates and this is what will happen to you.' Such stories were still being told in the eighteenth century, a time when mobility of labour was crucial and robust countryfolk were required to work in the new mills and factories. The tales of working-class pirates – female and male – may have reflected what the dominating forces wanted the potential labour force to know: that audacious *arrivistes* like Bonny and Read – or at least the idea of them – were not welcome in the new mill towns and cities.

Why have the legends of pirate women endured when the stories of other female criminals have long since faded from public memory? I suspect it is largely because of a fascination with the sea and with a milieu where all characters are seen as *picaresque* (unlike the homes, shops, lime quarries and woods that provide the setting for more ordinary land crimes). Women pirates also endure because of male obsessions with women whose interest is focused away from men. Women pirates such as Cheng I Sao and Lai Choi San were preoccupied by their work and did not need male attention, so men wanted them – or at least their mythologised selves. Women who behaved in this way had to be captured and their gaze adjusted; perhaps in writing about women robbers and transgressors, men were metaphorically taming them and restoring the approved balance.

Notes

1. Joan Scott, *Gender and the Politics of History*, Columbia University Press, 1988, p. 2.
2. Deidre Beddoe, *Discovering Women's History: a practical manual*, Pandora, 1983, p. 9.
3. Rudolf M. Dekker and Lotte C. van de Pol, *The Tradition of Female Transvestism in Early Modern Europe*, MacMillan, 1989.
4. Courts of admiralty trials at the Public Record Office, PRO, Co 137/14, x C18 757.
5. Captain Charles Johnson, *A General History of the Robberies and Murders of the Most Notorious Pyrates* (1724), published as Daniel Defoe, *A General History of the Pyrates*, Manuel Schonhorn (ed), Dent, 1972.
6. See David Cordingly and John Falconer, *Pirates: fact and fiction*, Collins & Brown, 1992, for good summaries of these.
7. They include Marcus Rediker, David Mitchell, David Cordingly and John Falconer. See 'Further Reading'.
8. Programme of the Amsterdam Summer University, 1993. I am grateful to Dian Murray for drawing this to my attention.
9. Christopher Lloyd, *The British Seaman 1200–1860: a social survey*, Paladin, 1970, p. 95.
10. Margaret Spufford, *Small Books and Pleasant Histories: popular fiction and its readership in seventeenth century England*, Methuen, 1981, p. 22.
11. *The Illustrated Police News*, 28 April 1883, p. 4. Thanks to Julie Wheelwright for showing me this reference.
12. Liz Stanley, *The auto/biographical I: the theory and practice of feminist auto/biography*, Manchester University Press, 1992.
13. Elizabeth Roberts, *A Woman's Place: an oral history of working-class women, 1890–1940*, Basil Blackwell, 1986.
14. Paul Thompson, *The Voice of the Past: oral history*, Oxford University Press, 1992.

15. Spufford, *op cit*, p. 12.
16. Peter Linebaugh, *The London Hanged: crime and civil society in the eighteenth century*, Allen Lane, The Penguin Press, 1991, p. 151.
17. *ibid*, p. 120.
18. *ibid*, p. 122.
19. Spufford, *op cit*, p. 22.
20. *ibid*, p. 221.
21. *ibid*, p. 51.
22. *ibid*, p. 9.
23. Jack Zipes, *Breaking the Magic Spell: radical theories of folk and fairy tales*, Heineman, 1983.

Section II:

Warrior women in command

5 Artemisia: adviser or Amazon?

Hyssop-haired and far from Cretan womb
you leave your widow's home and sail those seas.
Home you're rowed: victor-goddess-queen.
And when mothers mourn their oarsmen-boys
in inland orchards
what lie-scented song do you then sing?

This section explores the myths and lives of the early 'pirate queens': Artemisia, Alfhild and Grace O'Malley. Such women were born to privilege, often married to further consolidate their wealth and were powerful on land before they went to sea. In their times, plunder was not seen as an indefensible activity of outlaws, but as an almost reasonable practice.

But just because the sea warriors in this section were privileged does not mean that poor women without property were not sea warriors too. It is more a reflection of how history is recorded: people of noble birth are given more attention because the historian is usually of – or writing for – their social class (he is literate, and can arrange for his writing to be published); people who perform daring deeds in the role of leader are remembered whereas those who wash the plates are deemed too ordinary to record. In societies used to storytelling and mythology, gods and monsters, heroes and odysseys, women such as the pirate queens were an obvious focus, but may have been only a tiny part of the history of women's piracy. The women in these pages may be the exceptions that prove a rule – evidence that both women and men were involved in plundering on land and sea for as long as oceans have existed.

Artemisia, Queen of Halicarnassus, is the first recorded woman pirate. Sailing nearly 2,500 years ago, her name means 'spirit of Artemis' after the goddess renowned for independence, beauty and forcefulness. Artemisia, a wealthy woman in her middle years, captained a fighting ship in 480 BC, over four centuries before Christianity displaced the worship of beautiful and tyrannical gods and goddesses and 200 years after Sappho wrote loving poems about Greek women.

The sea at that time was still a crucial site of mythology. In different cultures, it was seen as an element made of menstrual blood or breast milk; a great womb chamber within an elemental mother-divinity that could give life to gods, monsters and mermaids; a place that could erupt into terrifying storms or smooth the way for favoured heroes, according to feminist readings of ancient myths.[1]

The waters round Greece, which Homer's epic poem *The Odyssey* had 300 years earlier evoked so richly, were a traditional site of monumental sea-battles and extraordinary events. Artemisia's story mirrors ideas of women as benign and bold protectors of men as well as destroyers. It was under the auspices of the goddess Athena, transformed into a sea eagle, that Odysseus came safely home from his ocean wanderings.[2] 'An inscription from the Greek island of Samos (just off the coast of present-day Turkey and still Greek) states clearly that in the 500s BC, plundering at sea was carried out with the approval of the goddess Hera, as well as with the consent of the state.'[3] Homer told also of wicked magic women, those of Cyrene (sirens) who lured Odysseus' sailors to the shallows where local Cyrenians pursued their trade as wreckers. The reality must have been that many coastal women – neither malign nor divine – were involved in sea-related work, as boat-owners and fishing people, sailors' and pirates' mothers and whores, quayside food-providers and shipboard service workers. But their history is absent.

Artemisia's experiences at sea are described in only one record: the story of her fight against the Greeks in the Battle of Salamis, a key battle in the Persian Wars in which she took a daring step to save herself – the kind of move a bold tactician, including a pirate, might attempt. Today this means that Artemisia has been given a place among women pirates, though it would probably be more correct to call her a naval leader, ship-owner and member of a ruling family. This transformation of a privileged but negligible widow into an Amazon heroine is a reflection of a particular male enthusiasm for, and fetishisation of, female ruthlessness. To regard Artemisia as a pirate also suggests moral confusion in which any woman who fights at sea becomes 'bad' and an outlaw. It is partly because she is operating in an ungovernable milieu which men have regarded as no fit place for a normal woman, and to place her as a 'pirate' – a lawless and glamorous reprobate – makes her easier to contain. It would be much more of a challenge to accept her as a relatively ordinary, if privileged person, who happened to be female and to use her competence and strategic judgement in sea-battle.

Artemisia is one of many women throughout history who have taken bold actions, including in battles, but she is not placed high in national myths or celebrated like Joan of Arc or Cleopatra, for example. Her relative invisibility means there is little danger of young Greek women watching Onassis vessels from waterfront cafes and asking, 'Well, if Artemisia can do it, why can't I?' Her sea action has not created a precedent, and the belated piratical tinge to her reputation has had no visible impact.

Herodotus, the main historian of the Greek area in that period, is the only source of our knowledge of Artemisia's fight at sea. Further details can only be guessed at from evidence of other Mediterranean women's lives at that time – be they priestesses depicted on urns or Frankincense-sellers referred to fleetingly in epic dramas and legal documents. Because Herodotus' records are so early and extensive, he has been called the 'Father of History',[1] a position that gives him a veneer of authority which should be treated with scepticism. Every history is just a collection of stories: and as some feminist historians have noted, history anyway is *his*-story, not *her*-story. Stories are told for a particular purpose; mythical ones are especially useful as a way of understanding the ideology of a period and societal preoccupations with power. But they cannot be taken at face value.

In describing Artemisia, Herodotus wrote as a male in a misogynist culture. But as a member of a wealthy family, coincidentally in Artemisia's native city, Halicarnassus, he was describing a leader of the power-holding group to which he belonged. His account necessarily reflects a view of the Persian Wars which suited the values and self-image of that group: had he wanted to criticise Queen Artemisia, he would have had to consider the social price he might be asked to pay.

Herodotus was born between 490 and 480 BC, so he was too young to have witnessed the Battle of Salamis first-hand, but instead drew up his account from what today would be called oral testimony. Aubrey de Selincourt, one of his translators, hazards that 'as a boy [he] listens to men who had sailed under Artemisia'.[5] Eyewitnesses 20 or more years after the event may well have garnished their narratives with battle glamour, designed to minimise humiliation and create a tale that fitted the ideology of the period, including the idea that any woman taking part in a war must be exceptional.

Herodotus wrote down hundreds of stories, with reed pen and ink made from lamp-black on rolls and rolls of papyrus. Commentators have since claimed that bits of his histories are fictional, bits partial and bits awry. More significantly for our purposes, there are things he did not see, or failed to see as important, including the daily round of women's lives. While assuring readers that the omission of women 'should not be taken as implying that Herodotus was anti-feminist',[6] K.H. Waters, a historian who analysed his work in the 1970s, points out, 'It is noticeable that a number of women who are prominent in minor episodes remain anonymous.'[7] This includes, for example, the woman whom one of the most important kings, Xerxes, adulterously loved.

So as we read about Artemisia, it is worth wondering, 'What would she have said about herself? Would other women have seen her as a pirate? Would non-privileged people have seen her as just another leader spending resources on yet another war? If pirates had not existed, what label would she have been given?'

Herodotus' story begins with Artemisia assuming the mantle of power from her dead husband. Then she decides to do something active herself instead of sitting at home watching the war.

On the death of her husband the sovereign power passed into her hands, and she sailed with the fleet in spite of the fact that she had a grown-up son and that there was consequently no necessity for her to do so. Her spirit of adventure and manly courage were her only incentives. She was the daughter of Lygdamis, a Halicarnassian; on her mother's side she was Cretan.[8]

Artemisia not only supplied five ships to the Persian effort to combat the Greeks but had a leading role in one of them. She made tactical decisions and was obeyed, despite being a woman commanding seafarers who were male (or women passing as male). 'She sailed in command of the men of Halicarnassus, Cos, Nisyra and Calydna, and furnished five ships of war. The places I mentioned as being under her rule are all Dorian...'[9]

Herodotus thought women in such roles were rare: 'It seems to me a most strange and interesting thing that she – a woman – should have taken part in the campaign against Greece...'[10] In keeping with other narratives about women pirates as much as 2,000 years later, her independence and confidence in her own judgement are subject to comment. She is praised by perhaps the greatest patriarch in her world: Xerxes (c.519–c.465 BC) who as king of Persia from around 485–65 BC invaded Greece, defeating the Spartans at Thermopylae in 480 BC. He withdrew from battle after his fleet was destroyed at Salamis. Xerxes visited the fleet at Phaleron

because he wished to talk to all the commanding officers and hear their opinions ... as they sat there in order of rank, Xerxes sent Mardonius [commander of the Persian infantry] to ask the opinion of each one about giving battle at sea ... the answers, with a single exception, were unanimously in favour of engaging with the Greek fleet: the exception was Artemisia. 'Mardonius' she said, 'tell the king for me that this is the answer I give – I, whose courage and achievements in the battles of Euboea were surpassed by none: say to him, "Master, my past services give me the right to advise you now upon the course which I believe to be most to your advantage."'[11]

She advised Xerxes at length against rushing into naval action, telling him that 'these people who are supposed to be your allies – these Egyptians, Cyprians, Cicilians, Pamphylians – are a useless lot.'[12] Such arguments sound as if they are based on strategic thinking rather than pacifism; Artemisia was a pragmatist: 'spare your ships and do not fight at sea, for the Greeks are as far superior to us in naval matters as men are to women.'[13] It appears from this male-authored statement that Artemisia saw herself as an honorary man, not as that 'inferior' thing, a woman. 'That Amazonian lady herself puts the view that men are far stronger – one thinks of that "weak woman" Elizabeth I – and this is no doubt of Greek origin, part of the Artemisia legend if not the original composition of Herodotus,' proposes Waters.[14]

According to Herodotus, other leading warriors in this sea-battle felt strong rivalry towards Artemisia.

> Artemisia's friends were dismayed when they heard this speech and thought that Xerxes would punish her for trying to dissuade him from battle; but those who were jealous of her standing among the most influential persons in the forces were delighted at the prospect of her ruin. However, when the other several answers to his question were reported to the king, he was highly pleased with Artemisia's; he had always considered her an admirable person, but now he esteemed her more than ever.[15]

Nevertheless, Xerxes ignored her advice and put to sea. In the ensuing battle at Salamis, a 36-square-mile island off the coast of Attica, west of the old port of Piraeus, Artemesia proved she could be ruthless. According to Herodotus: 'I must however mention Artemisia, on account of an exploit which still further increased her reputation with Xerxes. After the Persian fleet lost all semblance of order, Artemisia was chased by an Athenian trireme.' (A trireme is a war galley propelled by three banks of oars, so Artemisia could have been facing a ship powered by about 60 rowers. Such ships could do eight or nine knots – sea miles per hour – and were armed with long rams. Sometimes a few archers and soldiers were carried.)[16]

> As her ship happened to be closest to the enemy and there were other friendly ships just ahead of her, escape was impossible. In this awkward situation she hit on a plan which turned out greatly to her advantage: with the Athenian close on her tail she drove ahead with all possible speed and rammed one of her friends – a

ship of Calynda, with Damasithymus, the Calyndian king, on board. I cannot say if she did this because of some quarrel she had had with this man while the fleet was in Hellespont, or if it was just chance that that particular vessel was in her way; but in any case she rammed and sank her, and was lucky enough, as a result, to reap a double benefit.

For the captain of the Athenian trireme, on seeing her ram an enemy, naturally supposed that her ship was a Greek one, or else a deserter which was fighting on the Greek side; so he abandoned the chase and turned to attack elsewhere. That then was one piece of luck – that she escaped with her life; the other was that, by this very act she raised herself higher than ever in Xerxes' esteem [because bystanders including Xerxes assumed that it was an enemy ship she had sunk]. She was indeed lucky in every way – not least in the fact that there were no survivors from the Calyndian ship to accuse her.[17]

It is revealing that Artemisia is not criticised by Herodotus for ramming a ship from her own side. In common with other heroines of pirate stories, she is not called ruthless or a traitor. Nor is she derided with the kind of comments made today about the steering ability of women drivers: she is instead credited as a fine tactician.

Herodotus' next statement indicates that courage was seen as a male characteristic, not a female one. 'Xerxes' comment on what was told him is said to have been: "My men have turned into women, my women into men." '[18] Herodotus also implies that because she was a woman, some of the other leaders on both sides wanted desperately to outdo or overcome her. Among the Athenians, Ameinias of Pallene, one of the great leaders,

gave chase to Artemisia, and if he had known that Artemisia was on board, he would never have abandoned the chase until he had either taken her or been taken himself; for the Athenians resented the fact that a woman should appear in arms against them, and the ships' captains had received special orders about her, with the offer of a reward of 10,000 drachmae for anyone who captured her alive.[19]

She escaped. Ten thousand drachmae is approximately £300,000 in today's money,[20] a reflection of the extent of the gender divide in Athenian society, where expressions of male power ranged from plays ridiculing husbands who were under their wives' thumbs to laws which enabled fathers to marry off daughters to preserve family property.[21] Xerxes may have had an unusual respect for women or may just have decided that Artemisia gave sound or convenient advice (even though he had not taken it). He again sought her opinion on strategy: 'During the debate it occurred to him that it would be just as well to send for Artemisia to take part in the discussion, as she on a previous occasion had been the only one to give him sound advice.'[22] He asked her if he should follow Mardonius' counsel and attack the Peloponnese, the strategically crucial, mulberry-leaf-shaped Greek peninsula joined to the mainland by the tiny isthmus of Corinth. That attack would, he felt, enable his Persian troops to prove their worth. The alternative was that he allowed Mardonius to lead an expedition of 300,000 men while he, Xerxes, returned home. Artemisia advised him to take the latter course.

> Artemisia's advice was most agreeable to Xerxes, for it was the expression of his own thoughts. Personally, I do not think he would have stayed in Greece, had all his counsellors, men and women alike, urged him to do so – he was much too badly frightened. As it was he complimented Artemisia and sent her off to Ephesus with his sons – some of his bastards which had accompanied him on the expedition. To look after these children he also sent Hermontimus, his chief eunuch.[23]

On that motherly land-based note, Herodotus ends the story of Artemisia. There is no information about what she did at Ephesus, or whether Xerxes ever found out she had sunk an ally's ship, or whether she sought other opportunities for warfare at sea or on land.

If we look at the lives of other women of the period, as well as at the mythology of the time, we can develop a fuller picture of the kind of person Artemisia was. Some things must be guessed at: whether she was dark or fair, plump or thin, excitable or dignified. What was her voice like as she shouted commands to the people who sailed her vessel? Were her feet bare on the salty deck? Did she wear any sort of armour or sword?

Whether or not Artemisia was wearing men's clothes aboard ship, she had symbolically put on her husband's mantle of power. From records of wealthy women's sacrifices to Artemis, we know something about the clothes women of her class wore on land: a frog-green robe of silk covered by a white cape with an embroidered design on the border and a girdle, ivory earrings and gold and emerald rings.[24] Herodotus does not record the weather in which her sea-battle took place, but usual conditions in these waters suggest the sun warming her and the wind draggling her hair as she rammed the Calyndian ship. Being at sea might have been a great and unusual pleasure, the battle a thrill, or too tense a situation to be enjoyed.

Although no specific references to the women of Halicarnassus are available, documents collected by women historians reveal that privileged women in Athens at the time were educated and were skilled managers who supervised their slaves' weaving and their bread makers' baking. They appear to have spent time with friends, to have had lovers (dildoes have been found, too) and to have sought out entertainment, including music. Artemisia may have lived with friends, children, relatives. She had at least one adult son, who could have had children himself. Her life may have been a lively one in a house full of people including a number of servants. If recently widowed, she may have set off with the Persian fleet in some kind of mourning regalia, leaving behind a house sprinkled with drops of seawater and then hyssop. Women were usually disbarred from the public mourning rituals at the time,[25] which would have meant an uneasy grieving period. Or she may have been relishing life and rule without her husband. When she went to sea she would have had to leave whatever governing work there was – under Persian rule – to leaders with whom she would have had a complex relationship, as monarch but woman.

Where did Artemisia get the idea that she could command fighting ships and the social permission to do so? She grew up within a culture where 'traditions subordinating women were powerful but not all powerful', one that contained 'images and beliefs that gloried and empowered the female. In addition, exceptional circumstances occasionally allowed women of unusual ability to rise to prominence in fields usually reserved for men.'[26] Her mother was from the island of Crete, and Cretan women around 450 BC 'appear to have more independence' in law than Athenian women.[27] Following divorce or the death of a husband, women could keep the possessions they had brought with them, while heiresses had some degree of choice over whom they married. Artemisia also inherited the local 'woman warrior' tradition, especially that of Amazon women, who battled with men. These women were supposed to have besieged Athens in c.1200 BC, and the stories and vignettes of them in *The Iliad* have had a lasting effect.[28]

Named after the Amazonian moon-goddess Artemis/Diana, the hunter, Artemisia grew up in the knowledge that her namesake was one of the most important gods worshipped (along with Demeter, Cybele and Isis) in the Mediterranean area. The women priests of these cults had legitimate power – 'freed from the restrictions which confined ordinary women, priestesses shared the supernatural power accorded goddesses'[29] – before Christianity displaced this culture. In Sparta the name Artemis meant cutter or butcher; in Attica the goddess was 'ritually propitiated with drops of blood drawn from a man's neck by a sword, a symbolic remnant of former beheadings'.[30] In most myths, women of Artemisia's age – probably between 35 and 60 and past their fertile years – stand mythologically as the waning moon or destroying crone.[31] But as Artemis the goddess was seen as a patroness of nurture, fertility and birth, it may be that a mixture of these two ideas – crone and goddess – influenced the telling of the Artemisia story. The goddess connection may have predisposed seafarers and Herodotus to see her as a victorious and creative leader who protected their side rather than to deride her as an ageing fool.

As Queen of Halicarnassus, Artemisia was part of a network of people with economic, social and political power. Her grandson Lygdamis was 'a despot' who allegedly sent Herodotus into exile at Samos. Her parents or parents-in-law (her husband's name is not mentioned so we can only speculate as to whether her power was patrilineal or matrilineal) presumably had authority.

In these early cultures, strong women more often gained power by using their intelligence and their dynastic and familial connections to become rulers in their own right. Particularly in periods of political transition and uncertainty, inheritance of the throne even by a female seemed preferable to civil war and disorder.[32]

Because of her privilege Artemisia may well have been able to move around and take part in public life in a way that was possible for few other women. As Halicarnassus was under the rule of the Persian dynasty, she could have fought on the Persian side as a way of establishing herself following the death of her husband rather than as a powerful woman choosing political allegiances out of conviction.

No record exists of Artemisia involving herself in seafaring prior to the Persian Wars, and the story of these few weeks of her life is not told in a context of other women's bravery at sea. The nearest similar event took place in the fifth century BC in Sparta, when women on land took up arms under a privileged woman's leadership. Sparta was reaching the height of its power and was soon to defeat Athens in the Peloponnesian War (431-04 BC) to become the most powerful city state in Greece. Poet Telesilla, 'daughter of a famous house', led a fight by younger women to hold off Cleomenes, king of the Spartans, who was trying to take Argos, an important city 28 miles south of Corinth that had dominated the Peloponnese in the seventh century BC. The women took up arms, stood on the battlements and repulsed not only Cleomenes but also King Demartus.

To defeat Spartans, who were trained for war from an early age and taught to be indifferent to pain and death, was a significant feat for any warriors, whatever their sex. But the festivities that surrounded the commemoration of the event suggested that people believed that in their bravery the women were behaving like men – and were impertinent to boot – while the defeated men were like women: 'on the anniversary of [the battle] they celebrate even to this day the "festival of impudence", at which they clothe the women in men's shirts and cloaks, and the men in women's robes and veils', observed Plutarch 600 years after the event.[33]

Artemisia was not a pirate in the sense that she plundered ships to satisfy her own ends, but only in so much as she worked as a warrior at sea, bent on beating other vessels. Yet today she is judged not as a naval commander, but as an Amazon or virago,[34] an interpretation that demonstrates how judgements about job descriptions are coloured by ideas about gender. Had she been a man, Artemisia would have been remembered as a minor sea commander who behaved with an unremarkable mix of caution and audacity in pursuit of political victory.

Artemisia had successors. In 230 BC the Illyrian queen Teuta sanctioned a number of piratical attacks against Rome, including in one case against Roman envoys. She 'personally accompanied her Illyrian warriors on their raids, and directed them'.[35] Teuta was 'forced to sign a demeaning treaty in which she promised payment of tribute, the abandonment of piracy by her people, and the release of all Greek cities under Illyrian control.'[36]

Nearly 2,000 years later, a woman who is similarly treated as heroic, extraordinary and almost piratical, Admiral Lascarina Bouboulina (1771–1845), emerged. Bouboulina, whose 'name is synonymous with female courage and heroism', according to guide books to her home island of Spetsai,[37] was not a pirate but a sea warrior. Like Artemisia, she was a mother (of six children and three step-children). And as a woman who acquired sea skills and vessels from her father and two husbands – both killed by pirates – she fought with verve and ruthlessness in the War of Independence. She may have got her title because fleets from each Greek island had commanders or captains who called themselves admirals,[38] rather than having it conferred on her by naval authorities.

Spetsai was one of the main bases of naval operations throughout the war [39] and Bouboulina's reputation for breathtaking daring rests on several stories. When she was building her fleet, she had potential informants deported and bribed investigators to keep her operations secret. In appealing against later confiscation of these vessels by the Ottoman Empire in 1814, she bypassed the sultan and appealed directly to his mother, Valide Hanoum, 'whom she so impressed by her proud bearing and eloquence that the sultan guaranteed Bouboulina's right to her inheritance.'[40]

Eight ships which she commanded from her flagship the *Agamemnon* (the largest corvette in the Greek fleet) blockaded Nafplion in 1821. After 18 months the Turkish garrison there surrendered but Bouboulina was also involved in helping to supply the Greek forces surrounding the Ottoman administrative centre of the Peloponnesos, Tripolis. Then she committed an act that could be interpreted as treacherous and greedy, or as a recognition of other women's difficulties:

The Ottoman commander, Khurshid Pasha, was away fighting Ali Pasha in Yannina, but the ladies of the harem were besieged in Tripolis. When they heard of Bouboulina's arrival outside the Ottoman camp they begged her to take pity on them, offering their jewellery for safe conduct to Kurshid Pasha. Bouboulina accepted the offer and, at the beginning of October when the town fell, ensured that the harem escaped the ensuing massacre ... Bouboulina has been accused of greed and self-interest for the bargain.[41]

These high-profile and controversial figures suggest still more interesting stories to be uncovered. How were these brave and competent female warriors similar or dissimilar to the thousands of unrecorded women boat-owners, fisherwomen, sailors and perhaps pirates in one of the world's greatest seafaring regions?

Notes

1. Barbara Walker, *The Women's Encylopedia of Myths and Secrets*, HarperSan Francisco, 1983, especially entry on the goddess Mari, p.584.
2. For a useful discussion of this see Marina Warner, *Monuments and Maidens: the allegory of the female form*, Picador, 1987, pp.94-103.
3. Ralph T. Ward, *Pirates in History*, York Press, 1974, p.21.
4. For example, see K.H. Waters in *Herodotus the Historian, his problems, methods and originality*, Croom Helm, 1985.
5. Herodotus, *The Histories*, Book Eight, translated by Aubrey de Selincourt, Penguin, 1972, p.14.
6. Waters, *op cit*, p.129.
7. *ibid*, p.129.
8. Herodotus, *op cit*, p.474.
9. *ibid*, p.474.
10. *ibid*, p.474.
    ibid, pp.545-6.
11. Waters (*op cit*, p.139) suggests that this idea of an adviser borrows from epic drama, as well as being authentic. 'The "wise adviser" is said to be a figure from tragedy – which does not automatically exclude his or her appearance in real life.' So although the *story* of Artemisia may be helped by the existence of such a role, it may also have been true.

12. Herodotus, *op cit*, pp.545-6.

13. *ibid*, p.546.

14. Waters, *op cit*, pp.129-30.

15. Herodotus, *op cit*, p.546.

16. Peter Kemp (ed), *The Oxford Companion to Ships and the Sea*, Oxford University Press, 1992, p.890.

17. Herodotus, *op cit*, p.552.

18. *ibid*, p.553.

19. *ibid*, p.554.

20. A drachma, on what was the Euboean standard, weighed the same as a silver Swiss franc. One drachma was the top wage for a day's heavy or skilled manual work. An oarsman might get such a wage. By contrast, the most popular flute girls got paid one obol for an evening's entertainment (there were six obols to the drachma). Herodotus, *op cit*, p.36 (introduction by A.R. Burn).

21. Mary R. Lefkowitz and Maureen B. Fant, *Women's Life in Ancient Greece and Rome, a source book in translation*, Duckworth, 1982, p.20. For a general discussion of Greek women's authority today, by contrast, see Jill Dubisch (ed), *Gender and Power in Rural Greece*, Princeton University Press, 1986.

22. Herodotus, *op cit*, p.557.

23. *ibid*, p.558. Ephesus, just 30 miles SSE of modern Turkey, is the site of Artemis' majestic temple, one of the seven wonders of the world, looted and burned by Christians just after 406 AD, after fourth-century orator St John Chrystotom preached against her as part of a Christian campaign to vilify the cult of the goddess. He was deposed as Patriarch of Constantinople by the Empress Eudoxia, whom he angered. (Walker, *op cit*, p.60.) Ephesus was also a place where eunuchs were sold, so the eunuch might have come from there. A Chian called Panonius, 'made his living by the abominable trade of castrating any good looking boys he could get hold of and taking them down to Sardis or Ephesus, where he sold them at a high price – for it is a fact that in eastern countries eunuchs are valued as being especially trustworthy in every way.' (Herodotus, *op cit*, p.558.)

24. Lefkowitz and Fant, *op cit*, p.120.

25. *ibid*, p.35.

26. Bonnie S. Anderson and Judith P. Zinsser, *A History of Their Own, women in Europe from prehistory to the present*, vol. 1, Penguin, 1988, p.52.

27. Lefkowitz and Fant, *op cit*, p. 33.

28. See 'The Amazons of Ancient Athens' in Mandy Merck, *Perversions: deviant readings*, Virago, 1993, pp.121-61 for an interesting feminist discussion of Amazons and patriarchal ideology which summarises the main arguments about the legends, from Johann Jacob Bachofen to Joan Bamberger. For Amazon origin theories, see Susan Cavin, *Lesbian*

Origins, ism press, 1985, pp.63-81. It has a useful bibliography, including cross-cultural references.

29. Anderson and Zinsser, *op cit*, p.54.
30. Walker, *op cit*, p.58, citing among others Graves, *Greek Myths* 1.86; 2.79.
31. Walker, *ibid*, p.187.
32. Anderson and Zinsser, *op cit*, p.57.
33. Lefkowitz and Fant, *op cit*, p.21, citing Plutarch, *Moralia*, 245c-f, 2 AD, translated by F.C. Babbitt.
34. For example by Waters, *op cit*.
35. Ward, *op cit*, pp.34-5.
36. *ibid*, p.34.
37. Andrew Thomas, *Spetsai*, Lycabettus Press, Athens, 1980, p.8. Thanks to Brigit Davin for drawing this to my attention.
38. *ibid*, p.10.
39. *ibid*, p.63.
40. *ibid*, pp.63-4.
41. *ibid*, pp.63-4.

6 Arms and amours: Alfhild

Casting off from my snake chamber,
I sail with you in sable.
Maidens all, our shields shine and we
tack and win, then lose to anxious princes.
And now?
My sovereignty, packed in ice,
bleeds in the bay.
But my rudder, safely cured in kelp
awaits my daughter's bear-brave hand.

After Artemisia, no woman pirate appears in the records for 1,000 years. Then comes Alfhild, a Dane who sailed in the mid-fifth century AD. Like Artemisia, Alfhild was a privileged warrior rather than a pirate, a fairytale princess not a crook who happened to work at sea. But to conquer enemies, to defeat others, could be seen as theft: of their lives, their ships and their right to fight for a cause. Using this definition, coupled with the male tendency to create a pirate figure out of any combative woman maritime leader, we can see why Alfhild is included in pirate history. A feminist categorisation might place her as a cross-dressed woman sea warrior.

I discovered the first clue to Alfhild's existence in Boston stationer Charles Ellms' 1837 *The Pirates Own Book*[1] in the National Maritime Museum library in Greenwich. There I found a picture of 'Alwilda the

Danish Female Pirate' and a page about her. The original source was Saxo Grammaticus, who wrote the main text on Danish history, *Gesta Danorum* (Deeds of the Danes)[2] in the twelfth century. I could find no 'Alwilda' in the index to this work, and was about to give her up as a figment of a pirate-admirer's imagination, until I discovered she was spelt 'Alfhild' and was part of a Norse Amazon tradition.

Finding a way to understand such a phenomenon is difficult. What did she look like, smell like, feel like? How did she view her role? What would she and the other women have done on their ship? Did they menstruate in sync, did they have erotic relationships with each other? Did they learn sea skills together through trial and error? Was it a pleasure to be a Danish pirate or just a cold job with lean pickings? And ashore – would they languish on furry couches swigging stolen brandy or labour in cold forests hacking up more wood for their next voyage?

Saxo Grammaticus' writings offer no details of the experience of seafaring for these women and little that seems authentic about women's daily lives over a 1,200-year period. Instead, he tells of troll women who inspired whales to attack big boats; giantesses like versions of the Three Fates who bestowed gifts at Sleeping Beauty's christening; witches through whose bent arm someone making the right sign could spot a disguised god. As well as stories insisting that women are wicked and possess superhuman abilities, other tales almost deny their existence. Many heroes born from the gods were motherless or not-born, that is delivered by Caesarean section, like Macduff. This suggests that men felt so uneasy about women and their seemingly magical ability to reproduce that they preferred to pretend that males were capable of doing everything for themselves.

Nanna Damsholt, a feminist historian who specialises in medieval Danish women, believes that Alfhild – and shield maidens and other Amazons in Saxo's work – are 'pure fiction.'

Of course, no one can prove that female pirates or soldiers were non-existent, but I think they are men's imaginations. And as images I think they have meant a lot to people to whom these stories were told. So I think they are important not as examples of real persons but as impressive fictional characters. People in the Middle Ages did not distinguish as we do between myth and history.[3]

Saxo Grammaticus' account of Alfhild's life, then, has to be read in a particular way – as an interesting myth that reveals a man's desire to explore women who adventure, in male clothing, at sea; women who briefly choose 'arms not amours' (as his nineteenth-century translator has it). His book was written at the request of the Danish archbishop Absalon and its author saw it as a way of serving his country. In practice, Nanna Damsholt says, 'It functioned as propaganda for the Danish monarchy internally, as well as [being] a demonstration of Denmark's high cultural level which entitled it to a high rank in continental society.'[4] Saxo's long accounts, which mix up many periods, stretch from the first Danish King Dan to his own king, Canute VI. The volume in which Alfhild's story is told, Book Eight, is pivotal, Damsholt argues, because one of its main themes is the struggle between female and male supremacy. It deals with a period before Christianity, a time which Saxo would have been interested in portraying negatively as pagan and long-gone. In Book Eight:

> a number of women are powerful, trying to gain or actually gaining power. Female power seems to be a threatening possibility, coinciding with the appearance of other destructive forces in life such as darkness, famine and greed – and so women have to be thwarted as proof of progress, and as an example that patriarchal Christian power must prevail over women's wild ways.[5]

Saxo quotes maxims derived from Icelandic sagas and North Teutonic law which indicate the constraints limiting the possibility of women's piracy – for instance, 'it is disgraceful to be ruled by a woman'; a widow who marries her husband's slayer is bad, whatever her economic or emotional needs. He lists many significant customs: kings who were challenged to fight or to hand over their daughters; marriage by purchase; dowry systems; and 'in most instances the father or brother betrothed the girl, and she consented to their choice'.[6] Female captives were enslaved and put into brothels in one period. Independent action was limited.[7]

Saxo's story tells that Alfhild, the daughter of a Goth King, took to sea-roving after spurning a suitor. She first joined a ship of other cross-dressed women 'pirates', by implication fierce and untraditional, and was at some point elected by male pirates to be leader of their vessel.

The story closes on her – forcibly un-trousered – marrying Alf, the man she had been led to despise, and leaving her seafaring command to bear his daughter. Significantly, her fate is echoed by that of Groa, Alfhild's attendant on ship, who leaves to marry Alf's comrade.

In a seafaring area like Denmark there must occasionally have been women who slipped away to sea, and Alfhild's story offers an example of one way it might have been done – by a privileged lady. But Saxo's (unillustrated) text gives us no way of visualising Alfhild, if she even existed. The story's logic implies that she was in her late teens or early 20s; we could surmise that any seafarer in the North Sea, Baltic or Atlantic would have weathered, ruddy skin. Descriptions of life in that period suggest that as someone from a wealthy background she would have worn ermine, black or white fox, sable or squirrel. Her diet might have consisted of broth, rye bread, cheese, whale, seal or Polar-bear meat, washed down with beer or wine and accompanied by berries, apple or hazelnuts; sometimes meat in that region was preserved with whey or salt extracted from kelp.[8] A seafarer's eyesight needs to be sharp for navigation, so we might guess that this once-gentle maiden would have developed a direct gaze; looking out and at life rather than passively being beheld.[9] And she may have been long enough at sea to learn to walk with the rolling gait mariners develop to cope with the ship's movement. We might also deduce that she was either uncurvaceous or thickly enough clad to be assumed to be a youth. Or else we could ask, 'why is this a repeated fantasy: that a woman pirate could be mistaken for a male?'

The portrait of Alfhild (plate 2) is an engraving from an 1844 version of Ellms' book and demonstrates a nineteenth-century (presumably male) illustrator's response to a nineteenth-century male writer's text. North American and European marketing requirements must have demanded that Alfhild appear elegant and ungrotesque. Her tall slim body and long sword insist that she is a tough woman who can thrillingly dominate; a 'phallic woman'. The caption emphasises that she is exceptional: 'Remarkable Instance of Female Courage.'

Saxo Grammaticus' writings, by contrast, dwell on Alfhild's social position, contextualising her through her family and girlhood. A powerful early part of the long story suggests that the young Alfhild internalised the idea that she was responsible for men's sexual behaviour and that she must not incite their lust.

Sigar . . . had sons Siwald, Alf, and Alger, and a daughter, Signe.
Alf excelled the rest in spirit and beauty, and devoted himself to
the business of a rover. Such grace was shed on his hair, which
had a wonderful dazzling glow, that his locks seemed to shine
silvery. At the same time, Siward, the king of the Goths, is said to
have had two sons, Wemund and Osten, and a daughter Alfhild,
who showed almost from her cradle such faithfulness to modesty,
that she continually kept her face muffled in her robe, lest she
should cause her beauty to provoke the passion of another.[10]

Siward, Alfhild's father, wanted his daughter to remain an unsexual
young woman with her hymen intact. This obsession with virginity
was tied to property: wealthy men wanted to be sure that their heirs
were really their children and not the sons of any other man. In
different periods, virginity has been valued as something which would
make a father's property – a daughter – more marketable to potential
husbands. Saxo writes:

Her father banished her into very close keeping, and gave her a
viper and a snake to rear, wishing to defend her chastity by the
protection of these reptiles when they came to grow up. For it
would have been hard to pry into her chamber when it was barred
by so dangerous a bolt. He also enacted that if any man tried to
enter it and failed, he must straightway yield his head to be taken
off and impaled on a stake. The terror that was thus attached to
wantonness chastened the heated spirits of the young men. Then
Alf, the son of Sigar, thinking that the peril of the attempt only
made it the nobler, declared himself a wooer, and was told to
subdue the beasts that kept watch beside the room of the
maiden.[11]

This close guarding of Alfhild as potential reproducer, her chamber
symbolising her womb, stands in marked contrast to her later freedom
as captain of her own free-roving chamber/womb: her marauding
pirate ship. The guardians of her girlhood chamber are snakes, phallic
objects given her by her father. Yet she is expected to bring these to
manhood; her nurture will make them potent when fully developed.
So symbolically it was the males that Alfhild had mothered which then

protected her from the attacking maleness her father feared. But Alf did not win the victory he wanted. Siward proved remarkably respectful of his daughter's wishes – or perhaps he was obstructing the courting process in order to gain greater profit later. On Alf's appeal for Alfhild, in any case:

> Siward answered that he would accept that man only for his daughter's husband of whom she made a free and decided choice. None but the girl's mother was stiff against the wooer's suit; and she privately spake to her daughter in order to search her mind. The daughter warmly praised her suitor for his valour; whereon the mother upbraided her sharply, that her chastity should be unstrung, and she captivated by charming looks; and because, forgetting to judge his virtue, she cast the gaze of a wanton mind upon the faltering lures of beauty.[12]

What follows sounds like an extraordinary and traumatic transformation, even a breakdown. Suddenly the exceedingly shy, obedient and closeted young woman, who is attracted to this man, changes character. 'Thus Alfhild was led to despise the young Dane; whereupon she exchanged woman's for man's attire, and, no longer the most modest of maidens, began the life of a warlike rover. Having also enrolled in her service many maidens who were of the same mind . . .'[13]

We are not told of the family response to their good daughter suddenly cross-dressing, fighting and risking death, but certainly any resistance did not curtail her career. How did she set up the opportunity? How was the ship financed? How did she find the other like-minded 'maidens'? Such unanswerable questions suggest that we are in the realm of myth. But if Alfhild's companions were real, they would most likely have been the persevering daughters of landed parents or lower-born women who had become wanderers and were responsible to no one. Nanna Damsholt discovered that in Saxo:

> women seldom appear in groups except in one case: women as shield maidens. These girls live in chastity, and in a wish to be free of men. This is regarded as a provocation towards society, and in line with this the female warriors in Saxo's work are punished, in most cases by getting the worst of it from men. We

are not told much about [them] . . . but the whole idea has as its premise the will to stick together . . . it is not without intention that Saxo's shield maidens are ridiculed. He seems to know that the worst threat to patriarchy is sister-solidarity.[14]

The women's banding together is soon displaced by the story of Alfhild being elected a leader of men. The telling negates any idea that this company of female pirates had much long-term significance: while with the young women, Alfhild 'happened to come to a spot where a band of rovers were lamenting the death of their captain who had been lost in war; they made her their rover-captain for her beauty, and she did deeds beyond the valour of woman.'[15]

Again, the story seems implausible. No seafarer trying to make a living would choose a leader on the basis of appearance rather than ability to deliver booty, to command and to navigate. Yet Alfhild is shown not just to have been involved in a one-off venture, but commanding a pirate ship for perhaps months, committing several successful raids. Saxo also confuses the sequence of events: her crew of male rovers has disappeared by the time of her final venture in the ship full of women pirates. Indeed, her career as captain is given just a few words, and the account dwells more fully on her traditional female role of being wooed by a valiant man of the right caste, her rejected suitor Alf.

Alf made many toilsome voyages in pursuit of her, and in winter happened to come on a fleet of the Blackmen. The waters were at this time frozen hard, and the ships were caught in such a mass of ice, that they could not get on by the most violent rowing. But the continued frost promised the prisoners a safer way of advance; and Alf ordered his men to try the frozen surface of the sea in their brogues after they had taken off their slippery shoes, so that they could run over the level ice more steadily. The Blackmen supposed that they were taking flight with all the nimbleness of their heels, and began to fight them; but their steps tottered exceedingly and they gave back, the slippery surface making their footing uncertain. But the Danes crossed the frozen sea with safer steps and foiled the feeble advance of the enemy, whom they conquered, and then turned and sailed to Finland. Here they chanced to enter a rather narrow gulf, and, on sending a few men to reconnoitre they learned that the harbour was being held by a few ships.

For Alfhild had gone before them with her fleet into the same narrows. And when she saw the strange ships afar off, she rowed in swift haste forward to encounter them, thinking it better to attack the foe than to await them. Alf's men were against his attacking so many ships with so few; but he replied that it would be shameful if anyone should report to Alfhild that his desire to advance could be checked by a few ships in the path; for he said that their record of honours ought not to be tarnished by such a trifle.[16]

Alf thereby put his concern to impress the woman he desired ahead of the logistics of sea warfare (but was magically rewarded for his vanity).

the Danes wondered not a little whence their enemies got such grace of bodily beauty and such supple limbs. So, when they began the sea-fight, the young man Alf leapt on Alfhild's prow, and advanced towards the stern, slaughtering all that withstood him. His comrade Borgar struck off Alfhild's helmet, and, seeing the smoothness of her chin, saw that he must fight with kisses and not with arms; that the cruel spears must be put away, and the enemy handled with gentler dealings.

So Alf rejoiced that the woman whom he had sought over land and sea in the face of so many dangers was now beyond all expectations in his power; whereupon he took hold of her eagerly, and made her change her man's apparel to a woman's; and afterwards begot on her a daughter, Gurid. Also Borgar wedded the attendant of Alfhild, Groa, and had by her a son, Harald.[17]

This ending may have seemed a fairytale conclusion to Saxo: unproblematic capture of princess by prince, her abandonment of her career and male persona followed by proof of her equally unproblematic fertility. In fact, it tells of attack, stripping, rape and forcible destruction of her independence and choice of lifestyle. Off with the breeches, on with the pinafore. Sea-roving was a temporary lapse, a pre-marital adventure – even a titillation. The heterosexual balance is restored among these scions of the aristocracy.

The underlying fable is all too familiar: wild woman tamed. But whatever the improbability of the ostensible story, certain elements at least are based on fact. First, piracy did exist in this region and was well recorded several hundred years later in the Viking period (780–1070). Pirates travelled only short distances, specialising in small-scale local attacks on buildings rather than on ships, which meant there may have been more opportunity for women to be aboard. One brief reference claims that while no women took part in expeditions to the Atlantic or Mediterranean, women were on ships in the North Sea and the Baltic.[18] The relative ease with which short-term childcare and domestic duties could have been undertaken by a substitute would have made short trips a more real possibility than a six-month journey. Looting on land also meant that women companions could be left in safety on board.

Later sea plundering developed into large-scale, long-distance pillaging by gangs headed by captains with ferocious names such as Eric Bloodaxe, Harald Bluetooth, Swein Forkbeard, Bjorn Ironside. 'Danes and Norwegians ravaged the coasts of England, Scotland, France, Spain, North Africa and Italy . . . The overriding impression is one of traditional, full-blooded piracy – fire, slaughter, rape, loot, orgy, fierce and exultant irresponsibility.'[19] The causes of the flourishing of piracy include poverty, greed, habits of violence, opportunism and available targets. 'Scholars have proposed a four-fold classification of Viking adventures as developing from more or less random pirate raids to politically motivated expeditions, colonizing enterprises and commercial expansion; and have suggested overpopulation and famine as possible causes of the Scandinavian breakout,' David Mitchell points out.[20]

To Norse (North) seafarers, 'refugees from a stark land and a utility culture, "the West" was an Eldorado as lust-inflaming as the kingdom of the Incas to the boorish *conquistadores*.'[21] Not only did these marauders ransack extraordinarily wealthy targets, especially European monasteries such as Lindisfarne for gold, jewels, and finest brocades, they even stole the mundane but useful: horses from Loire and Thameside farms. But any economic motives for Alf and Alfhild's ventures are covered by a cloak of romanticism rather than exposed as a desperate struggle for material gain.

Nor was piracy seen as shocking, which may explain why no protest by Alfhild's parents is registered.

> In those days, trade and piracy went hand in hand. We should try to adjust our view of these matters to the standards of morality of the time . . . this was an age when everyone was his own master, when the power of the state was unknown and unchallenged . . . Imagine a ship on the open sea which had managed to survive several storms and on which provisions were desperately short: would not a raid on the nearest coast seem an urgent and obvious necessity? Or again, perhaps a fully laden ship appears in view: it is much easier to plunder this ship than to go south in search of goods. Each ship was a self-contained military unit, and the issue between peaceful commerce and sudden war was decided on the spur of the moment.[22]

References by male narrators to women being on board Scandinavian pirate ships could not necessarily be expected, for all the reasons discussed in Section I. But there is one other story of a woman on ship, primarily as a queen but also as a sea warrior. A French book from the 1930s, *Les Femmes pirates*,[23] describes Sigrid the Superb in the same mythical way as Saxo does, although without naming the original source. Operating in Sweden in 1000 AD, some 500 years after Alfhild, this 'fiery' woman was 'head of a group of unsatisfied subjects who ceaselessly harassed the king' – Erik, who had married then abandoned her. 'Sigrid the Superb knew how to battle on land and sea. Several one-time kings of Norway who dreamed of regaining their lands sought her hand in marriage. The fact that she burnt one of her suitors as unworthy tells us something about her.'[24]

In a sleight of major diplomatic manouevring to secure the lands she wanted when King Erik of Sweden died, Queen Sigrid tried to organise Olof, the king of Norway, into a marriage with her, and went to Kongfeld to see him for this purpose. However, he demanded that she become a Christian, which sparked an argument in which King Olof slapped her. 'She promises to kill him. He orders she be thrown into the sea.' Somehow this did not happen. Instead she married

Suenon, the future king of Denmark, and organised an alliance against Olof which included Sigrid's son by Erik and a group of rebellious Norwegians opposed to their king. Sigrid ordered a heavily armed group of ships to be prepared and then lay in wait for Olof's return from Vandal country, to which he thought he had a right. 'Sigrid's boat draws alongside Olof's and her sailors board; Sigrid appears on deck brandishing a weapon. Olof understands that all is lost and throws himself into the sea. Vengeance is done.'[25] The outcome of Sigrid's sea-battle, the Battle of Swoelderoe, was that the victors divided Norway among themselves, with Sigrid receiving the entire southern area.

Like Alfhild, Sigrid was a leader. But despite Nanna Damsholt's reservations, might there not have been bands of female buccaneers in the pagan period before Christianity imposed timidity on women? Saxo certainly wanted to persuade his readers that women pirates were not impossible:

> that no one may wonder that this sex laboured at warfare, I will make a brief digression, in order to give an account of the estate and character of such women. There were once women among the Danes who dressed themselves to look like men, and devoted almost every instant of their lives to the pursuit of war, that they might suffer their valour to be unstrung or dulled by the infection of luxury. For they abhorred all dainty living, and used to harden their minds and bodies with toil and endurance. They put away all the softness and lightmindedness of women, and inured their womanish spirit to masculine ruthlessness. They sought, more-over, so zealously to be skilled in warfare, that they might have been thought to have unsexed themselves.

> Those especially, who had either force of character or tall and comely persons, used to enter on this kind of life. These women, therefore (just as if they had forgotten their natural estate, and preferred sternness to soft words) offered war rather than kisses, and would rather taste blood than busses, and went about the business of arms more than that of amours. They devoted those hands to the lance which they should rather have applied to the loom. They assailed men with their spears whom they could have

melted with their looks, they thought of death and not of dalliance.[26]

Saxo gives another example of a band of women warriors during the Swedish War at Bravalla in an unspecified period.

> Now out of the town of Sle (Schleswig), under the captains Hetha (Heid) and Wisna, with Hakon Cut-Cheek came Tummi the Sailmaker. On these captains, who had the bodies of women, nature bestowed the souls of men ... Wisna, a woman, filled with sternness and a skilled warrior, was guarded by a band of Sclavs ... Hetha, guarded by a retinue of very active men, brought an armed company to the war ... So the maidens I have named, in fighting as well as courteous array, led their land-forces to the battle-field. Thus the Danish army mustered, company by company.[27]

Other tough women include Ladgerda, 'a skilled amazon who, though a maiden, had the courage of a man, and fought in front among the bravest with her hair loose over her shoulders. All on whose side she was fighting marvelled at her matchless deeds.'[28] Ragnar, a Norwegian prince, heard about Ladgerda, and 'declared that he had gained the victory by the might of one woman. Learning that she was of noble birth among the barbarians, he steadfastly wooed her by means of messengers. She spurned his mission in her heart' and set up obstacles, beasts that blocked the way. But Ragnar killed them and 'thus he had the maiden as the prize of the peril he had overcome. By this marriage he had two daughters.'[29]

Eventually Ragnar divorced her, but she carried on loving him and supported him in later battles – backed by Norwegians against the Jutes and Skanians, 'she brought herself to offer a hundred and twenty ships to the man who had once put her away.' Like other female plunderers in Saxo's myths, she was capable of killing those close to her in order to gain power. 'Ladgerda, when she had gone home after the battle, murdered her husband ... in the night with a spear-head, which she had hid in her gown. Then she usurped the whole of his name; for this most presumptuous dame thought it pleasanter to rule without her husband than to share the throne with him.'[30] Another 'Amazon' was Rusila, 'who aspired with military ardour to prowess in battle'. She was defeated by Hyrwil, the lord of Oland.[31]

Alfhild was not unusual in Saxo's chronicles in being allowed to choose or reject a suitor. Thora, daughter of Cuse, the king of the Finns and Perms, was permitted to make her own decision about a suitor Helgi, king of Halogaland, who 'was afflicted with so faulty an utterance that he was ashamed to be heard not only by strangers, but by those of his own house.' King Cuse said 'his daughter's wish must be consulted, in order that no parental strictness might forestall anything against her will. He called her in and asked whether she felt a liking for her wooer.' (She did.) Saxo also tells of women scorning the male partners assigned to them:

> Hildigisl, a Teuton of noble birth, relying on his looks and rank, sued for Signe, the daughter of Sigar. But she scorned him, chiefly for his insignificance, inasmuch as he was not brave, but wished to adorn his fortunes with the courage of other people. But this woman was inclined to love Hakon, chiefly for the high renown of his great deeds. For she thought more of the brave than the feeble; she admired notable deeds more than looks.[33]

Alfhild is placed in a flimsy tradition of Danish warrior women whose lives are closely bound up with the fortunes of male war leaders and political struggles for territory. These tales leave us in ignorance not only of whether such women existed, but also of their careers and lives. We can only speculate as to whether Alfhild's 'maidens of the same mind' went on to become pirate leaders, doing 'deeds beyond the valour of women'.

The flavour of all these stories oscillates between disgust at the utter ruthlessness of the warrior women and a persuasion that a woman's job is primarily to be weak and beautiful. Such an insistent message demonstrates that something politically significant was being conveyed in the stories of Alfhild, Sigrid the Superb and the other warrior women: society was being persuaded that lethal, wild, vengeful and free-roving ways of living should be given up and that women should accept a meek and home-based role, and a Christian one at that.

Notes

1. Charles Ellms, *The Pirates Own Book, or Authentic Narratives of the Lives, Exploits and Executions of the Most Celebrated Sea Robbers*, Sanborn & Carter, 1837.

2. Oliver Elton (translator), *The First Nine Books of the Danish History of Saxo Grammaticus*, David Nutt, 1894.

3. Letter to JS, 12 August 1993.

4. Nanna Damsholt, 'War, Women and Love' in *War and Peace in the Middle Ages*, Brian P. McGuire (ed), Copenhagen, 1987, p.2 of her typescript copy.

5. Nanna Damsholt, 'Women in Latin Medieval Literature in Denmark eg annals and chronicles' in *Aspects of Female Existence*, Birte Carle, Nanna Damsholt, Karen Glente and Eva Trein Nielsen (eds), Gyldendal, 1978, p.66.

6. Saxo Grammaticus, *op cit*, p.xxxi (introduction by Frederick York Powell).

7. *ibid*, p.362.

8. Kevin Crossley-Holland *The Norse Myths*, Andre Deutsch, 1980, p.xv.

9. We can think about this at length using psychoanalytic theories drawn from Freud and Lacan. In feminist art theory this includes women looking back at men, see S. Kent and J. Morreau (eds), *Women's Images of Men*, Writers and Readers, 1985. In feminist film theory on the female gaze, see particularly works by Laura Mulvey, and Linda Williams, 'When the Woman Looks' in *Re-vision, essays in feminist film criticism*, P. Mellencamp *et al* (ed), American Film Institute, Los Angeles, 1984.

10. Saxo Grammaticus, *op cit*, p.274.

11. *ibid*, pp.274-5.

12. *ibid*, p.275.

13. *ibid*, p.275.

14. Damsholt, *op cit*, p.12 of her typescript.

15. Saxo Grammaticus, *op cit*, p.275.

16. *ibid*, pp.275-6.

17. *ibid*, pp.276-7.

18. Henri Musnik, *Les Femmes pirates: aventures et legendes de la mer*, Le Masque, Paris, 1934, translated by Manuel A. Bermejo for this book.

19. David Mitchell, *Pirates*, Thames & Hudson, 1976, p.28.

20. *ibid*, p.28.

21. *ibid*, p.29.

22. Eric Graf Oxenstierna, *The World of the Norsemen*, Wiedenfeld & Nicolson, 1967, p.136.

23. Musnik, *op cit*.

24. Musnik, *op cit*, pp.16-18, translated by Bermejo.

25. *ibid*, pp.16-18.
26. Saxo Grammaticus, *op cit*, p.277.
27. *ibid*, p.311.
28. *ibid*, p.363.
29. *ibid*, p.364.
30. *ibid*, p.367.
31. *ibid*, p.367.
32. *ibid*, p.87.
33. *ibid*, p.278.

7 'The Pirate Queen of Ireland': Grace O'Malley by Anne Chambers

She had strongholds on her headlands
and brave galleys on the sea
and no warlike chief or viking
E're had bolder heart than she.

She unfurled her country's banner
High o'er battlement and mast
And 'gainst all the might of England
Kept it flying till the last.[1]

There came to me also a most famous feminine sea-captain called Grany Imallye and offered her services to me, wheresoever I would command her, with three galleys and 200 fighting men, either in Scotland or Ireland. She brought with her her husband for she was as well by sea as by land well more than Mrs Mate with him ... This was a notorious woman in all the coasts of Ireland.[2]

I had little idea that what began 15 years ago as a one-off voyage of discovery would make me forsake the security of a career in banking for the precarious existence of a writer. My quest was to release from the bondage of historical neglect and fictional misrepresentation an extraordinary woman, Grace O'Malley, or Granuaile as she is more familiarly known in Ireland. This quest had taken root subconsciously in my childhood. Holidaying each summer on the west coast of Ireland within sight of Clare Island and Achill, under the shadow of Croagh Patrick, beside the O'Malley abbey of Murrisk on the shores of Clew Bay, traditionally held to have been my heroine's base, spurred my resolve to know more. I grew up with an image of Granuaile fashioned by folklore stories told at family gatherings, by poetry taught at school and later by reading the many novels written about her. They presented the image of an Amazon performing incredible deeds of bravery by land and sea, a patriotic, godfearing woman beyond religious or ideological reproach. Yet in factual history books, Granuaile never received mention. Was this Amazon fact or fiction? As a child I could not tell.

But the fiction and folklore fuelled my desire to know more. A visit to Clare Island in July 1975 and a conversation with an American visitor who blithely informed me that she was in Ireland for two weeks to research the biography of Grace O'Malley convinced me I should begin my quest. It eventually took me four years to unearth the available information, and in the process I embarked on an exciting mission of discovery in unfamiliar territory. Daily after five o'clock I exchanged my chair in the bank for one in a library. Holidays and every free minute fell victim to the all-consuming Grace O'Malleymania for which there was no cure. As I commenced my search, I hoped that in disinterring Granuaile's bones the gorgeous legendary apparel with which she had been invested by folklore, fiction and poetry would not turn into rags under the stark light of reality.

The secrets of my quest lay locked inside age-darkened manuscripts whose spidery writing was evidence of the passing of the 400 years since their authors put quill to parchment. The records of that time were written on what was cream-coloured parchment paper but now is faded, brittle, mahogany-coloured relics that disintegrate at every touch. With patience I began to unravel the intricacies of sixteenth-century calligraphy, compiling an alphabet which with practice helped me to read the swirls and flourishes of sixteenth-century scribes. My treasure hunt unlocked an Aladdin's cave of information, and the remains I disinterred required no fancy fictional dress to conjure the image of a woman for whom the idiom 'stranger than fiction' must surely have been coined.

As I gingerly uncovered what could be approximately called 'the facts' about Granuaile, I also began a process of self re-education about her century. Contrary to what I had been taught, Ireland in the sixteenth century was largely devoid of ideological stimulus, either political or religious. Survival, not patriotism, was the spur of almost every Gaelic leader. Sixteenth-century Ireland was a tribal society, composed of a myriad of separate states ruled by independent chieftains continually at war with one another. Power was measured by the number of client lords over whom a chieftain held sway and from whom he could exact tribute and allegiance against his enemies. Outside the few walled cities and towns, it was mainly an agricultural society where wealth was measured in terms of the cattle that roamed the open pasture lands, the cow being the medium of exchange for the barter trade that predominated. The concern of the Irish chieftains was to hold fast to their power and position; to resist, if they were strong enough, the encroaching English administration which was pushing outwards from its centre in Dublin; or, if they were not, to ally with the English to ensure their survival. Confederation against a common enemy, when it did emerge towards the end of the century, was too little, too late.

Perhaps I had stumbled on one of the reasons why historians had debarred Granuaile: like her century, she did not fit comfortably into the mould. Irish heroines and heroes have been required to be adorned in the green cloak of patriotism, their personal lives pure, their religious beliefs fervently Roman Catholic, with an occasional allowance made for rebel Protestants. As Granuaile's main detractor, the English governor of Connaught, Sir Richard Bingham, wrote to Queen Elizabeth's secretary, Lord Burghley, she was the 'woman who overstepped the part of womanhood';[3] who superseded her first husband in his position as male chieftain; assumed command of her father's ships and hard-bitten male crews; traded and pirated successfully for the space of 50 years from Scotland to Spain; led rebellions against individual English administrators when they sought to overpower her; attacked her own son when he sided with her enemy; taught her youngest son the art of survival so well that he fought with the English at Gaelic Ireland's final stand at the Battle of Kinsale in 1601. Granuaile allowed neither political nor social convention to deter her; took a lover; divorced her second husband by right of the pagan laws of her ancestors; gave birth to her youngest son on her ship at sea. So she hardly fitted the rosy-hued picture of Gaelic womanhood painted by later generations of male, often clerical historians.

Politically the odds were stacked against her becoming an accepted leader in the male-dominated society into which she was born. Salic law, which debarred women from succession, was rigorously adhered to by the Irish clans. And socially the times were physically tough. Young men aspiring to power were required to prove their masculinity by raiding and plundering. Succession to the chieftaincy was not on the basis of the first-born son inheriting but by the selection of the fittest from among the ruling family. That Granuaile defied both law and convention to become a leader is an indication of both her physical and psychological abilities.

While other formidable sixteenth-century women, notably Eleanor Countess of Desmond, Maire Rua O'Brien and the Ineen Dubh O'Donnel, made their mark on the political scene in Ireland, they did so not as chieftains in their own right, but as wives of chieftain husbands. Perhaps Granuaile was a reflection of the time when Ireland was part of a Bronze-Age matriarchal culture in which the dominant divinity was the all-powerful Mother Goddess Dana. The earliest Irish legends, the stories of the Red Branch, contain fleeting but significant references to this prehistoric culture. The prime hero of the Red Branch cycle, Cuchulainn, learned his battle prowess under the tutelage of the woman warrior Scathach. In combat he could only overcome the warrior Princess Aoife by resorting to trickery. Many of the hero warriors of these stories used their mother's name in place of a patronymic, for example Conor Mac (son of) Nessa. The warrior Queen Maeve, of Granuaile's native province of Connaught, was a powerful, wilful and fearless woman who was prepared to go to war to achieve her ambition.

Without doubt it was the sea that cemented Granuaile's reputation as a notorious pirate, the 'great spoiler and chief commander and director of thieves and murderers at sea',[4] as the English President of Munster described her when he imprisoned her in Dublin Castle for a plundering foray on the lands of the Earl of Desmond in 1577. It was this picture of Granuaile as a freebooting pirate leader that enshrined her in legend as the Pirate Queen of Ireland and caused her memory to be preserved, if not by history, then by folklore. As official sources revealed, the facts relating to her maritime career far outweighed the fiction. They introduced me to an exceptional woman, vital and daring, a political pragmatist and tactician, a brave military leader by land and sea, a ruthless plunderer, a mercenary, a shrewd negotiator, a woman imbued with the necessary skills to survive in the competitive and dangerous trade of piracy for a period of 50 years. But what circumstances made her step outside the conventions of her sex and time? Did some traumatic event force her to assume her extraordinary role or was there some receptive spark within her that made her naturally incline towards perceived masculine territory?

Granuaile was the only daughter of Dudara O'Malley, chieftain of the kingdom of Umhall, the country around Clew Bay on the west coast of Ireland, and of his wife Margaret. The O'Malleys differed from the majority of Irish clans in that they derived their living in the main from the sea. Their motto, '*terra marique potens*', proclaimed them lords of the seas around Ireland. Irish annals would also claim that the O'Malleys sailed further afield to Spain, Scotland and Brittany. The fact that the merchants of nearby Galway City, then a major international port for the ships of England, Spain and France, prohibited the native Irish clans from trading there through the imposition of exorbitant taxes and racist bylaws, might have forced the O'Malleys to sell their salted fish and beef, hides, tallow and frieze cloth in more lucrative markets abroad.

But from earliest times, plundering by sea had supplemented the O'Malleys' income. Ancient histories record with regular monotony details of their raids on outlying coastal settlements from Kerry to Donegal. The isolated bays and coves of the local coastline have lent themselves readily as havens for plunderers and pirates from everywhere, right up to modern times. Names such as Broadhaven Bay, a great natural harbour in north Mayo, remote and outside the law, were familiar to the pirate communities of many countries. There the comforts of the pirate crews were catered for by a community reared to accept piracy and plunder as part and parcel of seafaring life. In the sixteenth century it was the O'Malleys who ruled the waves off the west coast of Ireland. They issued licences to English, Spanish and French fishermen to fish their fertile sea domain, traded and pirated, and ferried in Scottish mercenary soldiers, the Gallowglass, hired seasonally by the warring chieftains.

With this maritime background, it is perhaps easier to understand Granuaile's career. Had she been a boy, her life may have gone unrecorded. But the fact that she was a woman both helped and mitigated against her. It brought her to the attention of the English administration, who recorded disapprovingly her activities and her 'naughty disposition towards the state'[5] in their despatches to the English court. But her unfeminine, unholy and unpatriotic deeds ensured her dismissal from the pages of Irish history except as a footnote to her husbands and castles. Without the close attention paid to her activities by the English administration, Granuaile might have been written out of history.

There is little reliable information about Granuaile's childhood. Her father Dudara (Black Oak) conjures a picture of a swarthy, broad-shouldered chieftain, of great physical strength, his hair falling to his shoulders and cut in the traditional 'glib' or fringe across his forehead. He dressed in the customary tight worsted trews, a saffron shirt with loose sleeves pleated in folds at the waist under a jack of fine leather. His chieftain's 'brat' or cloak of wool was fastened with a gold pin and fell in folds to the ground. He was described as a proud man, one of the few Irish chieftains of the time who never submitted to the English crown. Perhaps her father's character, authority and even physical attributes drew Granuaile to emulate him, to dress like him, to adopt his lifestyle and to become in effect more like a son than a daughter. Given the unorthodox role she was to adopt, it is likely that as a child her interests lay not in the female domain of household management but in Dudara's world of ships, trade, politics and power. The arrival of Christianity in Ireland in the fifth century had gradually subdued all traces of matriarchy that may have survived from the previous millennium. A woman's place was definitely supposed to be in the home, not on the battlefield and certainly not on the throne. Women hit the headlines of the written annals of the day only as wives of chieftains or as doers of charitable works. The fact that Granuaile later assumed command of her father's fleet and crews implies that he accepted her unusual inclination and had faith in her abilities both as a seafarer and a leader.

Initially, however, as custom dictated, her father arranged her marriage at the age of 15 to a local chieftain, Donal-an-Coghaidh O'Flaherty, which obtained for him a politically advantageous alliance with a neighbouring clan. Whether against her wishes or not, for a time at least Granuaile would seem to have conformed to what her husband and society deemed a woman's role. She bore two sons, Owen and Murrough, but her husband was immature and reckless, and he intensified his aggressive activities, wasting his clan's resources. His clansmen turned to his wife for help in surviving the famine-like conditions which resulted from their chieftain's excesses. Disregarding legal convention which debarred her from the chieftaincy, Granuaile emerged as *de facto* leader of her husband's clan. While her contemporaries might well have been astounded that a woman should usurp male power and prerogative, the Irish bards, keepers of clan genealogies, legends and folk history, could testify that Granuaile merely followed in the tradition of the woman warrior rulers of her Celtic ancestors.

Her husband's warring disposition finally brought about his downfall, and his death gave rise to one of the many stories that contribute to the legend of Granuaile. According to the folklore of the area around Lough Corrib, her husband died while attacking an island fortress on the lake, then known as Cock's Castle, which had been taken from him by his bitter enemies, the Joyces. On Donal's death, the Joyces imagined the castle securely theirs, but they reckoned without O'Flaherty's wife. Granuaile led the O'Flahertys in a sudden reprisal and regained the castle, demonstrating such personal courage that it was hurriedly renamed Hen's Castle.

Following the death of her husband, Granuaile experienced the discriminatory dictates of Irish law. Despite her competence, bravery and success as *de facto* chieftain, the law would not countenance a woman chieftain, and her husband's cousin was elected to succeed him. Having tasted power, Granuaile was determined that she would not be denied either by law or convention. She had proved her worth as a leader and a leader she intended to remain. Taking with her the O'Flaherty men who wished to continue to serve under her, she returned to her father's territory and settled on Clare Island. With her father's ships and a private army of 200 men, she launched herself on a career of piracy which she later euphemistically described as 'maintenance by land and sea'.[6] In her highly manoeuvrable galleys, one of which was described as being 'rowed with thirty oars and sail and had on board ready to defend her one hundred good shot',[7] she set about making herself both a fortune and a reputation.

The merchant ships plying their way along the west coast from England, Spain and France, heavy with cargoes of wine, Toledo steel, salt, damask, silk and alum, made rich pickings. In vain did the merchant princes of Galway report her activities to the English crown, accusing her of 'taking sundry ships and barks bound for this poor town which they have not only rifled to the utter overthrow of the owners and merchants but also have most wickedly murdered divers of young men to the great terror of such as would willingly traffic'.[8] The English had neither the ships to apprehend her versatile galleys nor sufficient geographical knowledge of the remote coastline over which she held sway. Clew Bay, with its myriad of islands, dangerous reefs and currents, was as much unknown territory as the far-off Americas. Many years later the English sent an army which entrapped her in one of her castles and laid siege. In a remarkable military feat after enduring a siege of 21 days she dislodged the besieging army and routed them from her territory.

To achieve even part of which she is accused of by her English contemporaries in Ireland, Granuaile had to be accomplished in the skills of seafaring. Even with her maritime background, it was no mean achievement to survive on the wild Atlantic. Her ability to sail her ships to Scotland, England and further afield to Spain and Portugal must rank her with her contemporaries Raleigh and Drake. Knowledge of navigation, of the dangerous coastline, sound judgement of the elements and the capabilities of her ships were basic requirements. The threat of English warships out to capture her or competitors in the piracy trade out to relieve her of her cargo and her life augmented the hazards.

Her capacity to endure physical privation was remarkable. Seafaring in the sixteenth century was not for the fainthearted. Conditions on board were primitive, privacy non-existent. Poor personal hygiene was endurable if you were a man; for a woman, menstruation added additional hardship. Skin toughened under the barrage of wind and salt spray, hands and nails were hardened and split by hawser and canvas, bare feet became chafed from the rough swaying boards, sodden woollen trews and linen shirts itched, cold food lodged undigested. To give birth on a bucking galley on the high seas, as Granuaile did her third son, thereafter known as Tibbott-ne-Long (Toby of the ships), is unimaginable. To retain control of her wild crewmen, to enforce her

will, it was essential that she led by example, outenduring and
outdoing her men, leading them personally by land and sea, as a later
poem claims:

. No braver seaman took a deck in hurricane or squalls
   Since Grace O'Malley battered down old Currath castle's wall.

Something more than allure kept her 200 male followers in thrall over
half a century. That she was successful at her trade undoubtedly
helped, but there must have been some additional spark, some
charisma that forged such a lasting bond between her and her men that
they were willing to be led by a woman contrary to native mores and
chauvinistic pride. She is reputed to have been proud of her men and
to have said 'go mh'fear lei lán loinge de Cloinn Conroi agus Cloinn
Mic an Allaidh na lán loinge d'ór'. (That she would rather have a
shipful of Conroys and MacAnallys than a shipful of gold.)⁹ The fact
that her followers were made up of members of different clans, each
bearing tribal grudges, whom she had to mould into a force loyal only
to her was an added difficulty. That she could offer Sidney an army of
'two hundred fighting men' willing to fight wherever she ordered is
testimony to her absolute control.

   Though far from the centre of English power, international events
eventually began to affect Granuaile's operations. Fearful that Spain
would use Ireland as a back door to England, the English administration, with its sheriffs, governors and military men, was pushing west-
wards into remote areas such as Mayo. To obtain a more sheltered
haven for her ships and men, Granuaile decided to marry again. This
time she did the choosing and the castle rather than its owner was the
reason for her choice. Rockfleet Castle on the north shore of Clew Bay
was owned by Richard-in-Iron Bourke, tanaiste (deputy) to the Mac
Williamship, the position of most power in the area. Rockfleet was a
safer haven for Granuaile's ships and crews than Clare Island.

   Folklore maintains that Granuaile married Richard for 'one year
certain' and that if after that period either party wished to withdraw
they were free to do so. In no social sphere was Ireland more apart
from the rest of Europe than in the area of marriage, which was a
largely secular event adhering to Celtic pagan rites rather than to the
Christian ethos. Under Brehon law, the ancient, native law of Gaelic

Ireland, divorce was permitted and was the right of either party. Brehon law also sheltered women from the economic effects of divorce, protected the dowry they brought with them and permitted married women to own and administer their own property independently of their husbands. This ran contrary to the common law of England, for example, where a husband had absolute control over his wife's property. As English common law gradually replaced Brehon law in Ireland in the seventeenth century, so divorce and the rights of women as individuals within marriage were negated.

When Granuaile's marriage to Richard Bourke reached a year's duration, she installed her men in Rockfleet Castle, locked the castle against him and shouted from the ramparts 'Richard Bourke I dismiss you', thereby divorcing herself of a husband and obtaining a fine castle in lieu of her dowry. But Granuaile and Richard were reunited and their son born at sea. The day after his birth, her ship was attacked by an Algerian corsair. According to stories, as the battle raged on deck, her captain came below where she lay with her new-born son and begged for help. 'May you be seven times worse off this day twelve months, who cannot do without me for one day,'[10] she upbraided him and stormed on deck. The Algerian pirates allegedly stood transfixed at the dishevelled female apparition. Roaring her men into action, she led them to victory.

In 1576 Sir Henry Sidney became the first English deputy of the English monarch to venture into the west of Ireland. During his visit to Galway City he encountered 'the most famous feminine sea captain, Grany I Mallye'. Why Granuaile risked capture and imprisonment by meeting Sidney is open to speculation. She knew that most of the neighbouring chieftains, including the Mac William of Mayo, had submitted to Sidney on promise of restoration of their powers and lands.

These submissions had major implications for two principles of Irish law: ownership of land and succession to the chieftaincy. By Brehon law, a chieftain held a life interest only in the lands of his lordship ruling them in trust for the members of the ruling sept. On his death the lands became entrusted to his successor for his lifetime. A new chieftain was elected from among members of the ruling family of the clan, so a brother could succeed a brother, a nephew an uncle, a younger son a father, and so on. The chieftain's tanaiste was also elected during the lifetime of the chieftain. By submitting to the English crown, the chieftains in effect agreed to rule by English rather than native law and thereby accept the principle of primogeniture whereby an eldest son succeeded and inherited from his father.

This had a major bearing on the position of Granuaile's husband Richard, who was tanaiste to the Mac Williamship. If on the Mac William's death, English rather than Irish law prevailed, then Mac William's son, not Richard, would succeed. By establishing good relations with the English deputy, Granuaile sought to secure Richard's position. That Richard was well ruled by Granuaile is evident by Sidney's comment, though she is also said to have made a pleasing and 'most feminine' appearance. Her meeting at the same time with Elizabethan courtier and poet Philip Sidney must have given him an extraordinary story to relate on his return to court.

During her stay in Galway, Granuaile agreed to take the deputy out into the bay on her galley so that he might better examine the city's fortifications. Business being business, however, she ensured that he paid her for the privilege. In the event her mission to Sidney was successful, for on the death of the Mac William, despite opposition from his son, Richard succeeded to the title. But to put an English gloss on so Irish a title, he was also knighted and Granuaile became an unlikely Lady Bourke. At the investiture in Galway, the English Governor Malby, noting Granuaile dressed for once in female finery, wrote to court that 'Grany O'Mally thinketh herself to be no small lady'.[11] But Granuaile gave her promise of loyalty to Sidney a broad interpretation and continued as before, a scourge of the seas, taking tolls and raiding and pirating the ships that ventured within her domain.

In 1577, on a plundering expedition on the lands of the Earl of Desmond in Munster, she was captured and imprisoned in Limerick gaol. Desmond delivered her to the English governor, William Drury. From Limerick, Drury brought her to Dublin where she was imprisoned in Dublin Castle for 18 months. She was eventually released on condition that she would bring her husband, who was implicated in the rebellion in Munster, to heel. But shortly after her release, when an English official was sent to collect crown dues from the Lord and Lady Bourke, he met with unusual opposition. 'I went there towards the place where Mac William was, who met me and his wife Grany O

Mallye with all their force and did swear they would have my life for coming so far into their country, and specially his wife who would fight with me before she was a half mile near me.' [12] On Richard's death in 1583, Granuaile 'gathered together all her own followers and with a 1,000 head of cattle and mares became a dweller in Rockfleet.' [13] She was now 53 years old and looked set to continue as before had it not been for the arrival in Connaught of the *bête noire* of her life, Governor Richard Bingham.

As the hostility between England and Spain intensified and Elizabeth, from the safety of her court, sent her sea dogs to harry and plunder Spanish shipping, English control of Ireland took on a new urgency. Bingham was one of the new breed of English administrators sent to Ireland. Ruthless and domineering, he sought to compel the Irish chieftains into submission. He was particularly antagonistic to Granuaile, whom he accused as being 'nurse to all rebellions for forty years'.[14] Three times Granuaile was actively involved in rebellion against Bingham's cruel rule in Connaught, ferrying in the Gallowglass from Scotland. Bingham eventually captured her and as she later related to Elizabeth, he 'caused a new pair of gallows to be made for her last funeral'.[15] At the last moment the chieftains of Mayo, by submitting hostages, obtained her release. This was a tribute to her standing among them and to their acceptance of her as a chieftain. But Bingham retaliated by confiscating her enormous cattle and horse herds. Once more her ships were her only salvation.

Bingham eventually subdued the rebellion and set about exacting revenge. He took Tibbott-ne-Long hostage for Granuaile's good behaviour and her eldest son, Owen O'Flaherty, was killed while in the custody of Bingham's brother. Her second son, Murrough, incurred Granuaile's wrath by siding with Bingham. In fury she set out to teach Murrough a sharp lesson and 'manned out her navy of galleys, landed in Ballinahinche where he dwelleth, burned his town and spoiled his people of their cattle and goods and murdered 4 of his men who made resistence.' [16]

In 1592 Granuaile experienced a further blow to her power when Bingham penetrated her pirate haven of Clew Bay and impounded part of her fleet. Despite the setbacks she had encountered in running the gauntlet with individual English administrators, she had always retained control of her fleet and thereby the freedom of the seas. This had enabled her to remain in power. But time was catching up with her. The more distant parts of Ireland were slowly being brought within the English net. A new map of the country had been drawn which more accurately depicted the remote havens of the west coast. It reflects Granuaile's status as leader that her name appears on the Boazio map above the area over which she ruled, the only woman so mentioned. And she was no longer young. It is one of the extraordinary features of her life that she managed to attain old age in such a dangerous occupation at a time when female life expectancy was no more than 50 years.

But when Bingham imprisoned her son Tibbott-ne-Long on a charge of treason for conspiring with the Ulster chieftains who were plotting a rebellion with Spanish assistance, there was little alternative but to go over Bingham's head. Granuaile's first petition to the queen of England is dated July 1593. The daring and cleverness of its author is evident in its tones. Knowing that the queen has full knowledge of her piracy and rebellious career, Granuaile sets out her version of events: how circumstances 'constrained your highness fond subject to take arms and by force to maintain herself and her people by sea and by land the space of forty years past.'[17] She seeks Tibbott-ne-Long's release from prison. She requests that Tibbott and her other son Murrough O'Flaherty be allowed to hold their lands by right of English rather than Irish law, an astute move now that it seemed likely that the demise of native Irish law was at hand. In return, she offers 'during her life to invade with sword and fire all your Highness's enemies wheresoever they are or shall be without any interruption of any person or persons whatsoever',[18] a cunning ruse to circumvent Bingham. By appealing directly to Elizabeth, Granuaile played her trump card. She bargained on Elizabeth's parsimonious nature and it paid handsome dividends. Pardon was less expensive than war.

Intrigued by Granuaile's petition, Elizabeth dispatched 18 'articles of interrogatory to be answered by Grany Ni Maly'.[19] The answers provide an informative résumé of Granuaile's life, though she wisely concentrates on aspects least objectionable to the English. Her deft replies are a match for the subterfuge of the Elizabethan court and demonstrate an astute political mind. Leaving nothing to chance, however, in July 1593 Granuaile followed her correspondence to court, sailing her ship from Clew Bay to Greenwich, determined to put her case face to face to the woman whose avaricious male servants had so drastically altered her life.

The details of the meeting between these two women, each an outstanding leader in a male-dominated society, remain in the realm of folklore. Curiosity about each other may have been a major motivation: for Granuaile to meet the woman whose policies had wrought such drastic changes on her country and herself; for Elizabeth to marvel how this weatherbeaten woman, as old as herself, had fought her way by sea and land for over 40 years. Elizabeth had inherited her kingdom and a well-oiled political machine to facilitate her task as ruler; Granuaile had single-handedly, in defiance of law and society, carved out her own 'kingdom' and had earned her right to rule by example. Unlike Elizabeth, Granuaile did not dictate policy from the protection of her castles but actively effected it at the head of her army. Despite her claims of sovereignty over much of the world's oceans and the riches that fell into her lap from piracy, Elizabeth had never sailed further down-river than Greenwich.

Whatever words were spoken, possibly in Latin, Elizabeth was sufficiently impressed by the 'Pirate Queen' to disregard the weight of evidence against her and to go against the advice of her own governor. The queen in her letter to Bingham ordered Tibbott-ne-Long to be released and he and his step-brother Murrough O'Flaherty to be favoured. Unwittingly she accepted Granuaile's offer 'to employ all her power to offend and prosecute any offender against us . . . and to fight in our quarrel with all the world' [20] which in effect gave Granuaile licence to return to her old trade of 'maintenance by land and sea'.

Granuaile took her leave of Elizabeth with her burden much lightened and returned to Mayo in the middle of September to confront Bingham with the queen's letter. In horror Bingham believed that the queen had been hoodwinked into underestimating the capabilities of the 'aged woman' [21] who had appeared before her, and that she had neglected to obtain any pledge for Granuaile's further good conduct. To circumvent what he perceived as the queen's rashness, he released Granuaile's son but quartered English soldiers on her land and ordered others to accompany her on her every voyage. In 1595 Bingham was recalled in disgrace and at the age of 66, Granuaile returned to her plundering ways, in 1597 sailing as far as Scotland in a reprisal attack on MacNeil of Barra.

Political events were rapidly reaching a climax in Ireland. The Ulster chieftains O'Neill and O'Donnell had joined forces against the English and were awaiting help from Spain. Granuaile and her galleys were eagerly sought after by both sides. Initially she and Tibbott-ne-Long sided with the Ulster chieftains against the English. But when O'Donnell came into Mayo and created his own favourite the Mac William instead of Tibbott, Tibbott sought terms with the English and for the duration of the war sailed his mother's ships under the English flag, fighting on the English side at the Battle of Kinsale (1601). He was knighted in 1603 and created Viscount Mayo in 1627.

Granuaile left her struggle for survival in her son's hands. The final reference to her appears in the State Papers 1601, when one of her galleys is apprehended off the coast of Mayo by an English warship. She is thought to have died in Rockfleet Castle in about 1603 and to be buried in the abbey of Clare Island, beside the sea which had sustained her throughout her life.

The faded manuscripts of Granuaile's time, letters, petitions and despatches, reveal the glories and tragedies of this eventful age. Through her I have become part of a century of exploration and exploitation, of war and intrigue, of armadas and invasions, of empires at the pinnacle of their power, of the demise of ancient civilisations and the birth of new orders. More than anything else, Granuaile has made me realise that history is not as black and white as it has been painted, but is made up of many shades of grey, with few black villains and fewer white heroes.

Notes

1. Extract from 'Granuaile', a song which originated in County Leitrim around Ballinamuck about 1798, with the survivors from Mayo of the Battle of Ballinamuck between the Franco-Irish Forces and the English. It presents her as nationalist heroine rather than pirate. Found in J. Hardiman, *Irish Minstrelsy*, vol. II, London, 1831. See also my own *Granuaile, The Life and Times of Grace O'Malley, 1530–1603*, Wolfhound Press, Dublin, 1991 and *Chieftain to Knight, Tibbott-Ne-Long Bourke, 1567–1629*, Wolfhound Press, Dublin.

2. Sir Henry Sidney, calender of Carew Mss, no. 501 of 1583.

3. State Papers, Ireland, 69/19, no. 56.
4. *ibid*.
5. State Papers, Ireland, 62/66.
6. State Papers, Ireland, 63/170.
7. Calender State Papers, Ireland, vol. CCVII, p.436.
8. Calender State Papers, Ireland, vol. CCVII, p.5.
9. Ordnance Survey, Mayo, vol. 1, p.1.
10. *ibid*, p.1.
11. Calender State Papers, Ireland, vol. CLXX, p.102.
12. Calender State Papers, Ireland, vol. XC1X, p.425.
13. Calender State Papers, Ireland, vol. CLXX, p.132.
14. State Papers, Ireland, 63/158, no. 37.
15. Calender State Papers, Ireland, vol. CLXX, p.132.
16. State Papers, Ireland, 62/66.
17. State Papers, Ireland, 63/170.
18. *ibid*.
19. Calender State Papers, Ireland, vol. CLXX, p.132.
20. Calender MSS Marquis of Salisbury, pt.IV p.368.
21. *ibid*, p.368.

Section III:

Working for a living

8 *In the right place at the right time*

Breasts seaward, babes leeward,
I serve each wave of rovers,
salt in my eye,
expecting bruises or the brightest lace.

Fish, my son, for gold, for me.
Fins have faded. Gills are gone.
Take the morning tide
and net me molasses, ivory.

It was one of the more lurid twentieth-century books on piracy, the 1935 *Pirate Harbours and Their Secrets* by Basil Fuller and Ronald Leslie Melville,[1] which first made me realise that women met pirates simply because they lived and worked by the sea: they were the coastal providers of what could be called 'visitors' amenities'. The sea was the focus of the lives of many women, but it was mainly men who sailed on it. For the most part, women stayed at home, waiting anxiously for vessels to return, bearing the babes and gazing out on to the waves that custom forbade them cross.

A chapter called 'The Women's Havens of Mayo' in Fuller and Melville's book almost fetishises the idea of women offering services to pirates, as if they were fairytale maidens thrillingly giving sanctuary to devils. Central to the story is the dubious fancy that seventeenth-century pirates were lured to Broadhaven, County Mayo, just because Cormac, a jovial but cowardly chief, had 'unusually beautiful' daughters. The authors report the account of the British Admiral Monson's visit to Cormac's house, disguised as a famous pirate leader in order to trap some pirates.

> [Cormac's] 'three hackney daughters rose to entertain me, and conducted me to the hall newly strewed with rushes, as the richest decking their abilities or the meanness of the place could afford. In the corner was a harper who played merrily to make my welcome the greater.' The girls eagerly asked after their pirate lovers and demanded to see their presents . . . soon the party spirit took firm hold, and the girls suggested a dance.[2]

A disarming picture of girlish contact with wild sea-rovers. But a more serious reading of pirate literature suggests that although the story contains an important truth about shore women's support work for pirates (as lovers and hospitality-providers), it may also be full of twentieth-century gentlemanly euphemisms for a more forthright and exploitative seventeenth-century situation. We could try reading 'unusually beautiful' as 'available'; 'lovers' as 'former sexual contacts'; 'presents' as 'payment in kind'; and 'party spirit' as 'alcoholic carouse'.

Sex, drink, abuse and bribery were the common ingredients of life on cluttered American docksides, in peaceful Caribbean fishing villages and in lively African ports, where numbers of working women took part in a waterfront economy that survived thanks to seafarers, including pirates. Thousands of land-based seamstresses and prostitutes, cooks and traders, laundresses and landladies, daughters, mothers, sisters, wives, sweethearts, grandmothers and aunts were connected with the thousands of men who sailed pirate vessels. If you lived on the notorious Jamaican waterfront of Port Royal or in the wild and rebellious dive of Nassau in the seventeenth and eighteenth centuries, it would have been impossible to avoid pirates. Indeed, living cheek-by-unshaven-jowl with them, you could find out how a woman might get on to a pirate ship, or at least benefit from the industry's proceeds. In some cases, women gave their services out of affection or for money, but often, especially in Africa, their bodies and goods were stolen from them. Sometimes they stole in return.

At the basis of the relationship between women and pirates is the material fact that pirates, like fugitives or travelling armies, needed to eat and arm themselves. Between attacks or while searching for targets, they had to recuperate and prepare. Their requirements included potable water and nourishing food; physical nurture – be it nursing, listening, bought intercourse or nuptual embraces; shelter free from sea mist and storm dangers; local hardwoods for rebuilding rotted hulls and decks; recycled cannons for refitting ships; skilled help including technical expertise from blacksmiths and shipwrights; and intelligence about when profitable cargoes might sail by. The arrival of pirates could be at best a mixed blessing, at worst a nightmare.

When the two sides met in a situation of negotiation rather than rape, the women worked with pirates in the same way as female camp followers did with soldiers: as sutlers (providers of cooked food), laundresses, nurses and seamstresses, they provided support services for groups of men bent on fighting and prepared to pay for services rather than look after themselves. Women tavern-keepers, relatives, lovers, whores and traders became part of a subculture, in a climate of casual and intermittent brutality and plunder. In the same way, hard-pressed coastal people of both sexes took – and still take – advantage of other opportunities to earn money from the sea: wrecking, beachcombing or smuggling.

What impact did the eighteenth-century Anglo-American pirates have in the years when the English Civil War was over and the slave trade had begun? Did the arrival of pirates draw women and men on coasts from Madagascar to North Carolina into piracy and smuggling? How many coastal people were already used to plundering the sea in whatever way they could? Were women ready accomplices, shrewd exploiters or terrified victims? What did the women who cooked for ravenous pirates, washed sea-drenched canvas breeches and knew the right herbs for poultices make of the invaders? How did different pirates handle their different views of women as consolers or fickle exploiters, suckers or predators?

Pirate histories do not tell much about these women: almost all that is available in secondary sources is assembled in this chapter. Collected together, it makes something fairly substantial, but in Captain Charles

Johnson's 700-page *A General History of the Pyrates* (1724)[3] there is at best one reference to women every 15 pages; the often derogatory fragments about women involved with Anglo-American seafaring appear merely as background, as part of the taken-for-granted foreign scenery. Johnson at least tries to give an honest account, but popular nineteenth- and early twentieth-century stories about piracy, including the best-known ones by Charles Ellms and Philip Gosse,[4] make sadistic, romantic and objectifying allusions in words and pictures to ripe exotic 'native' women, ready for the plucking, who welcomed pirates with trusting embraces on palm-fringed beaches. Like snuff movies today, these say much about contemporary male attitudes towards women, especially black women, but mask basic truths about interdependence and power.

Pirates had as many different ways of behaving towards people on land as those people had of handling the lawless invaders from the sea. Possible scenarios can be pieced together using twentieth-century feminist theories and a range of different and overlapping histories. At the brutal end are accounts like Alexander Exquemelin's 1678 tales of coastal villages where women and men were raped, terrorised and killed and descriptions by modern scholars such as Hilary McD Beckles of how Caribbean slaves were used by European navies.[5] At the less dramatic end are sociological works such as Judith Fingard's history of nineteenth-century Canadian sailortowns, which offers a way to understand earlier lifestyles.[6] John C. Appleby has gathered information from High Court of Admiralty papers and other official documents which explain Irish women's connections with piracy 200 years after Grace O'Malley's time.[7] Such documents make it clear that women met pirates because they were in the right place at that right time. As Johnson pointed out:

> Pyrates at Sea, have the same Sagacity with Robbers at Land; as the latter understand what Roads are most frequented, and where it is most likely to meet with Booty, so the former know what Latitude to lye in, in order to Intercept Ships . . . Pyrates generally shift their Rovings, according to the Season of the Year; . . . they follow the Sun, and go towards the Islands, at the approach of cold Weather.[8]

Jamaica, Tortuga and Hispaniola (now Haiti and the Dominican Republic) were popular sites for pirates waiting to attack Spanish ships going from the New World to Seville. Islands offered the safest seclusion. While lone pirates who had committed offences were marooned on uninhabited islands (Alexander Selkirk, on whom Defoe's *Robinson Crusoe* is based, was cast on the Chilean island of Juan Fernandez), piratical operations required coastal dwellers to supply both the ships' and the pirates' needs. Some pirates tried to establish idealistic communities: ex-privateers moved to Nassau in the Bahamas in 1716 and formed a 2,000-strong colony, a kind of pirate republic or commonwealth.[9] Maritime historian Marcus Rediker believes that the 'communitarian urge was perhaps most evident in the pirate strongholds of Madagascar and Sierra Leone' at the start of the eighteenth century.[10] What little evidence we have about women there portrays them as wives and supporters rather than communards in their own right.

Madagascar, off the eastern seaboard of Africa, had a reputation for being the archetypal tropical pirate isle, with its bananas and honey, tamarinds and dates, ebony, gum of Dragon's Blood and aloes.[11] Above all – according to the imaginative illustrators of Charles Ellms' popular nineteenth-century book – it was full of beautiful women happy to lie all day on pirates' laps under surfside palm trees. Madagascar's position meant it was a useful haven from which pirates could attack ships crossing the Indian Ocean from India and the Far East to Europe. Although it was a principal pirate base between 1690 and 1730, only several hundred pirates can have settled there at any one time: 'A visitor at the end of the seventeenth century counted 17 pirate vessels and an estimated population of 1,500',[12] which suggests that hundreds but certainly not thousands of women might have profited from the outlaws' presence. Eighteenth-century pirate Captain's Tew's delighted quartermaster wrote in his papers: 'This island of Madagascar affords all the Necessaries of Life . . . The Seas around it are well stor'd with Fish, the Woods with Fowl, and the Intrails of the Earth are enrich'd with Mines of excellent Iron.'[13] Indeed, it was not uncommon for a ship to leave a notice: 'Gone to Madagascar for Limes.'

Other pirate bases, by contrast, were wild, rebel-filled, corrupt towns. Nassau, the main gathering place of New Providence in the Bahamas, was a shanty town of driftwood and palm fronds and old sails draped over spars to make tents . . . every other hovel was a grog shop or brothel with Negro and mulatto prostitutes. Favourite drinks were rumfustian (a mixture of beer, gin and sherry, heavily spiced) and rum and gunpowder . . . the general atmosphere resembled that of Hogarth's Gin Lane in a balmy climate, or of a resurrected and even sleazier Port Royal [Jamaica].[14]

Jamaica was the base for major English operations against the Spanish, especially Spanish treasure ships heading for the Windward Passage. By the mid seventeenth century, many buccaneers had moved into Port Royal, a southern town with a hell-raising reputation. From 1672 until it was destroyed by an earthquake in 1692, the fortified harbour port had a population of 6,500, with wharves 'lined with merchant ships and storehouses filled with spices, tobacco, sugar, beef, and barrels of wine. The residents of the town included 4 goldsmiths, 10 tailors, 13 doctors . . . 44 tavern keepers . . . and "a crew of vile strumpets and common prostitutes."'[15] Pirates chose the port not because of its halcyon island landscape but because it was safe. 'The English governors of Jamaica encouraged buccaneers (originally based in nearby Tortuga) to base their ships and crew at Port Royal. They believed correctly that their presence would protect the island from the return of the Spanish and would also discourage the French from attempting to seize the colony.' Governors would give out letters of marque to buccaneers, licensing them to attack Spanish ships. It was also a good place to fence goods: 'Governor D'Oyley even organised prize courts for the sale and disposal of captured ships and their cargoes.'[16]

While the myth of pirates enjoying strange and gorgeous luxuries on tropical isles endures, 'In reality, much of these riches – silk, spices, jewels – were funnelled straight back to Europe and America by traders who in turn were only too willing to prey on the pirates, flocking to their hideaways (under the pretence of the more respectable trade of slave-gathering) to provide them with the basic necessities of life at hugely inflated prices.'[17] In St Thome, off the African coast, the clergy too were involved in fleecing the pirates, according to Johnson: 'A ordinary Suit of black will sell for seven or eight Pound; a Turnstile Wig of four Shillings, for a Moidore; a Watch of forty shillings, for six Pound, &c.'

But the poor could not afford to haggle. 'As these Refreshments lay most with people who are in Want of other Necessaries, they come to us in Way of bartering, very cheap: A good Hog for an old Cutlash; a fat Fowl for a Span of Brazil Tobacco ... But with Money you give ... a Testune and a half for a Fowl; a Dollar per Gallon for Rum ... half a Dollar for a Dozen of Paraquets.'[18] (A moidore was a Portugese gold coin worth about 27 shillings then, £1.35 in today's terms; a crusado, of gold or silver, was worth about one-tenth of a moidore.)[19] Some self-sufficient cultures did not welcome the pillaging interlopers who used up essential resources such as food and brought only baubles, disease and the mixed blessing of guns. Other coastal people, including women, had to adapt in their struggle to survive and could develop a profitable co-operation based on varying degrees of discomfort and familiarity.

In different places and times, welcomes for pirates as big spenders might have been cautious, opportunistic or wholehearted. The notorious Blackbeard in North Carolina:

> often diverted himself with going ashore among the Planters, where he revell'd Night and Day: by these he was well-received, but whether out of Love or Fear I cannot say; sometimes he used them courteously enough, and made them Presents of Rum and Sugar, in Recompence of what he took from them; but, as for Liberties (which 'tis said) he and his Companions often took with the Wives and Daughters of the Planters, I cannot take it upon me to say, whether he paid them *ad Valorem*, or no.[20]

Culture shock on both sides, racial terror, even innate friendliness may have played their part. When pirate Captain North's boat was upset by a squall near the Main of Madagascar:

> Being now ... quite naked, he frightened the Negroes he went with, as he got out of the water, they took him for a Sea-Devil; but one woman, who had been used to sell fowl at the white Men's houses, had the Courage not to run away ... she gave him half her Petticoat to cover his Nakedness ... [and] help'd him perform his Journey to the Dwellings of some white Men.[21]

When pirate sloops hove into view, took down their mighty sails and dropped their anchors, not all crew members had to make radical adjustments to new conditions, because not all were strangers. In Ireland and England in the sixteenth and early seventeenth centuries, 'The business of plunder . . . was deeply rooted within the maritime community. Mariners, fishermen and even landsmen usually turned to piracy as a way of supplementing work and wages. Such men tended to retain close connections with communities ashore, seeking aid and assistance from women when the need arose.'[22] These women might have been involved with piracy because the pirates were their brothers, husbands, fathers (maybe even secretly their sisters); the histories of many societies show that people stay loyal to their relatives, however 'criminal' their occupations, unless they butcher their own kind or put the community at risk from another group's attacks.

Nor was piracy something foreign pirates brought with them as a novel practice to adopt. It existed already. Piracy among major landowning families such as the O'Malleys and the O'Flahertys in Ireland, as Anne Chambers showed in Chapter 7, consisted of short-distance raids on passing merchant vessels: local work, carried out opportunistically. There was no need for support from strangers in other coastal communities. These were families who had already established their territorial rights, for example selling permission to fish in certain waters. Women who served the people from such vessels may well have had a similar role to those in service to lords of the manor.

In sixteenth-century Cornwall, the infamous Lady Killigrew, though not a sea-based pirate, was nevertheless a plunderer (ironically and significantly, her son Sir John Killigrew was the president of the Commissioners for Piracy in 1582). I first found her story in a lively pamphlet on Cornish smuggling, on sale in a tourist tearoom. Out in the windy sun of that coast, eating cream scones and surrounded by moorland flowers, I read a tale which implicitly described her as leading attacks in the same way as Artemisia had – as a woman born to it. Members of the Killigrew family were reputedly 'the mainsprings of Cornish piracy'.[23] Historians present them as vultures preying on every ship that landed on their coast, their sense of entitlement the result of centuries of privilege. In one attack, it is reported that the ageing Lady Killigrew 'had quite lost her conscience . . . and led a boarding party to a German ship in the roads to commit two murders for the sake of a hoard of pieces of eight. John Killigrew succeeded in obtaining her acquittal when the case came before the judges at Launceston but this verdict cost him his fortune.' [24] Although she was not hanged, two of her employees were executed. [25]

It is likely that those who benefited most from the presence of pirates, whatever the coastal community, were the privileged, well connected and literate. Next in line would have been unprivileged men, who could sell their own labour and that of their wives and children; unprivileged women who had only their own labour and bodies to sell were at the bottom of the pile. Links in some cases may have run along the lines of the local smuggling network romanticised by Rudyard Kipling in 'Brandy for the parson, baccy for the Clerk; laces for a lady, letters for a spy, and watch the wall, my darling, while the Gentlemen go by!' [26] Complicity certainly operated at the highest level. The Minister of Killybegs in Ireland apparently had pirates glutting themselves with whoring and drinking in his house. [27] Lord O'Sullivan of Berehaven was 'A notorious friend of the English pirates, he bought their spoils, which he stored in his castle. He helped fit out pirate captains for their cruises and protect them when Queen Elizabeth sent ships to try and arrest them.' [28]

The people who had power, whether local landowners, tribal leaders or the governors of British colonies, had most resources to offer to pirates. These included legal or political protection, accommodation, spare, good-quality food, the ability to command local labour to serve the pirates' needs, be it repair worm-eaten bands on waterbarrels or stock a vessel with coconuts, wild hogs and goats. [29] Some greedy local landowners may have gained prestige by having men of violence on their side, while in places and periods where there were gaps between local power and regional, national and colonial authority – for example in some Caribbean islands, where the English crown's tax demands were hated – pirates may have found friends in high places. If the authority was remote and resented, for instance a big landlord or representative of foreign domination, local big wigs might well turn a blind eye to piracy or allow pirate activity up to a certain threshold. Head-on collisions with pirates were risky when local policing power was limited and local leaders more inclined to show loyalty towards buccaneers than towards jumped-up princes.

Loyalty faced even more complex tests if rival pirate clans appeared. Locals would have to calculate 'Who can pay most? Who is the more terrifying? Strategically, who should be shown respect?'

Women's involvement with pirates ashore

Throughout history people have swallowed hard and given a no-questions-asked hospitality to invaders simply because it has not paid to cross cut-throats or those in power, whether pirates in the west of Ireland or Nazis in 1940s France. In the case of pirates, local peoples' decision to co-operate enabled the sea-rovers to carry on with their adventuring and fighting, but may have divided the community into those who collaborated more and more, and those who resisted. In that sense some women were complicit with piracy, and very integrally involved in the whole structure of the piracy business.

In many cases, both parties needed to exploit each other for survival. Although shore-based women were not central to pirate crimes at sea, they were pivotal to the pirates' survival between voyages. Women and men offered pirates essential services at a time when the line between hospitality to strangers and business practice was not as fiercely drawn as it is today. The help offered would often have been informal, sometimes intermittent and as likely as not given by women with their children (by pirates) balanced on their hip in between their own domestic work.

Seventeenth-century pirate captain's wife Mistress Suxbridge ran a lodging house near Dublin with her daughters.[30] By the eighteenth and nineteenth centuries, coastal women were recorded as naval landladies, owners of ships' chandlers, madams, marine victuallers, crimps, shareholders of whaling boats, philanthropic founders of seamen's missions and organisers of the Ladies Seamen's Friends Society.[31] After working on a man-o-war, Mrs Cola ran an East End sailors' pub in 1782;[32] the fictional Mrs Hosea Hussey in *Moby Dick* in the 1840s ran the Nantucket whalers' inn, the Try Pots, wearing 'a polished necklace of codfish vertebra'.[33] So it seems inevitable that earlier women would have had been landladies for pirates too.

Although the main healthcare references in Johnson are to (male) ships' surgeons, women probably performed at least auxiliary duties in their traditional role of carers. When in 1681 buccaneer surgeon Lionel Wafer stayed with Cuna Indians on Darien, Panama, he 'took part in tremendous drinking bouts where the effects of huge quantities of palm liquor and corn beer were slept off in hammocks while women sponged the men's overheated bodies to keep them cool.'[34] One of the main problems for women as healers and sexual partners was sexually transmitted diseases. On St Thome, for instance, Johnson recorded that:

> The women (not unlike the Mulatto Generation every where else) are fond of strangers; not only the Courtezans, whose Interest may be supposed to wind up their Affections, but also the married Women, who think themselves obliged when you favour them with the Secrecy of an Appointment; but the Unhappiness of pursuing Amours is, that the Generallity of both Sexes are touched with venereal Taints, without so much as one Surgeon among them, or any Body skill'd in Physick, to cure or palliate the progressive Mischief: The only Person pretending that Way, is an Irish Father, whose Knowledge is all comprehended in the Virtues of two or three Simples, and those . . . is what they depend on, for subduing the worst of Malignity . . . few are exempted from the Misfortune of a Running, Eruptions, or the like.'[35]

Sex with seafarers

The boundaries between physical ministering, hospitality, love and paid sexual intercourse are unclear in all the accounts – as they may have been in reality. When pirates landed in tiny coves and busy harbours, the local women they met must have had different levels of knowledge, interest in men and assertiveness about their own needs. Throughout history, women have wanted information about the worlds they have been excluded from. For women dealing with better-behaved pirates, a sloop in their bay – whether or not it flew the Jolly Roger – may have been a rare opportunity for economic gain or just for excitement. New Zealand criminologist Jan Jordan found that

1960s 'ship girls' who rushed down to greet ships were not primarily avid for sex (whether for profit or not) but thrilled by second-hand contact with the adventurous world of the sea. They liked being with men from far away who travelled to exotic places, told extraordinary stories and led seemingly unfettered lives (a few ship girls who married their seafaring contacts were quickly disappointed to find that their roving heroes were feckless, boring or unable to make contact with other human being).[36]

Old Irish public records indicate something of the stigma attached to such women, some of whom were married: 'In August 1610 the council of Munster complained of the number of desperate and dishonest men joining the pirates, as well as "such shameless and adulterous women as daylie repaired unto them . . . [in] divers Taverns, Alehouses and victualling houses" in Baltimore, Inisharking and other places along the coast.'[37]

Certainly one way for less privileged women to have access to pirates' booty was by selling sexual favours. Seamen, because of long confinement on ship, 'slaves for 46 weeks and lords for six', were more ready to roister ashore than perhaps any other group of cloistered workers, even monks. We can imagine that pirates, with their sometimes vast earnings, were even more reckless than the eighteenth-century mariners who behaved 'with greater Licentuousness than is Customary to be allow'd to others . . . You may . . . see them accompanied with three or four Lewd Women, few of them Sober, run roaring through the streets by broad Daylight with a Fiddler before them: And if the Money, to their thinking goes not fast enough these ways, they'll find out others, and sometimes fling it among the Mob by Handfuls.'[38] However, even pirates could tire of sex. Johnson described the pirates' readiness to move on 'after six Weeks Stay . . . [they became] weary of whoring and drinking'.[39]

One of the most famous pirate stories is told by Exquemelin: 'I have seen a man in Jamaica give 500 pieces of eight to a whore, just to see her naked.'[40] (This translates into about £1,500 in today' terms because there were eight reales to the dollar and a dollar was worth between £2.50 and £3 around 1670). Pirates coming ashore in Ireland with pockets 'full of Spanish silver and Duckettes [found their] wealth [was] too much for such hoores', as Sir Basil Brooke told the Lord Deputy in 1627.[41] One effect of this was that women apparently became rivalrous:

pirate Captain Roberts reported that in the Caribbean island of St Bartholomew, women 'endeavour'd to outvie each other in Dress, and Behavior, to attract the good Graces of such generous Lovers, that Paid well for their Favours.'[42]

As well as being a good base from which to attack transatlantic shipping, the stated main reason for many English pirates' visits to Ireland, increasingly after 1604, was the plentiful supply of sexually available women. Captain James Henry Mainwaring, a pirate who was later pardoned and knighted, claimed that pirates frequented Ireland because of 'the good store of English, Scottish and Irish wenches which resort unto them'.[43] At a time when few working-class women made sea journeys, this is fascinating evidence of mobility, suggesting that prostitutes may have migrated to Ireland for the specific purpose of work and that the sex industry, like the piracy industry, had developed a good underground intelligence network concerning sites of the richest pickings. Historian John Appleby found:

> In some places piracy fed off the hidden support of women. But by the same process it could easily turn women into victims; wherever piracy flourished so did the business of prostitution. The relationship between the two is clearly revealed by the spread of prostitution into the remote coastal communities of south-west Munster in the early seventeenth century, when large numbers of English pirates were regularly visiting the coast.[44]

Not all prostitutes were free agents. Women had sex on instruction, including by order of pirate 'masters'. In Guinea in 1721 Captain Roberts found about 30 English men who:

> have been either privateering, buccaneering or pyrating, and still retain and love the Riots and Humours common to that Sort of Life. They live very friendly with the Natives, and have many of them of both Sexes, to be their *Gromettas* or Servants: The Men are faithful, and the Women so obedient, that they are very ready to prostitute themselves to whomsoever their Masters shall command them.[45]

Networking and fencing

Women could place themselves in a more powerful position by using their local knowledge of networks and prices to help dispose of stolen booty. In writing about plunderers on land, Eric Hobsbawm makes the point that: 'It is . . . a mistake to think of bandits as mere children of nature roasting stags in the greenwood. A successful brigand chief is at least as closely in touch with the market and the wider economic universe as a small landowner or prosperous farmer.' [46] The business of piracy is to acquire and dispose of the best possible goods with the greatest possible ease and profit. This means pirates valued whispers about merchantmen sailing in areas where they could be attacked and might reward those who could pass on such intelligence. They would also pay those who acted as emissaries for ransom demands, transmitted threats to pillage, or knew about the policing plans of local officials. Local people may have wanted payment in cash or food, rather than bales of Spanish hide or bushels of cloves fat as fingers, but they had to accept the currency that was on offer. Its inappropriateness may have allowed them to demand a better bargain. Pirates needed contacts not just with local victuallers but with those in the wider world able to afford the captured spoil – gold dust and elephants' teeth, molasses, tobacco and gum – and with those able to dispose of stolen goods without question. In some cases they needed moneylenders or informal pawnbrokers to finance new voyages and refittings. Women must have been involved in such pirate networking, as fences, receivers and informants. In 1740, all London indictments show that:

> the *only* felony for which a greater number of women were indicted than men was the offence of receiving stolen goods . . . Males thieves frequently formed partnerships with female receivers. In the eighteenth century, marriage was a business partnership. In the proletarian life of London as revealed by felony records it is interesting that the most frequent male-female relationship was that between the thief and the receiver. [47]

John Appleby's research in Ireland found that many local women received pirate booty. In 1610, silverware, linen and canvas was given to Mrs Henry Skipwith, wife of the captain of the Fort of Kinsale. Donor Captain William Baugh hoped to marry her daughter. Irishman John Bedlake's kinswoman was presented with a parcel of striped canvas and blue starch, which could be used to make a waistcoat. On Long Island blacke dermod (*sic*) and his wife gave pirates food, gaining wine, broadcloth and steel in return.[48] There was a whole system of trading and those with most access to it would have been the women from families which already had power and privilege.

Love and Marriage

When people from a shore-based community accepted some sort of exchange with the pirates (or smugglers), based on an approximate equality of interests and power, then they implicitly entered the outlaw world. Sometimes a symbiotic relationship developed, and one way this could be expressed was through friendship, courtship or marriage. Johnson's eighteenth-century tales of local women befriending, loving and marrying English and American pirates sometimes show real inter-racial tenderness with pirates who might be confused about – but fitted in with – very different lifestyles. Wives and mistresses have often played a crucial role in the acclimatisation of foreigners: early twentieth-century local women acted as 'sleeping dictionaries' for English rubber planters in Malaya, while Canadian Indian women in the eighteenth century functioned as social bridge-builders between foreign fur traders and indigenous hunters in a mix of temporary and permanent relationships.[49] Decision-makers in the pirate band had to find ways to assess whatever arrangements were already in place on arrival ashore and determine whether and how to co-exist with local people, if they were not going to attack. Women's information about cultural patterns must have been crucial.

Pirates, like the crew of Captain Davis at St Nicholas in the Cape Verde Islands, sometimes remained for months and years, 'So charm'd by the Luxuries of the Place, and the free Conversation of some Women, that they staid behind; and one of them . . . married and settled himself and lives there to this Day.'[50] Local women appear sometimes to have welcomed the changes these outsiders brought to the place, in the same way as Jane Austen describes nineteenth-century gentlewomen appreciating the officers quartered near them, who helped fill the long evenings with dances, gossip, flirtation and dinners.[51] It is possible that some of the more glib and educated pirates were welcomed with fervour and regularity, for pirates did have favourite haunts. For instance, 'In May 1627 the crew of a Dutch pirate ship were apparently always drunk ashore with the Queanes of Killybegs.'[52] At least 20 pirate ships regularly dropped anchor by the south and west Irish coastal communities in the early seventeenth century, which could mean as many as 1,000 men visited.[53] In 1690 the 'Pirate Round' (of attacks in the Indian Ocean on Mogul and Arab vessels passing between the Red Sea ports of Jeddah and Mocha, then disposing of the goods in America, especially Rhode Island) had a marked effect on women ashore in Madagascar. The 'Round' 'operated so smoothly during the decade or so of its existence that pirates went in for domesticity and sometimes offered wives and children as pledges of their return. There was little need for such hostages, who would probably have been abandoned without a qualm anyway.'[54]

Women married to pirates could still have been involved in crime in their own right. A number of women topped at Tyburn gallows in London had been connected with or married to sailors and there is no reason to assume that pirates were any different in this respect:

> Anne Hazard, termed a 'prostitute' who married a sailor and was hanged in 1743 had been a 'Bomb-boat woman' – that is, one who plied small craft alongside the moored ocean-going vessels to sell groceries and other wares ... Ruggety Madge, the famous Dublin lady of Rag Fair and Drury Lane ... often passed as an Indiaman's widow ... Hannah Dagoe ... was married to a Spanish sailor whom she met in debtor's spunging house in Wapping ... Elizabeth Fox ... the wife of a sailor ... was described by the Ordinary of Newgate as ... 'being one of the most scandalous, Creatures and notorious Pickpockets in Town.'[55]

Johnson calls some male pirates' women partners 'wives' and twentieth-century writers, for example Philip Gosse, confer posthumous marital status on live-in lovers. But there were many forms of unofficial working-class marriage, some of which continued into the nineteenth century among isolated communities, especially travelling and scavenging ones, Peter Linebough adds.

Although hundreds of 'Dalilahs' made permanent liaisons with men they knew to be pirates, others plighted their troth to males who only later took up the profession. High-born Captain Nelson initially sailed a regular schooner loaded with potatoes and fruit to Halifax, but became wilder and lost his commission through drinking. Leaving his wife on Prince Edward Island, 'to look after his estates, which brought him in £300 a year', he went a-pirating to the West Indies. When he returned home, 'to visit his wife and family . . . no one dared to molest him', according to Gosse.[56]

Sometimes pirates who settled down to marriage found themselves behaving with care in regard to sexual matters – by choice or by force. When Captain North's pirates took up residence in Ambonavoula, eastern Madagascar, they 'grew continent and sober, as no doubt they esteemed their Security to depend on shewing the Blacks they could govern those Passions to which they themselves were Slaves.'[57] Local black people often showed themselves critical of the morals of white pirates who became involved with women. Eighteenth-century pirate Captain England 'liv'd there very wantonly for several Weeks, making free with Negroe Women, and committing such outragious Acts that they came into an open Rupture with the Natives.'[58] On occasions the community policed domestic violence: Captain Howard, off the coast of India, 'married a woman of the Country, and being a morose ill natur'd Fellow, and using her ill, he was murder'd by her Relations.'[59] In the 'Sierraleon' trial of Mate William Davis, a witness deposed that Davis 'consorted to idle Customs and Ways of living among the Negroes, from whom he received a wife, and ungratefuly sold her one Evening, for some Punch to quench his Thirst.' Her relations and friends angrily decided that the best punishment was to sell him in turn – to a 'Christian Black', for two years' service.[60]

Pirates who became tired of the sea would naturally abide in places that gave them ease, possibly as traders or landowners. Many a poacher has turned gamekeeper, and this appears to be true of some pirates who joined the forces of law and order rather than just settling down. Marriage to a former pirate could bring a woman new social status. Maria Cobham, according to Ellms, was socially ambitious and she and her pirate captain husband became pillars of the community (see Chapter 11). Plymouth-born pirate Captain Condent married the Mauritius governor's sister-in-law. 'A few years later the captain and his wife left the island and sailed to France, settling at St. Malo, where Condent drove a considerable trade as a merchant.'[61] But some black wives of retired Anglo-American pirates were treated as second-class citizens and their mixed-race children taken away from them for rearing in the capital cities of empires. South Sea pirate Thomas White, from Plymouth, 'settled down with his crew at a place called Methelage in Madagascar, marrying a native woman and leading the peaceful life of a planter . . . In his will, he . . . appointed three guardians for his son, all of different nationalities, with instructions that the boy should be taken to England to be educated, which was duly done.'[62] In the 1760s, Captain Joseph Thwaites had two wives. A Mohamedan convert who worked for the Ottoman Empire, whenever he 'happened to be near Gibraltar, he would go ashore and through his agents, Messrs. Ross and Co., transmit large sums of money to his wife and children in England. But Thwaites had another home in Algiers fitted with every luxury, including three Armenian girls.'[63] (He later bought himself a handsome mansion near New York, but 'retribution came in an unlooked-for quarter, for he was bitten by a rattlesnake and died in the most horrible agonies both of mind and body.')

With their men away at sea for long periods, coastal women connected with seafarers have long learned independence. Studies of twentieth-century Liverpool seafarer's wives[64] show women taking the major responsibility for breadwinning and day-to-day decisions. In seventeenth- and eighteenth-century Irish coastal communities, the women owned ships, organised markets for fish, as at Claddagh near Galway, and arranged 'wage protests and demonstrations on behalf of absent husbands'.[65] This suggests that many women who co-operated with or married pirates were spirited and had learned sound judgement within the boundaries of knowing what they had to do to avoid incurring wrath.

Occasionally, significant local women may have given pirates status by marrying them. In Johnson's fantasy account, Signor Caraccioli, a renegade priest turned pirate, and Captain Misson, married the Madagascan queen's niece and daughter respectively and Caraccioli 'was appointed Secretary of State', Gosse told readers of *The Pirates'*

Who's Who.[66] They also lavished much love on the men. Sometimes women saved pirates' lives in courtrooms: 36-year-old Irish widow living in Havana, Elizabeth Berrow (Isobel Verroa), deposed in favour of pirate Don Phelipe Ybanes in the case of La Virgen de Rosario and del Santo Cristo de Buen Viage. Her testimony was one of the factors that enabled a judgement to be reversed in the appeal court, and her pirate friend was released.[67] In Charlestown, South Carolina, at privateer Stede Bonnet's trial, 'His piteous Behaviour under Sentence, very much affected the People of the Province, particularly the Women, and great Application was made to the Governor for saving his Life, but in vain.'[68] But not all women were so generous: the wife of Boston Captain Knot in 1699 'gave information to Governor, the Earl of Bellomont, of the wherabouts of a pirate called Gillam, who was "wanted".'[69]

Coastal women on pirate ships

Because of their connections on land with pirates, women sometimes sailed with them – as whores, wives and workers. Despite men's fears of the disruption to the crew and bad luck women's presence aboard might bring, lust overrode qualms. In at least one case women who may have been captives rather than members of a local community served as sex slaves. Johnson reports that when pirate Charles Vane was sailing north Jamaica waters, the crew captured a turtle sloop, and put their captives aboard another captured ship, 'except the two Women, whom they kept for their own Entertainment, contrary to the usual Practice of Pyrates, who generally sent them away, lest they should occasion Contention.'[70] In 1609 a merchant ship trading with pirates at Baltimore in Cork '"hoysed sayle and went away with . . . two of the pyrattes and some of their whores, about fyve in number" still aboard, in order to evade the local Admiralty officials.'[71] Prostitutes who worked with pirates had the opportunity to make short excursions: at best jaunts, at worst a floating incarceration, these were a means to earn a lot from a captive market down in the bowels of the heaving ships. Young women who were not prostitutes but had taken a fancy to a pirate (and vice versa) might have needed permission from parents and other crew members in order to sail. Poverty-stricken parents throughout history have agreed to much in order to lessen family hardship; Cormac (see page 112) was said virtually to have acted as his daughters' pimp. Accounts mention he was so friendly to pirates that he 'spared not his own daughters to bid them welcome'.[72]

It seems likely that crew resistance to having women aboard might have lessened if the visitors wore breeches for the duration. Seeing the women dressed as men however notionally, might have enabled the superstitious to dodge the idea that there were omens of bad luck aboard, as well as giving a clear sign that they were not sexually available to the entire crew. Another way women could have been overlooked might have been if they were seen as of too low a status to count; as objects that could be kicked and dis-counted, like dogs. Aboard pirate Captain Williams' vessel off Madagascar, a black woman advised a seaman not to let the allegedly friendly messengers aboard 'with Goat and some Calabashes of Toke.' The seaman, 'Giving the Wench a kick, cryed "D-m ye, must we have no fresh Provisions for your Whimsies."' (In fact, she was right. Once aboard the tricksters shot the seaman in the head, threw his colleague overboard, and took the ship. No mention is made of what happened to the woman.)[73]

Women could also be counted as 'not really women' if they were officers' wives. Johnson indicates this possibility in his fantasy about Captain Misson, living on the island of Johanna, who proposed a short cruise to Zanzibar. Misson's wife and the wife of his *confrère* Caraccioli issued threats at the prospect of being left behind, saying:

If they were not allowed to keep them company on the Voyage, they must not expect to see them on their Return . . . In a Word, they [the officers] were obliged to yield to them, but told them, if the Wives of their Men should insist as strongly on following their Example, their Tenderness would be their Ruin, and make them a Prey to their Enemies; they answer'd the Queen should prevent that, by ordering no Woman should go on board, and if any were in the Ships, they should return on Shore: This Order was accordingly made.

When the pirates attacked a rich Portuguese ship, 'The two Women never quitted the Decks all the Time of the Engagement, neither gave they the least Mark of Fear, except for their Husbands.'[74]

Unlike these non-battling heroines, some Algerian women are said to have worked as pirates and taken the initiative sexually with their English male captives, fascinated by their foreskins. According to a story in *Les Femmes pirates*,[75] Penmal, an English seafarer, was captured by Djoamite pirates off Algeria in 1804:

> He noticed . . . the presence of several pirates who stood out from the others. They were appreciably smaller both in waist and breadth of shoulder, with their voices and cheeks completely devoid of hair . . . [Penmal took them to be adolescents, but then] dumfounded, learnt that it is not uncommon for a widowed and childless woman to take her place on board a pirate ship in order to make a living. This was seen as preferable to the precarious life of a widow with no means of support. The women Djoamite pirates were as courageous in battle as men, perhaps more so when in the heat of the moment, after boarding, it came to killing the victims.[76]

One woman pirate noticed that Penmal was limping, and offered to have him taken home with her to be treated.

> The man would normally have accepted the situation . . . but his seductress really was not very appealing. She wore on her head a kind of turban whose colour it would have been foolish to try to define; in truth it was greasy and it is quite probable that she, just like all the Djoamite people, knew or cared little about personal hygiene, lest it be an accidental fall into the sea!

However, Penmal did go off with her, for a month. When he came back cured,

> he refused point blank to comment on the nature of his relations with the woman pirate. All he would say was that her name was Jossabee and she had helped him get better by the use of herbs and ointments . . . One can however deduce that the woman had

obtained what she desired, for how else would one explain the sudden upsurge of interest in the sailors shown by her colleagues, who, as a result of her revelations, came and demanded something not inconsiderable? They wanted quite simply to find out what possible difference there could be between followers of Mohammed and the uncircumcised! . . . like it or not, the uncircumcised were obliged to submit themselves to the will of these ladies.[77]

The racist and reticent tone of this account leaves many important questions open. How could the women be so sexually free? How could such a society permit women to be pirates? Above all, how typical were they? But it does let us know that some women in the right place at the right time took the initiative in relations with men and sailed as pirates themselves.

Victims of pirate barbarity

Accounts of piracy mainly refer to women as victims of pirates' wanton cruelty. A whole book could be written based on extracts about such violence. Women suffered sexual barbarities all the more ferocious because they were female victims of men and in some cases black victims of white abuse. Many descriptions, for instance Exquemelin's in 1678, tell of the kind of European plundering of less-developed countries and their peoples that has become familiar from accounts of early imperialism. These instances of mass-slaughter, enslavement and depredation are not so much pirates being wickedly piratical as European men doing what Europeans did in places they thought they had a right to despise.

At the Laccadive Islands, in the Arabian Sea west of Malabar, pirate Captain England's men found the men had gone, leaving 'the Women and Children to guard one another. The Women they forced in a barbarous Manner to their Lusts, and to requite them, destroyed their Cocoa Trees, and fired several of their Houses and Churches.'[78] Captain Morgan in Latin America in 1670 sent out relays of 200-strong raiding parties to scour the countryside each day.[79] Precious food stores were depleted to satisfy current and future hunger, and local wives and daughters brutally taken for sex. 'The rovers had ways of dealing with the women who held out. They would let them leave the church, which was being used as their prison, as if giving them the chance to wash themselves – but once a woman was in their hands they would work their will upon her, or beat her, starve her or similarly torment her. Morgan, being the General, should have set a better example but he was no better than the rest. Whenever a beautiful woman was brought in, he at once sought to dishonour her.'[80]

Nor were local leaders respected. When Monmouthshire pirate Captain Howel Davis found that the governor and chief men of Princes Island had sent their wives to a village a few miles away, he walked there with 14 of his men 'intending, as we may suppose, to supply their Husbands' Places with them; but being discover'd, the Women fled to a neighbouring Wood, and Davis and the rest retreated to their Ship, without effecting their Design.'[81] Captain Edward Teach even set up the assault of one of his own wives, a young woman of 16. 'While his Sloop lay in Okerecock [Ocracoke] Inlet, and he ashore at the Plantation, where his Wife lived, with whom after he had lain all Night, it was his Custom to invite five or six of his brutal Companions to come ashore, and he would force her to prostitute her self to them all, one after another, before his Face.'[82]

Nor were the depredations all committed thousands of miles away. Captain John Smith, alias Gow, was plundering off the coast of Scotland. At Calf Island, 'Here the Boatswain went ashore again, but, meeting with no Plunder, carry'd off two young Women, the Mother of whom, crying and begging of them to let alone her Daughters, was knock'd down by the Villain with a Pistol, of which 'tis said she died the next Day, and the poor Girls were hurried on board, and used in a most inhumane manner.'[83]

Plate 8, from Ellms' nineteenth-century anthology on pirates, shows a toned-down version of what may have been an orgy or a mass-rape in Carolina. Captain Charles Vane, renowned for his ventures off the North American coast, met the crew of the famous Blackbeard 'whom he saluted with his great guns loaded with shot. This compliment of one pirate chief to another was returned in like kind, and then "mutual civilities" followed for several days between the two pirate captains and their crews, these civilities taking the form of glorious debauch in a quiet creek on the coast.'[84] Although twentieth-century writer of pirate yarns Philip Gosse described the incident as a 'glorious debauch', local women could well have experienced it as a nightmare. Any brutality that took place is denied by the image.

Plundering from the shore

Some coastal women plundered the sea from the safety of the shore. For at least the last 500 years British women have smuggled goods and taken part in wrecking parties (shining a false light to lull an unwary ship on to rocks in order to get its cargo). Wrecking reached its height in the eighteenth century, and the proliferating newspapers reported a number of cases, especially in Devon and Cornwall. 'Mistress Edgecumbe was not above looting wrecks in Mount's Bay while at Padstow, on the north coast, the Prideaux family had their own hide-outs in the cliffs for "rich merchandise."'[85] The cargoes recovered ranged from the useful, like fruit, flour, tar, cork, deerskin or staves, to the luxurious, like wine, coffee berries, saffron, indigo, licorice, rum or brandy.

Although Daphne du Maurier's novel *Jamaica Inn* presents wrecking and smuggling as men's trade, it appears to have been more a community activity. In 1817 in Mullion:

> Thousands of people are instantly collected near the fatal spot . . . men, women and children are working on her to break her up by night and day. The precipices they descend, the rocks they climb and the billows they buffet to seize the floating fragments are the most frightful and alarming I have ever beheld; the hardships they endure, especially the women in winter, to save all they can, are almost incredible.[86]

In 1826 in Hale Bay, people plundered a distressed ship, *The Ocean*, which was *en route* from Campeachy to Havre de Grace. A disgusted Plymouth newspaper revealed that women were in the lead.

> On the first intimation of the disaster, a number of persons from the adjacent villages crowded down with the view to plundering

the stores. The greater part of these miscreants were women who carried off whatever they could lay their hands on, and were very dextrous in concealing bottles of wine, and other things, so as to elude a search . . . As the day advanced, the plunderers, male and female, became intoxicated, and a variety of contests, some of them of the most ludicrous description, took place . . . Every exertion was made by the respectable inhabitants to check this most disgraceful scene of rapine . . . We state these facts in shame and sorrow.[87]

Given the precarious nature of making a living and women's responsibility for fending off starvation, it can be seen how and why coastal women would be drawn into piracy and wrecking. They could not afford the luxury of conforming to distant ideas about respectable womanly behaviour.

Notes

1. Basil Fuller and Ronald Leslie Melville, *Pirate Harbours and Their Secrets*, Stanley Paul, 1935.
2. Fuller and Melville, p.184.
3. Captain Charles Johnson, *A General History of the Robberies and Murders of the Most Notorious Pyrates* (1724), published as Daniel Defoe, *A General History of the Pyrates*, Manuel Schonhorn (ed), Dent, 1972.
4. Charles Ellms, *The Pirates Own Book, or Authentic Narratives of the Lives, Exploits and Executions of the Most Celebrated Sea Robbers*, Sanborn & Carter, 1837 and Philip Gosse, *The Pirates' Who's Who*, Dulau 1924.
5. See A. O. Exquemelin, *The Buccaneers of America* (1678), The Folio Society, 1969 and Hilary McD Beckles, *Natural Rebels: a social history of enslaved black women in Barbados*, Zed Press, 1989.
6. Judith Fingard's *Jack in Port: Sailortowns of eastern Canada*, University of Toronto Press, 1982, takes a sociological approach to seafarers as labourers within an economic system.
7. See John C. Appleby, 'Women and Piracy in Ireland: from Grainne O'Malley to Anne Bonny' in Margaret MacCurtain and Mary O'Dowd (eds), *Women in Early Modern Ireland*, Wolfhound Press, 1991, p.66, which has a full and useful bibliographic list.
8. Johnson, *op cit*, p.5.
9. David Mitchell, *Pirates*, Thames & Hudson, 1976, p.84.

10. Marcus Rediker, *Between the Devil and the Deep Blue Sea: merchant seamen, Pirates and the Anglo-American maritime world, 1700–1750*, Cambridge University Press, 1987, p.275.
11. Johnson, *op cit*, p.130.
12. David Cordingly and John Falconer, *Pirates: fact and fiction*, Collins & Brown, 1992, p.82.
13. Johnson, *op cit*, p.435.
14. Mitchell, *op cit*, p.84.
15. Cordingly and Falconer, *op cit*, p.38.
16. *ibid*, p.36.
17. *ibid*, p.82.
18. Johnson, *op cit*, p.179.
19. *ibid*, p.675 (footnote by editor Manuel Schonhorn).
20. Johnson, *op cit*, p.76.
21. *ibid*, p.520.
22. Appleby, *op cit*, p.54.
23. Neville Williams, *Captains Outrageous*, Barrie & Rockiff, 1961, p.74.
24. *ibid*, p.75.
25. Mitchell, *op cit*, p.39.
26. Rudyard Kipling, 'Smugglers' Song'.
27. Appleby, *op cit*, p.61, especially note 21, based on C. Senior *A Nation of Pirates*, 1976 and PRO SP 63/244/659b and 678b.
28. Gosse, *op cit*, p.288.
29. Johnson, *op cit*, p.467.
30. Appleby, *op cit*, p.60.
31. Fingard, *op cit*, pp.198, 230.
32. Julie Wheelwright, *Amazons and Military Maids: women who dressed as men in pursuit of life, liberty and happiness*, Pandora, 1989, p.111.
33. Herman Melville, *Moby Dick* (originally published in Britain 1851), Wordsworth Classics, 1992, p.68.
34. Mitchell, *op cit*, p.78.
35. Johnson, *op cit*, p.199.
36. Jan Jordan, 'Ship Girls: the invisible women of the sea' paper to the 'Women and the Sea' conference, Wellington Maritime Museum, New Zealand, December 1993.
37. Appleby, *op cit*, p.59, note 16.
38. Bernard Mandeville, quoted in Peter Linebaugh, *The London Hanged: crime and civil society in the eighteenth century*, Allen Lane, The Penguin Press, 1991, p.131, note 22.
39. Johnson, *op cit*, p.228.
40. Exquemelin, *op cit*, p.68. (Other translators call her a common strumpet.)
41. Appleby, *op cit*, p.61.
42. Johnson, *op cit*, p.218.
43. Appleby, *op cit*, p.59.

44. Appleby, *op cit*, p.55.

45. Johnson, *op cit*, p.226.

46. Eric Hobsbawm, *Bandits*, Pelican, 1972, p.74.

47. Linebaugh, *op cit*, p.145.

48. Appleby, *op cit*, p.61.

49. Charles Allen (ed), *Tales from the South China Seas*, Futura, 1991 p.100; Sylvia Van Kirk, *'Many Tender Ties': Women in Fur-Trade Society, 1670–1870*, Watson & Dwyer, 1980, p.53.

50. Johnson, *op cit*, p.170.

51. See Jane Austen's description's of the Bennett daughters' reception of officers in *Pride and Prejudice*, MacMillan, 1895, p.73.

52. Appleby, *op cit*, p.61.

53. *ibid* (estimate), p.59.

54. Mitchell, *op cit*, pp.101-2.

55. Linebaugh, *op cit*, p.140.

56. Gosse, *op cit*, p.235.

57. Johnson, *op cit*, p.527.

58. *ibid*, p.117.

59. *ibid*, p.494.

60. *ibid*, p.280.

61. Gosse, *op cit*, p.85.

62. *ibid*, p.316.

63. *ibid*, p.299.

64. Pat Ayers, *The Liverpool Docklands: life and work in Atholl Street*, Liverpool Docklands History Project, 1992.

65. Appleby, *op cit*, p.54.

66. Gosse, *op cit*, p.74.

67. John Franklin Jameson, *Privateering and Piracy of the Colonial Period*, MacMillan, 1923, p.564. A. Hyatt Verrill also writes about the woman, constructing a long and implausible romantic tale, in *Love Stories of the Pirates*, Collins, 1924.

68. Johnson, *op cit*, p.111.

69. Gosse, *op cit*, p.186.

70. Johnson, *op cit*, p.620.

71. Appleby, *op cit*, p.60.

72. *ibid*, p.59, citing Captain Monson.

73. Johnson, *op cit*, p.504.

74. *ibid*, p.415.

75. Henri Musnik, *les Femmes pirates: aventures et legendes de la mer*, Le Masque, Paris, 1934, translated for this book by Manuel A. Bermejo.

76. *ibid*, p.121.

77. *ibid*, p.121.

78. Johnson, *op cit*, p.126.

79. Exquemelin, *op cit*, p.166.

80. *ibid*, p.167.
81. Johnson, *op cit*, p.192.
82. *ibid*, p.76.
83. *ibid*, p.365.
84. Gosse, *op cit*, p.304-5.
85. Williams, *op cit*, p.75.
86. Quote from Rev G.C. Smith, 'The Wreckers', cited in John Vivian, *Tales of Cornish Wreckers*, Tor Mark Press, 1970, p.21-2.
87. Vivian, *ibid*, p.31-2.

9 Criminals, communards or crumpet?

With jacket blue and trowsers white
Just like a sailor neat and tight
The sea was the heart's delight
of the rambling female sailor . . .
From stem to stern she'd boldly go
She Brav'd all dangers, feared no foe.[1]

What kind of women became pirates in the seventeenth and eighteenth centuries, when Anglo-American piracy was at its height? Were they breeched lesbians attracted to the idea of pirate vessels as floating egalitarian communities, petty thieves changing their field and scale of operation or waterfront prostitutes putting in a stint on a ship instead of a bawdy house? In Chapter 11, the stories of Ann Bonny, Mary Read and Maria Cobham stand as examples of what scores or hundreds of other women may have done. The early eighteenth century was a time of greatly increased mobility for women, with pirate vessels in plenty, so there was more likelihood of women going a-pirating during that period than at any other time. I have come across two buried references to women on privateers, but how many women pirates and privateers went unrecorded? Out of between 1,500 and 2,000 Anglo-American pirates sailing between 1719 and 1722,[2] surely at least 20 were women in disguise? Surely at least 50 of the men took women to sea? Surely at least ten were female workers known to be women? Although some maritime historians[3] believe that women on pirate ships were prostitutes rather than participants, the evidence about cross-dressed seafaring women on ordinary ships suggests a more complicated picture:

> the virtual absence of a relationship – between cross-dressing and prostitution, is striking. For many lower-class women, prostitution was a last resort . . . in view of the fact that prostitutes and female cross-dressers were very much alike in age, class, and background, the choice for cross-dressing when confronted with difficult circumstances implied a clear rejection of the alternative of prostitution . . . those who became prostitutes followed the female, passive, sexual path, while those who 'became men' followed the male, active and sexless path, [and] at the same time preserved their sexual honour.[4]

The two sorts of women may not have been so drastically different, in all cases. We can work out what kind of women were likely to become pirates by looking at the population pirates were drawn from (itinerant, resistant, prone to crime, sometimes violent); at accounts of criminal women in London in that period; and at the limited pirate biographies. And we can understand something of their relationship to the systems of social regulation by using as a guide feminist studies of marginalised women such as prostitutes today.

A time of opportunity

Urbanisation changed hundreds of thousands of lives in the eighteenth century. Women in the expanding cities and towns, most of them domestic servants, had new opportunities – and reasons – to wander in search of work. Increasingly prohibited from the trades they had practised for centuries, including tailoring, inn-keeping, blacksmithing, butchering and milling,[5] wives, widows and daughters of craftsmen were also largely excluded from the new, less household-based, lifestyles. It is no accident that these changes brought resis-

tance: dissent, combinations of workers, and the publication of Mary
Wollstonecraft's *Vindication of the Rights of Women* towards the end of
the century, just after the French Revolution.

Historians of transvestism Dekker and van de Pol found widespread
evidence of women cross-dressing in Western Europe in the seventeenth and eighteen centuries, especially in Holland and Britain.
Women cross-dressed because they wanted to rove safely – usually for
love, money or out of patriotism[6] – at a time when women's roles were
subject to increasingly hostile scrutiny. By the middle of the eighteenth century, 'spinster' had begun to take on a derogatory meaning
(as a threat to 'men's' jobs) and marriage had come under increased
state control, with greater gaps between the status of legitimate and
illegitimate children and the married and unmarried. The increased
surveillance of working peoples' lives and growing gulf between the
sexes was worsened by a division between waged employees and
those with more organically structured lives. The gap between 'a
dangerous incomprehensible secret underworld, and an honest, plain-
spoken orderly world of labouring dependents' is revealed by the first
cant dictionaries: 'By the 1790s the association between civilisation
and correct English implied that speakers of vulgar English were
"savage" . . .'[7]

Maritime life grew enormously in the course of the eighteenth
century, especially with the expansion of Britain's overseas territories.
Working at sea was one of the three biggest trades (agriculture and
textiles being the others). Not only was the sea a site of valuable booty
that could be appropriated by theft, but it also offered an ideal opportunity for retaliation by people feeling deprived and resentful. In 1721,
the year Ann Bonny and Mary Read were operating, Britain had
20,533 seafarers. The nation's combined imports and exports were
£14.5 million, but a sailor's wage was only 30s (£1.50).[8] The total wage
bill for the country was £360,000 which suggests the extent to which it
was profiting from the low wages of its seafarers.

Robbery was one way for seafarers to survive. Pirates were part of a
huge sailor population which was deeply involved in crime, often less
out of malevolence than as needy people faced with opportunity at a
time when it was 'a wicked world in all meridians'.[9] Thief Richard
Eades, for example, when discharged from a man-o-war on to which
he had been press-ganged, hung around with ' "A Parcel of the most

abandon'd Wretches" . . . [and] stole buckles, watches, wigs and money of the wealthy people in Cable Street' [10] in 1741.

Different people had different access to the bounty from this trade. If women could not sail, then at least they could profit from those who did. While boys might sell stolen oranges on the dockside streets and people with property could charge high rates for overcrowded rooms in verminous boarding houses, women could provide sex and other female services. One combined laundering and prostitution. 'Chatting about common friends in Liverpool and taking off the pants of a seafaring man she had picked up, Catherine Davies, who also did his washing, swallowed six of the sailor's guineas.' [11] Six guineas was two-thirds of a year's pay for a live-in woman domestic worker, who might receive at most £10 for a year's washing and cleaning. As many women had dependents as well as themselves to feed, piracy, prostitution and crime were options that had to be considered if the opportunity arose.

Piracy was one way for low-waged people to get a slice of the profitable action. Captures of cargo vessels could yield as much as £100,000, not only in gold and silver, wine and brandy, but in indigo, silk, linen, spices and cotton. Privateer Sir Francis Drake made a 4,700 per cent profit on one trip, [12] while pirates on Thomas Tew's ship in 1693 got £3,000 each as a result of capturing a Bombay merchantman in the Indian Ocean. [13] It would take three lifetimes for a regular seafarer to earn this sum, [14] so it is perhaps no surprise that of the 700 people tried for piracy in the period 1600-40, 73 per cent were sailors. [15]

Despite traditional hostility to the idea of women at sea, several sorts of women seemed to be sailing on non-pirate ships during this period. On family-owned vessels, wives, mothers and daughters worked in various degrees as they continued to do on whalers in the next century, as members of a family work-team with the father as the 'employer'. [16] On naval vessels, officers took wives on trips and there is evidence that babies were born on ship. Such women would have been more like guests than workers, though of course they would have provided unwaged wifely services.

Cross-dressed women, especially in the great seafaring and soldiering nations England and Holland, joined ships as independent rovers rather than protected wives or daughters. [17] And there is a much less substantiated group of women whose large-scale presence at sea maritime historians suspect rather than are able to prove: waterfront prostitutes who sailed with the ship. Such women may have worked with the whole crew or been attached to a leading member as a temporary mistress or potential wife.

Pirate vessels, by contrast, were not floating family work-teams and the women who worked on pirate ships would not have been daughters or wives but either transvestites or women there because of their sexual availability. (Mary Read belongs to the first category; Ann Bonny and Maria Cobham to the second.) But there is no indication as to what brought women to work on privateers. Flora Burn is listed without comment on her sex as one of the 35-strong crew of the privateer *Revenge*, sailing off the American coast in 1741.[18] And in summer 1805, among the French privateers 'annoying British shipping in the Windward Passage' was a 100-person vessel, *La Baugourt*, 'commanded by a woman' according to a Baltimore gentleman who had been held prisoner in Cuba.[19]

How did these working women pirates pull it off? In times of labour shortage, employers cannot afford to be choosy and may not have looked too carefully at new crew members. Certainly the tales of press-ganging in wartime suggest that anyone might have been lifted, and a woman who wanted to sail might have managed to do so by walking in the streets in her breeches when the press-gang was on the prowl. As in the world wars in the twentieth century, necessity may have forced men to allow women to take on formerly prohibited roles. Another explanation 'lies in the strictness of the differentiation between the genders at the time. A sailor, in trousers, smoking a pipe, with short and loose hair, would not easily be thought of as anything but a man,'[20] according to Dekker and van de Pol.

On the other hand, 'Piracy emphatically was not an option open to landlubbers, since sea robbers "entertain'd so contemptible a Notion of Landmen".'[21] So how could women lose their landlubber position and qualify themselves for respected status on a pirate ship? The answer has to be that they learned their skills as 'boys' on a merchant or naval vessel. Cross-dressed women often looked more like boys than men and so would have been allowed to be learners rather than experts.

Why become a pirate?

Maritime social historian Marcus Rediker sees piracy as for the most part voluntarily chosen by large numbers of people, 'who directly challenged the ways of the society from which they excepted themselves'.[22] He regards pirates 'as free wage labourers and as members of an uncontrolled, freewheeling subculture [which] gave pirates the perspective and occasion to fight back against brutal and unjust authority and to construct a new social order where King Death would not reign supreme.'[23] Women dissatisfied with their position and attracted to the egalitarian ideals and relative freedom of a roving life may well have been drawn to pirate ships for similar reasons. But they would also have been there for the better money: transvestism was a woman's solid and valid route to access to higher-paid male jobs.

B.R. Burg suggests that people became pirates because they were working on a ship captured by pirates or privateers and decided to join their captors.[24] Rediker explains the process:

> The seizure of a merchant ship was followed by a moment of great confrontational drama. The pirate captain or quarter-master asked the seamen of the captured vessel who among them would serve under the death's head and black colors, and frequently several stepped forward. Many fewer pirates originated as mutineers who had boldly and collectively seized control of a merchant vessel.[25]

The choice for a cross-dressed woman working on such a ship would be the same as that of the men; going over to the enemy paid. Since pirates often gang-raped women captives, most would try either to continue to pass as men or perhaps would seek the protection of an officer. In Hollywood movies such as *Blackbeard the Pirate* (RKO, 1952, see plate 13), the tempestuous aristocrat's daughter resists but finally succumbs to the pirate leader's charms, only to discover that he is really a gentleman in disguise. In reality, such patronage was unlikely on pirate ships: 'One has to assume that they [crew members] . . . would immediately have invoked the basic pirate principle of fair shares. The captain, whose privileges were so closely circumscribed, would have been the last person to be allowed a private concubine – or catamite'.[26]

People also became pirates when leading vagrant lives out in the Caribbean, not necessarily as seafarers but as convicts or 'wastrels'. Such sources of labour were valuable when pirate ships were recruiting. Mary Read was in the West Indies after having been captured by pirates who then settled down to enjoy an amnesty. When she heard that privateers were being fitted out in Providence, she and several others sailed off in search of a new job.[27] This is also a way Caribbean women – perhaps runaway slaves – might have been recruited; pirate ships had crews of many races.

Burg also suggests that pirates who joined up in England were people who wanted to get far away from home, to sail long distances. This would appeal particularly to women discontented with life ashore and to lesbians for whom abroad meant an escape from family surveillance.[28] Soldiers learned camaraderie and opportunism so the prospect of carrying on an itinerant life by joining a travelling band of rogues may have been appealing. Philip Gosse sees pirates as people already adrift and motivated by economic needs as well as available opportunities.

> When, at the conclusion of hostilities, peace was declared, the crew of a privateer found it exceedingly irksome to give up the roving life and were liable to drift into piracy. Often it happened that, after a long naval war, crews were disbanded, ships laid up, and navies reduced, thus flooding the countryside with idle mariners and filling the roads with begging and starving seamen. These were driven to go to sea if they could find a berth, often half starved and brutally treated, and always underpaid, and so easily yielded to the temptation of joining some vessel bound vaguely for the 'South Sea', where no questions were asked and no wages paid, but every hand on board had a share in the adventure.[29]

Pirates, like seafarers, saw the life they had chosen as a way of fending off unemployment, hardship, alienation and despair. Their motives might be compared to those of some mini-cab drivers today: the free-lance job was dodgy, *ad hoc* and often illegal but in the absence of anything else, it was a way out. Many (male) pirates are described as drifters, some driven to the life by their 'bad' wives. Major Stede Bonnet, one of the most famous pirates, was said by Gosse to have turned from land-owning to pirating because 'his mind had become unbalanced owing to the unbridled nagging of Mrs Bonnet', an excuse Gosse concocted from a range of complex psychic reasons that might be guessed at from Johnson's founding statement that Bonnet 'was afterwards rather pitty'd than condemned, by those who were acquainted with him, believing that this Humour of going a-pyrating proceeded from Disorder in his Mind . . . which said to have been occasioned by some discomforts *he* [my italics] found in the married state.'[30]

Loss and need were the factors that initially pushed Mary Read on the travels that led her to piracy: the loss of her husband and of their garrison-town eating-house which was her means of support. Because of their proximity to highly paid men, women in pirates' and privateers' milieux could see ways to make more money than those women who lived near – or off – ordinary seafarers. For some, flight to sea may have seemed a more positive option than the suicide, hanging or transportation that was the end for many wandering women. The range of problems women wished to escape might have included the law, abusive partners or the legacies of unwanted pregnancies. If the women were lesbian or unwilling to fit into expected patterns of female behaviour, then a pirate ship was one of the places where nonconformity was more possible.

Joining a criminal underworld could bring additional pleasures. Modern studies show that one of the primary attractions of crime is the excitement of high-adrenalin situations leading possibly to wealth. It also offers isolated women a sense of belonging to what can be a surprisingly loyal and kind group, even if the price is conformity to standards that are not theirs. Women certainly worked in criminal gangs in the eighteenth century. London's Black Boy alley gang, which specialised in violent robbery and controlled a further 7,000 people, had four women members (one an orphaned laundress; one a receiver; one the daughter of a black sword-maker).[31] A life of theft by teamwork can offer an illusion of power and the means to transcend the restrictions that limit ordinary people: pirate gangs could make things happen in a way a solo pastry cook or dairyhand could not.

Taking Mary Read as an example, we can see that according to Johnson's story, economic necessity led her mother to crime ashore – defrauding her own mother-in-law – and drove Mary to itinerant occupations such as soldiering which predisposed her to a life within a criminal subculture. She had no settled community when an adolescent, an uncertain gender identity (because she had had to pass as a boy from an early age), no high-earning skills, and had lost at least a brother, father and husband. Mary Read was adrift from her family, as many young women by at least 1650 were. Studies of that period have found a 'prevailing custom of adolescents leaving home before 15 and spending ten years before their marriage away from home', often sexually active years.[32] Of the 92 women hanged at Tyburn's triple tree between 1703 and 1772, 65 per cent were born outside London (19 per cent were from Ireland).[33]

Being in care, poverty, drug addiction (including alcohol abuse) and a desire for excitement are four common features identified in a recent study of modern women criminals.[34] While pirate molls and women seafarers may or may not have visited dockside Chinese opium dens, cheap drink – without censure – would have been relatively easy for working-class women to get in low-life bars. The price of a night's gin or porter might well have been sex with men who were part of criminal subcultures, including pirates. Sexual connection draws people into closer membership of new cliques. Casual prostitutes driven by alcohol addiction to increased work may have joined seafarers and ships as a way to pay for their habit, or as an attempt to kick it. Waterfront bars such as The George at Billingsgate were places in which to find out which ships were recruiting – a kind of labour exchange frequented by pirates who permitted disaffected women to participate in their culture. If the women were already part of a floating population, it would have been easier to move on to a ship. (In this scenario, ships themselves may have been a logical – though less intensively drunken – extension of the waterside bar.) No well-paid permanent job, no satisfying relationships, no status – what was there to lose?

While no recorded woman pirate publicly admitted to a desire for excitement as motivation, certainly 1970s 'ship girls' have been found to be attracted to the docks and to relationships with seafarers. One of them, Desna, told an interviewer:

'Magic. You know, at 15 years old you're listening to somebody who tells you stories that include every single part of the world . . . and the presents they bring back from overseas and everything.' . . . As Lisa explained it: 'For centuries sailors have gone to sea and it's the whole legend connected with it; the sea is such a combination of beauty and terror. It's wild and free, so wild it can kill . . . and these men go out and conquer it.' [35]

The possibility of money, revenge and escape must have excited many eighteenth-century 'roaring girls' too.

Men (and women) of desperate fortunes?

Pirate histories tell of a range of male pirates. Captain Kidd in 1696 sailed 'with a company recruited from the dregs of the waterfront, "men of desperate fortunes and necessities", thirsty for treasure and with few scruples about how they obtained it.' [36] Others saw pirates as the cream of skilled seafarers. Some descriptions of male pirates make them sound emotionally disabled, the kind of tedious companion who would frustrate any lively woman. When an English seafarer met pirate leader John Ward in 1808 he reported that far from swashbuckling, Ward 'speaks little, almost always swearing, drinks from morn to night . . . sleeps a great deal and often on board when in port'. [37] To us today, women pirates automatically sound remarkable, but it is possible that some of them too were socially awkward, boring, snoozed their miseries away and rarely ventured ashore.

'Almost without exception, pirates, like the larger body of seafaring men, came from the lowest social classes. They were, as a royal official condescendingly observed, "desperate Rogues" who could have little hope in life ashore.' [38] There is no reason to assume that women pirates belonged to a different class from the men, especially as historians of women's transvestism have found that cross-dressers who faced courts were women of the common people who had been doing the kinds of work characterised by a low degree of schooling, limited prospects and poor pay: 'servants, seamstresses, twine makers, sheet burlers, knitters or street peddlars.' [39] Mary Read was certainly from a low position on the social ladder; Ann Bonny, with her attorney father, was a little more privileged.

No women pirates' ages are given, but from biographical information about men found in Johnson we might deduce that they were typically in their early 20s. Cross-dressed women tended to be between 16 and 25 when they decided to change their appearance – a time when 'women of the lower classes generally had to look after themselves, to earn their own living, and, ideally, to accumulate a dowry.'[40] Rediker's study of 117 pirates active between 1716 and 1726 shows that they ranged from 17 to 50 years, but that most were between 20 and 29: 'three in five were 25 or older. The age distribution was almost identical to the merchant service as a whole, suggesting that piracy held roughly equal attraction for sailors of all ages.'[41]

Some male pirates were married – to women in Britain and America or in the more exotic locations to which they retired. Captain Teach (Blackbeard) had 14 wives. After Lorne-born Captain 'Jack the Batchelor' was found dead in the Ferdinand Hotel, Naples, it was discovered that in spite of his nickname, he had three wives.[42] Upper-crust buccaneer George, Third Earl of Cumberland, was married at 19 in 1577, presumably before he took his MA at Trinity College Cambridge. 'Cumberland was greatly esteemed by Queen Elizabeth, and always wore in his hat a glove which she had given him.'[43] Deptford boatswain John Upton was a widower who had turned to seafaring because he was in danger of being arrested by creditors for debts accrued by his wife.[44] Buccaneer, explorer and naturalist Captain William Dampier, from East Coker, married a member of the Duchess of Grafton's family in 1678;[45] Captain Pete Eston, who headed a fleet of 25 vessels in 1612, bought his titled wife.[46] By contrast, at least one pirate is reported to have been a manager in the sex industry; Walter Kennedy retired to Deptford in 1721 where he 'prospered as a brothel keeper until one of his whores informed on him and he went to Execution Dock'.[47]

Most seem to have had few ties. 'Wives and children were rarely mentioned in the records of trials of pirates, and pirate vessels, to forestall desertion, often would "take no Married Man."'[48] All three women pirates described in Chapter 22 had once had husbands; none is reported as having a child with her, though Ann Bonny had had a child who may have been left in Cuba, where it was delivered.[49]

Captain Tew left his children with his wife in Newport Rhode Island, while Captain Kidd's daughters lived with their mother in New York.[50]

Some of the characteristics of women pirates may be guessed at from accounts (usually male-authored court reports) of other criminal women of the period. The connections of sex, loneliness, seafarers, poverty and crime (by women and men) are strong. Historian Ivy Pinchbeck found that women in street jobs, especially selling and prostitution, were prominent among those hanged at Tyburn Tree and that, 'it was their dependence upon casual and pauper trades that explains the large number of suicides, prostitution, starvation and crime among lone women.'[51] Londoner Anne Baker had five children by a seafarer before she was 19; when he went to sea she went into the workhouse which put her out to make shoes in Rosemary Lane. 'She could not live on such an income and took to street walking. In January 1764 she stole a guinea and was hanged two months later.'[52] But women's land-based crimes were different from mens':

> Deprived of the social power of money, men might resort to their training in violence . . . In general, women lacked such freedom of action and consequently resorted to different methods . . . While the outdoor robberies of men required alacrity, physical strength, boldness, bravura and speed, women tended to work indoors and relied upon quiet, intelligence, stealth and quick-ness.[53]

Seventeenth and eighteenth-century records show that women stole on a small scale – a sister lodger's linen gown, a potage pot, bread, a kettle, flat irons or money.[54] This suggests that women who became pirates might have had different expectations about both the adventurousness of the methods they would use and the size of the booty they might acquire.

Women – and men – were operating at a time when ruthless brutality could ensure survival. Delicacy of stomach would not have stopped women attending public hangings. The taste for – or habit of – violence is indicated in an implausibly lurid broadsheet story of eighteenth-century women who turned cannibal when most of the men on their ship died of thirst after 22 days. Not only did they cut up and eat the corpses, but when Ann Saunders, the master's wife's maid, heard of her fiancé's death, she snatched a cup from the mate, 'cut her late intended husband's throat, and drank his blood, insisting she had a greater right to it and a scuffle ensued and the heroine got the better of her adversary, and then allowed him to drink one cup to her two!' [55]

Leaving piracy

Pirates' time in the job was often brief: 'The careers of pirates using Madagascar as a base were usually short, lasting only a year or two. In fact, this was the case with most oceanic pirates.' Leaders' careers are better recorded than workers', and we know that 'during the 1700's, one, Captain Lowther, captured 33 ships during his seventeen month career; Edward Low took 140 vessels in 29 months; Captain Bartholomew Roberts took 400 prizes in three years.' [56]

Sometimes pirates were drowned in high seas or killed in battle; occasionally the job ended with jail or hanging. But more often pirates would go on to work on non-pirate vessels – privateers and merchant-men – or would find work on land, perhaps as soldiers or thieves. Others returned to shore life because they were caught, the opportunities dried up, or perhaps because they felt they had earned enough or were no longer physically fit. According to Gosse, 'not a few drank themselves to death with strong Jamaican rum, while many of the buccaneers died of malaria and yellow fever contracted in the jungles of Central America.' [57]

Mary Read stopped pirating and then resumed before her career was ended when she was caught. Women may also have given up because they were pregnant, although studies of hard-pressed twentieth-century women seafarers – stewardesses – show that they left children at home with parents or in the Seamen's Orphanage; they could not afford to let babies affect their employment. Dekker and van de Pol reveal that eighteenth-century seafaring women transvestites traditionally abandoned their lives on the high seas because they were discovered to be women and were expelled, at least from that ship. Some got away with their disguise for as long as 20 years, but many more were unmasked within a few months. [58] They might well have had to leave their ships rather than face verbal disrespect or mass rape. We know that many cross-dressed women on land had their sexual identity exposed when they were caught as felons and handled by the authorities, or undressed by surgeons following an injury. Others let their disguise slip, for example when drunkenly lying naked on their bunk or when urinating. Some were challenged by suspicious male colleagues, for instance if acting implausibly in a brothel, while in other cases people from non-European countries less accustomed to reading clothing codes and more attuned to body language pointed out to seamen that their colleague was a woman. (While there are no reported stories about pirate women being exposed in this way, cases in foreign countries may have gone unrecorded.)

It would have been hard to move out of piracy when a woman's friends and lovers were in the same business, as tends to be the case with women in crime. 'The life' becomes a trap, as modern sociological studies of prostitution have shown.[59] There are pleasures in recounting shared crimes together, while each new crime committed makes it difficult for a woman to fit back into straight society. Becoming used to independence creates an obstacle to adjusting to a non-roving life. Having openly renounced ordinary social standards, stepping back into a straight world would often have offered nothing but misery – motivation would have to be very strong.

Criminality and cruelty

Women who worked with – or as – pirates must have felt they had nothing at all to lose; there might even have been something to gain from piracy, as if all else fails, crime pays. When women have suffered a welter of misfortunes – bereavement, loss of home, ill-health, isolation, identity problems – they are more likely to commit desperate actions. Mary Read often said, 'the Life of a Pyrate was what she always abhor'd, and went into it only upon Compulsion.'[60]

Sociological studies today show that most people do not consider the 'crime' they commit to be a crime. They usually have an excuse or justification, or else regard it as a crude way of getting justice. Coal-heavers on the Thames riverside in the 1790s saw taking two or three bushels of coals 'a perquisite and "a custom of their predecessors", that

they had "fair title to such coals".' Similarly dockyard workers kept
their families fed on stolen naval stores: 'After the naval defeats of the
War of American Independence it was remarked that more ships were
lost piecemeal in women's aprons than to enemy action at sea.' [61] Today
some office workers similarly assume that free photocopying and
personal telephone calls are part of the wage – or are just revenge.
Piracy under some circumstances was almost socially acceptable
(privateering was licensed and legitimised), so it is easy to believe that
pirates may have had trouble in regarding their plundering as wrong
when they were doing the same work as privateers although not under
licence. In eighteenth-century trials, Anglo-American pirates usually
said they did not consider themselves to be sinners: many felt they
were acting for their Christian God and King against the infidels.

Pirates may not even have thought of themselves as particularly
cruel or vicious. Studies of people in groups and institutions such as
armies and mental hospitals[62] show that newcomers can be easily and
rapidly trained to commit the most appalling acts – including murder
in the armed forces' case – with a sense of pride and appropriateness as
they strive for belonging and acceptance. They believe such acts not
only to be condoned, but expected of them. Women in male work
groups are particularly under pressure to conform. Women and men
who were pirates by choice as well as by accident of fate were implicitly
trained in all those months closeted at sea as to the appropriate codes
of behaviour. Deprived of any frame of reference other than the standards of those already working as pirates, who had found their own
ways to justify what they did, piracy must have begun to seem the only
way, even the sane way, to go about life. Moreover, foreign places
could easily be left behind – there was no sense of consequence to
actions since another person's nest had been fouled, not their own.

Cross-dressed women who had been soldiers – like Mary Read – had
experience of fighting foreigners in the name of a greater good. One of
the main ways people who violate and plunder adjust to their inhumane acts is to perceive the person they are attacking as Other. This
was particularly easy in a period when xenophobia and racism were
strong, and seafarers were at the cutting edge of this. The ideology
that engendered slavery enabled white people, especially from imperial powers, to think that everyone else was Other and lesser.
Empathy was seldom on the agenda in a time characterised by the

lordly maltreatment of others. Around 1.4 million slaves are thought to have been taken to the West Indies in the 60 years before 1700.[63] Both the thousands of seafarers who transported them for months and the people on land who had contact with them would have been habituated to dehumanising practices.

White women as well as men in Barbados leased out slaves for sex to men on passing vessels[64] and 'coloured' and white women owned brothels staffed by black women slaves. This suggests that shared gender did not bring humanity but that any human body was disposable. Seafarers could have learned cruelty partly as victims of vicious mates and masters. And when a merchant vessel hove into sight, loaded to the gunwhales with goods that no mantlemaker or serving maid could ever own, the idea of the victim ship as 'not our ship' may well have led pirates to think it was fair game and should be taken by whatever means necessary. It could seem all the more noble and right – in a Robin Hood way – to rectify the imbalance by appropriating the prize of foreigners. However, the way in which racially mixed crews dealt with attacks on members of their own race is open to question. And how might a woman pirate have felt if she drew her sword and then discovered that her potential victim was a woman? Complex nightmares about mixed loyalties may well have had to be drowned in brandy and bravado.

Facing the law

Only two eighteenth-century women are known to have stood in dock for their buccaneering on the high seas: Mary Read and Ann Bonny. In the courtroom, all those who sailed beneath the Jolly Roger had to face the reality that however innocent, justified or mild they felt their actions to have been, others with more power could now decide to take their lives. If 'these monsters in human form'[65] were seen as deviant and criminal, then pirate women were regarded as doubly 'monstrous'. What could be worse than a woman who took to piratical crime, especially in *his* appropriated trousers?

These women were acting in ways that were a hindrance to those who organised social structures and attitudes: kings, MPs, landowners, bankers, captains of industry and their brothers – dons, headmasters and newspaper-owners. Pirates could also make useful scapegoats for the bigger crimes committed by companies and national leaders. Historians have pointed to the case of Captain Kidd, a privateer and unsuccessful New York businessman who was hanged, as an illustration of this: 'There is little doubt that Kidd committed a number of outright piracies in the Indian Ocean ... [but] it is equally clear that his trial provided a scapegoat for the establishment figures who had employed him: a full investigation would have exposed both their greed in organising an anti-piracy mission for their own profit, and their incompetence in choosing a commander so unsuited to the task.'[66]

The past two decades of profound feminist thinking about the ways women are controlled offer a lens through which we can view the treatment of women pirates by the judicial system. For instance, today we can see such women as among the many ordinary, impoverished victims of changed political attitudes towards piracy and unregulated women. We can also see that they could not have hoped for justice or respect from white male juries of slave- and plantation-owners licensed by the admiralty to 'judge' those who jeopardised their wealth. Women pirates were part of a category of unruly characters including highwaywomen, murderers and prostitutes seen as in need of control and punishment for their non-conformity. But unlike prostitutes, pirate women were not in men's service: a woman pirate was not 'under' a judge, but out of his grasp – at sea.

The subtle social regulation of female and working-class behaviour was – and is – so effective that the mores involved seem natural and invisible. A trial of pirates was an expression of the power of social leaders as well as of their needs: freedom to move goods without impediment; the acceptance of their values; freedom to expropriate wealth in whatever way they chose, supported by a flexible and acquiescent workforce. If the hypocritical structure of controlling ideas in British society was to remain intact, then only one verdict was possible: guilty. As with witches accused of consorting with the devil, the lesbian imputation put on Read and Bonny may have been a way to devalue them further, though their lesbianism may also have been real and an additional reason for hauling them before the bench.

Women generally receive less judicial attention than men.[67] Early theorists argued that women were not biologically strong enough to commit crimes,[68] while later theories claimed that women were biologically predisposed to be more cruel, and culturally trained to have an underdeveloped sense of moral responsibility. But the main concern of the eighteenth-century courts was social and economic: women whose unruliness affected the maritime workforce were a menace to shipowners' and traders' profits. From the late 1690s in London prostitutes were imprisoned in great numbers and jails were filled with women who were spared death provided they agreed to transportation (which cost the government £8 a head). 'One reason for the extraordinary repression of women, prostitutes particularly, was undoubtedly the encouragement they gave to sailors to desert . . . women often took the lead in opposing the press-gangs.'[69]

Rediker found admiralty trials of seafarers in this period badly biased. 'Judges rendered numerous verdicts that supported the interests of merchants and captains even when the evidence and the law stood firmly on the side of the common tar . . . After all, the admiralty court system was part of a general design to rationalize the imperial trading network, and a major part of this project was to confine social conflict to legal channels.[70] Jurors on piracy cases had to take into account their public-relations role in discouraging piracy by administering exemplary sentences and the strategic needs of trade. (Buccaneer Bartholomew Sharp was apparently freed because he brought back an invaluable captured Spanish document about coastlines and ports at a time when charts meant power.)[71] The jurors women pirates faced were likely to hold superstitious views about women's 'dark passions' and hypocritical notions about females' proper place. And since such views were facing challenge in a world often described as being 'turned upside down' – and people usually uphold ideas all the more fiercely when they are under threat – women pirates must have aroused personal anxiety and hostility among the 'Twelve Good Men and True'.

Not all jurors in all trials were men; juries of women were sometimes used when defendants – as Ann Bonny and Mary Read did – claimed to be pregnant (judicial officials did not want to take an innocent life along with a guilty one). In the case of burglar Anne Davies, the first woman to be hanged in Australia (1789), 'A Jury of Twelve Matrons were then impanelled and sworn to try if the prisoner is

Quick with Child. On their return into Court, the Foreman [sic] delivered in their Verdict that the Prisoner at the Bar is not with Child.'[72] The fact that a jury of women was not set up for Read and Bonny suggests that they were small fry and that there were enough other pirate victims available to prove that miscreants always faced the gallows.

It may be that no women buccaneers other than Bonny and Read were brought to the courtroom because there were fewer Anglo-American pirates of either sex to be caught. After many waves of hangings and pardons for piracy, opportunities were being stamped out: 'A royal proclamation of 1698 declaring a general amnesty to all pirates east of the Cape (with the exception of Avery and Kidd) persuaded a number of pirates to abandon their old way of life, while a new Act of Parliament for the more effective suppression of piracy of 1700, and the hanging of many . . . were also measures that gradually reinforced the message that the game was no longer worth the candle.'[73] The wave of piracy trials in the 1720s that involved Bonny and Read was the biggest and one of the last.

Part of the romantic attraction of Bonny and Read's generation of pirates is that they are seen as representing one of the last flings of a type of British renegade. Outside Europe the wildness carried on in various ways, for example with the growing Maratha 'piracy' off the west coast of India between Goa and Bombay, where vessels including East India Company ships faced attacks because of their refusal to accept local customs control.[74]

In various later 'trials by story-writer', women pirates did not die, but nor did they carry on fighting bloodily. They were restored to womanly lifestyles. Was a life sentence at the eighteenth-century equivalent of the kitchen sink punishment enough? Or does women pirates' imputed sexiness excuse them from the harsher judgements that might be made on women whose age, plain appearance or lack of seductive breeches and Robin Hood aura make them clearly humdrum thieves; needy human beings rather than tasty artefacts? When the real danger of piracy is gone, the figure of 'a woman pirate' can be put above the law – and on to celluloid.

Notes

1. From a popular broadside ballad printed by W. Fordyce, Newcastle, c.1830 in Harvard University, Houghton Library (Misc Prints, no. 57-784, vol. I, no. 536), quoted by Dianne Dugaw, '"Rambling Female Sailors": the rise and fall of the seafaring heroine', *International Journal of Maritime History*, IV, no. 1, June 1992, pp. 179-94.

2. Marcus Rediker, *Between the Devil and the Deep Blue Sea: merchant seamen pirates and the Anglo-American maritime world 1700-1750*, Cambridge University Press, 1987, p. 256.

3. David Mitchell, *Pirates*, Thames & Hudson, 1976, p. 87.

4. Rudolf M. Dekker and Lotte C. van de Pol, *The Tradition of Female Transvestism in Early Modern Europe*, MacMillan, 1989, pp. 38-9.

5. Dian Leonard and Judy Lown, *Open University Chronological Chart: the changing experience of women*, OU, 1983.

6. Dekker and van de Pol, *op cit*, especially p. 27.

7. Peter Linebaugh, *The London Hanged: crime and civil society in the eighteenth century*, Allen Lane, The Penguin Press, 1991, p. 429.

8. *ibid*, pp. 127-8. A voyage – say to Jamaica – might net a seafarer between £2 and £3 plus another £10 to £20 made on the rum they brought back to England to sell.

9. *ibid*, p. 126.

10. *ibid*, p. 126.

11. *ibid*, p. 434.

12. Mitchell, *op cit*, p. 44. But not all heists were of treasure or resaleable goods: pirate John Gow in 1774 captured a ship out of Newfoundland from which he lifted anchors, cables and sails, according to David Cordingly and John Falconer, *Pirates: fact and fiction*, Collins & Brown, 1992, p. 35.

13. Cordingly and Falconer, ibid, p. 35.

14. *ibid*, p. 84.

15. *ibid*, p. 115.

16. See the chapter describing the extent to which fishing was family business in Harriet Bradley, *Men's Work, Women's Work*, Polity Press, 1989 and books on whaling, for example Joan Druett, *Petticoat Whalers: whaling wives at sea, 1820-1920*, Collins, New Zealand, 1991.

17. Dekker and van de Pol, *op cit*.

18. John Franklin Jameson, *Privateering and Piracy of the Colonial Period*, MacMillan, 1923, p. 94, citing the journal of the sloop *Revenge*, 5 June to 3 October 1741.

19. *Mariner's Mirror*, vol. IX, 1923, p. 96. The information is in a reader's query reporting on a letter from the Baltimore gentleman in the Times, 17 September 1805. The *Mariner's Mirror* query is 'is anything known of

HISTORIE DER ZEE-ROOVERS.

1. Ann Bonny, or female piracy embodied?, 1725.

2. Alfhild, the American nineteenth-century version.

ANTHOLOGIA HIBERNICA.
VOL. II.

GRANA UILE introduced to QUEEN Elizabeth.

W. Beauford delin.   Clayton sculp.

3. LEFT: The 'Pirate Queen' meets the English Queen, July 1593.

5. TOP RIGHT: The earliest and most widely used version of Ann Bonny and Mary Read.

6. BOTTOM RIGHT: A non-sexualized 1844 image of Mary Read.

4. Passengers on the *Morning Star* facing attack by pirates in 1827.

Mary Read killing her antagonist.

THE
PIRATES OWN BOOK,
OR
AUTHENTIC NARRATIVES
OF THE
LIVES, EXPLOITS, AND EXECUTIONS OF THE MOST CELEBRATED
SEA ROBBERS.

Gibbs carrying the Dutch Girl on board.

WITH
HISTORICAL SKETCHES
OF THE
Joassamee, Spanish, Ladrone, West India, Malay, and Algerine Pirates.

PORTLAND:
PUBLISHED BY SANBORN & CARTER.

PHILADELPHIA:
THOMAS, COWPERTHWAIT, & CO.

7. LEFT: Women play a crucial role in pirate tales, as victims.

8.BELOW: Community celebration or sentimentalized eighteenth-century orgy?

The cr s of Blackbeard's and Vane's vessels carousing on the coast of rolina.

9. RIGHT: 'Mrs Ching in action', as Gosse describes it.

HISTORY OF THE PIRATES
SMUGGLERS, &c.
OF
ALL NATIONS.

No. 29.   SATURDAY, SEPTEMBER 17, 1836.   PRICE 1d.

Engagement between the Chinese Pirates and the Mandarins.

But the fleet of Mistress Ching and her bold lieutenant were too quick for the Imperial forces. They came up with them near a place called Olang-pae, and there, their vessels being rendered motionless by a dead calm, the daring pirates threw themselves into the sea, and swimming to the Mandarin's ships, boarded and took six of them. The mandarin was killed.

In the next adventure on record, a party of the pirates sustained a rude check from a lofty argoisie, laden with goods from Cochin-China and Tung King, and were compelled to retire to their boats: " a circumstance (saith the historian,) which never happened before."

In the action after this, they were still more severely handled. The great Admiral Tsuen-Mow-Sun, proceeded with 100 vessels to attack the pirates, who did not retreat, but drew up in line of battle, and made a tremendous attack on the Imperial

10. BELOW: 'Lai Choi San: she was now to be obeyed, and obeyed she was.'

11. BELOW: Cover of the first-known book about female pirates: *Les Femmes pirates: aventures et legendes de la mer*, 1934.

HENRY MUSNIK

LES FEMMES PIRATES

AVENTURES ET LÉGENDES
DE LA MER

" LE MASQUE "
23, RUE MARBEUF, 23
PARIS

12. ABOVE: Jean Peters as Ann Bonny, in the 1951 film *Anne of the Indies*.

13. BELOW: Linda Darnell is taken prisoner in the 1952 film *Blackbeard the Pirate*.

14. Tabea Blumenschein as the piratical figurehead in *Madame X, an absolute ruler.*

If you thought Bonnie and Clyde were dangerous, wait until you meet Bonny and Read.

PIRATES
Exhibition at Greenwich.

15. The National Maritime Museum's *Thelma and Louise* version of women pirates, 1992.

16. Sara Mair-Thomas as Mary Read faces the press-gang in a 1992 S4C version of piracy.

17. Captain Connie Blackheart (Helen Atkinson Wood) takes a break from shooting *Tales from the Poop Deck*.

this privateer, and are there any recorded instances of women having actually commanded ships which have engaged in warlike operations?' I can trace no reply.

20. Dekker and van de Pol, *op cit*, p. 23.
21. Rediker, *op cit*, p. 260.
22. Rediker, *op cit*, p. 255.
23. *ibid*, p. 286.
24. B. R. Burg, *Sodomy and the Pirate Tradition: English sea rovers in the 17th century Caribbean*, New York University Press, 1984.
25. Rediker, *op cit*, p. 260.
26. Mitchell, *op cit*, p. 88.
27. Captain Charles Johnson, *A General History of the Robberies and Murders of the most Notorious Pyrates*, (1724) published as Daniel Defoe, *A General History of the Pyrates*, Manuel Schonhorn (ed), Dent, 1972, p. 133.
28. Dekker and van de Pol, *op cit*.
29. Philip Gosse, *The Pirates' Who's Who*, Dulau, 1924.
30. *ibid*, p. 52, and subsequently citing Johnson.
31. Linebaugh, *op cit*, pp. 149-50.
32. Premarital pregnancy was as high as 20 per cent and tolerantly treated (as was adultery). See Margaret Spufford, *Small Books and Pleasant Histories: popular fiction and its readership in seventeenth century England*. Methuen, 1981, p. 161, referring to studies of North Essex by Dr A. McFarlane.
33. Linebaugh, *op cit*, p. 143.
34. Pat Carlen, *Women, Crime and Poverty*, Open University Press, 1988, pp. 7, 12. For further reading on feminist approaches to crime, see Carol Smart, *Feminism and the Power of the Law*, Routledge, 1989. For a good early 1980s introduction to the debates and theories, see Eileen B. Leonard, *Women, Crime and Society: a critique of criminology theory*, Longman, 1982, and the more recent work edited by Loraine Gelsthorpe and Allison Morris, *Feminist Perspectives in Criminology*, Open University Press, 1992, especially a discussion by Marcia Rice giving a black feminist critique. See also Michel Foucault, *Discipline and Punish*, Allen Lane, 1977.
35. Jan Jordan 'Ship Girls: the invisible women of the sea' paper to the 'Women and the Sea' conference, Wellington Maritime Museum, New Zealand, December 1993, pp. 3, 8.
36. Cordingly and Falconer, *op cit*, p. 90.
37. *ibid*, p. 12.
38. Rediker, *op cit*, p. 261.
39. Dekker and van de Pol, *op cit*, p. 12.
40. *ibid*, p. 13.
41. Rediker, *op cit*, p. 260.
42. Gosse, *op cit*, p. 94.
43. *ibid*, p. 95.

44. *ibid*, p. 302.

45. *ibid*, p. 101.

46. Mitchell, *op cit*, pp. 141-2.

47. *ibid*, p. 134.

48. Rediker, *op cit*, p. 261.

49. Johnson, *op cit*, p. 165.

50. Cordingly and Falconer, *op cit*, p. 115.

51. Ivy Pinchbeck, *Women Workers and the Industrial Revolution, 1750-1850*, (1930), republished by Virago, 1981, p. 61.

52. Linebaugh, *op cit*, p. 232.

53. *ibid*, pp. 338-9.

54. *ibid*, p. 339.

55. Story of the *Frances and Mary*, travelling from St John's, NB, to Liverpool, broadsheet no. 595, *Bristol Broadsheets 1700-1840*, vol. 2, BL 1880c20.

56. Ralph T. Ward, *Pirates in History*, York Press, 1974, p. 176.

57. Philip Gosse, *op cit*, p. 23.

58. Dekker and van de Pol, *op cit*, p. 10.

59. A range of reading on prostitution and its relationship to institutions includes Judith Walkowitz, *Prostitution and Victorian Society: women, class and the state*, Cambridge University Press, 1980; Myna Trustram, *Women of the Regiment: marriage and the Victorian army*, Cambridge University Press, 1984; *Women of the Streets: a sociology of the common prostitute*, ed C. T. Rolph for the British Social Biology Council, New English Library, 1961; Jess Wells, *A History of Prostitution in Western Europe*, Shameless Hussy Press, 1982; Eileen Mcleod, *Women Working: prostitution now*, Croom Helm, 1982.

60. Johnson, *op cit*, p. 156.

61. Linebaugh, *op cit*, p. 376.

62. See Erving Goffman's illuminating study, *Asylums*, Pelican, 1961.

63. Hilary McD Beckles, *Natural Rebels: a social history of enslaved black women in Barbados*, Zed Press, 1989, p. 8.

64. *ibid*, p. 142.

65. Charles Ellms, *The Pirates Own Book, or Authentic Narratives of the Lives, Exploits and Executions of the Most Celebrated Sea Robbers*, Sanborn & Carter, 1837, p. 3.

66. Cordingly and Falconer, *op cit*, p. 91.

67. Carlen, *op cit*, p. 4. In 1987 there were 59,000 women in the indicted British population compared with 385,200 men.

68. Luke Owen Pike in 1876, Ely van de Warker in 1876 and Caesar Lombroso in 1900, then Otto Pollak in 1950.

69. Linebaugh, *op cit*, p. 59.

70. Rediker, *op cit*, Appendix F, p. 316.

71. Cordingly and Falconer, *op cit*, p. 26.

72. Judith Cook, *To Brave Every Danger*, MacMillan, 1993, p. 130.
73. Cordingly and Falconer, *op cit*, pp. 93, 96.
74. *ibid*, p. 96.

10 Living beneath the Jolly Roger

Beneath King Death,
my silvered horn and silenced moon
sail on no man's sufferance.
My sisters, skirts aloft, speak from womb.
Differently, our teeth test diseased reales.
Differently, our legs await
the next myrrh-laden tide.

Male pirates' unease about women meant that only a limited number of eighteenth-century Anglo-American pirate ships carried female crew members over the blue oceans towards heists and havens. On some vessels, such as pirate John Phillips' *Revenge*, the whole (male) complement had to swear to abide with a set of rules that included: '"No boy or woman to be allowed among them. If any man were found seducing any of the latter sex, and carried her to sea disguised, he was to suffer Death." These articles were written out and "all swore to 'em upon a hatchet for want of a Bible."'[1] The pledge may have been as much about stopping sexual relationships as about prohibiting women mariners *per se*. But maritime historians are divided as to how often the rules were ignored and women openly travelled on pirate ships.

The much-vaunted bold women whose histories are best known sailed in the classic age of piracy. Between 1714 and 1724, the fields of operation were 'the Caribbean, along the coasts of the Carolinas and Virginia, in the Gulf of Guinea, and again in the Indian Ocean. Blackbeard and Bartholomew Roberts, Howard Davis, Edward England and John Taylor are the big names, with a large supporting cast, among them Charles Bellamy, Henry Vane [and] "Calico Jack" Rackham'. . .[2] Their Anglo-American ships bore names redolent of vengeance, noble principles, enjoyment and bravado: *Batchelor's Delight*, *Liberty*, *Night Rambler*, *Queen Ann's Revenge*, *Cour Valant*, *Scowerer*, *Flying Dragon*, *Most Holy Trinity*, *Happy Delivery*, *Bravo*, *Black Joke* and *Blessing*.[3] But rather than being the standard lavish galleons of Hollywood movies, pirate ships reflected the period and area of operation. In China, pirates used 600-ton war junks; in Indonesia, native canoes; on the Barbary Coast, oar-powered galleys.[4] The ships on which Anglo-American pirates sailed in the reigns of Queen Anne (1702-14) and King George (1714-27) were chosen because they were effective: 'Size was less important than speed because the essence of a pirate attack was to hit and run. Vessels of shallow draught, which could hide in shallow creeks and be easily beached for repairs were also favoured.'[5] These were ships that needed wind and oars if they were to move; dependent on the elements and on labour, they could not easily zoom after a likely-looking cargo vessel as a speedboat can today. Pirates on the North American coast and Caribbean in the eighteenth century preferred two-masted, 214-ton schooners, 76 feet long with 22 guns, a type that Robert Louis Stevenson's *Treasure Island* schooner, the *Hispaniola*, was supposed to resemble.[6] Other pirate ships were as small as 50 tons.[7]

Flying high on the masts of a pirate ship, flags were both the owners' statement of identity (like a customised car) and a signal of horrifying intent, a threatening signal visible from afar and an indication of the pirates' awareness that they were fighting 'beneath the sombre colours of "King Death"'.[8] The black flag embellished with a white skull and crossedbones (usually limbs) was a symbol pre-literate mariners could understand; captains' logs marked death by drawing a skull in the margin.[9] Some skeletons were accompanied by an hour-glass and cutlass to show that violence was nearby, time was running out, the possibility of death loomed.[10] The skull-and-crossbones flag came into use at the end of the seventeenth century as a sign that the vessel was a pirate one, but also as a way of telling the enemy that negotiation was possible. Pirate historians David Cordingly and John Falconer report that earlier a red flag – meaning no quarter would be given in battle – was used in a more widespread way. The scarlet is probably the root of the word 'Jolly Roger', from the French 'Joli Rouge', although 'Old Roger' was also a synonym for the devil in the early eighteenth century. The frightening meaning of the red flag was transferred to the black flag by 1724.[11] In one case at least it was a woman's underpaid labour that created these flags: in the seedy shanty town of Nassau in the early eighteenth century, 'A sailmaker's widow sewed black jacks to order in return for a generous ration of brandy . . .'[12]

The ships on which women set foot were complex workplaces with their own lifestyles. Like mobile camps for soldiers, they contained all the tensions about boundaries, rights, conditions and goals that living together in confined quarters can bring. Ships were also machines that controlled the workers within them: mariners worked round the clock, though shifts were shorter on privateers than on naval vessels.[13] Boring, strenuous, done in difficult weather and sea-dampened clothes, pirates' work – like work on any ship – comprised maintenance, sailing and fighting on demand. And, ' . . . the pirate did not just cruise the ocean aimlessly waiting to come across his prey by chance: he had to position himself across the known trade routes, which in the days of sail were determined by prevailing winds.'[14] But equipment was patchy and primitive; navigation was achieved with whatever inadequate charts, compasses, quadrants and astrolabes had been captured. A huge degree of co-operation was required between those on board: tasks were specialised, with navigation the province of the captain and mates; ordnance and ballistics the responsibility of the gunnery crew; and repairs taken care of by the carpenter, sailmaker, cooper and so forth.[15]

Crew members had to be fit, strong and agile to deal with the work, including constantly taking down sails and putting up new ones, even in gales. A seafarer had to be 'proficient in knots and the intricacies of running and standing rigging . . . and to know the languages needed for trade and survival in a world of intercontinental communication.'[16] These were skills that women who worked at sea for some time might develop, if they were passing as men or if men – as fathers, lovers or brothers (or other cross-dressed women) – were prepared to teach them. Unlike press-ganged merchant seafarers, many pirates were not amateurs but 'sea-artists'. As workers in a profit-sharing co-operative, their competence could bring them riches; a bungling pirate team would not necessarily get booty. A woman would have to earn her place on board. Parts of the work were unskilled; on non-pirate ships, 'Probably the largest proportion of the ship's crew were those "waisters, men without art or judgement". They were the do-ers of all the dirty work on ship, and acted as scavengers, swabbers, pumpers, pigsty and livestock keepers, poulterers, butchers, etc etc.'[17] It may well be that some women, with low status on land, laboured at these degraded tasks.

Because speed was crucial in pirate operations, a ship had to be well prepared. According to buccaneer Basil Ringrose's journal, work ashore involved beaching the ship on a secluded shore to careen it (scrape the barnacles and weed off the bottom), repainting it with some form of anti-fouling layer, and repairing spars, sails and rigging. While some seafarers were occupied in this way, others went off in search of water and food: goats, turtles, monkeys and snakes, some of which were salted for future consumption.[18] The fast pace and erratic diet meant that according to maritime historians, most seafarers' deaths were caused by appalling working and living conditions. The joke is fondly told that more (male) pirates died in brothels than in battles, though the difficulties of keeping an under-crewed ship afloat in bad conditions could be more hazardous than any fracas or 'nanny house'. Mariners' illnesses included deadly diseases such as malaria, yellow fever, typhus and scurvy (early Portuguese explorers knew from at least the sixteenth century that citrus fruit was a cure for scurvy, though it was not introduced into the navy until 1785; the extent to which pirates took lemons and oranges aboard would depend on their initiative or on the captain's knowledge).[19] Pirates also faced gonorrhoea, gangrene, dysentery (which killed Sir Francis Drake) and the effects of exposure, sunburn, vermin, thirst and malnutrition. In overcrowded and under-cleaned quarters, infections and fevers could quickly take hold and wipe out whole sections of a shipboard population. On top of these dangers came the risk of occupational injury, from slipping on a wet deck to falling from the crow's nest. Eyes or limbs were more likely to be lost in this way, or in drunken brawls with fractious shipmates, than in the rare hand-to-hand combat and head-on engagement with enemies. Women would have to cope not only with menstruation but perhaps with pregnancy, post-natal or post-abortion symptoms.

There was no travelling village wise woman to offer cow's spleen for the feet of typhus patients or red nettle for piles,[20] but ships necessarily carried a doctor's chest or even a surgeon. A ship could be weeks or months from quacks and sawbones ashore, and so developed, probably, remedies for everything from *mal de mer* to gangrene as well as prosthetic limbs for the injured. One of the most significant stories is that Blackbeard held some Charleston dignitaries hostage until the Governor of Carolina agreed to give him a shopping list of medicines the ship's surgeon said he needed: these were probably mercury-based remedies for syphilis.[21] As pirates sometimes had a lot of money, they could afford more paid sex than other mariners, which could have caused a disproportionate rate of infection by sexually transmitted diseases.

Unfortunately, illness and examination by a doctor often caused cross-dressed women to have their identity exposed.[22] Any sick woman on ship who wanted to keep her sex secret would have to choose silent suffering or the untutored assistance of a collaborator.

Myths have it that pirates caroused at celebratory banquets of captured venison and Portuguese wine; buccaneer William Dampier, for example, spoke of a dish of flamingoes' tongues. But a pirate's meals were more likely to have been an irregular mix of feast and fast, with poor-quality provisions the norm if a ship could not put into port or had not captured food-bearing vessels. Seafarers already belonged to a malnourished section of the population, so shipboard fare may not have been much worse than the food they were used to ashore. The difference between Wapping and the Windward Islands, however, was that in the latter fresh protein was available in the form of flying fish, dolphins, mackerel, skate, oysters, turtles and grilled ships' rats.

Victualling a ship for long journeys was a major feat of planning. When food was already substandard before it was salted or brought aboard, a few days in bad conditions could worsen it substantially, with firkins of butter going rancid and vermin infesting the stores. When the archetypal ships' hard biscuits were decorated with lacy patterns, it was a sign that weevils had got to them. Seafarers found that, 'Weevils tasted bitter and made the throat feel dry but maggots (flat with a big head and nicknamed "bargemen") felt cold as they went down.'[23] Hard salt beef could be carved into boxes that looked like mahogany; cheese could be carved into buttons. Drunkenness has an understandable cause: wine or beer remained drinkable whereas water became putrid in the casks within a few days of being grubbed up from river beds, went sweet, then after several weeks in the hold became thick, slimy, stagnant and 'full of green things'.[24]

Rivalry over food – one of the main causes of mutiny in the navy – may have been less ferocious on pirate ships, where victuals were usually better. On British naval vessels, routines to stop the crew cheating were devised: for instance, the cook of the day had to whistle while preparing a raison duff, on the grounds that you cannot whistle and eat raisons at the same time. But 'youngsters were sometimes bullied and deprived of the best victuals by older men.'[25] While pirate ships were more egalitarian, such patterns of abuse suggest that any woman who shared a low status with such lads would have had to fight to ensure the fair shares that would enable her to survive.

Eighteenth-century seafarers counted themselves fortunate if they had a dry mattress to sling in their narrow canvas hammocks – beds that explorer Christopher Columbus copied from Bahamian people.[26] For centuries, 14 inches was the permitted breadth of a hammock and no sheets or pillows were used. Seafarers in the navy shared hammocks between two (because one of them was always working).

The miserable quarters between decks were cramped, noisy, under-ventilated and dungeon-dark, with little space to stretch out freely and no privacy. Food was eaten by light of tallow, on deal tables sometimes covered with stout oilcloth slung between two guns,[27] and since the crew's living space doubled as sleeping quarters, what limited recreation there was took place with a smell of food, vermin and excess cargo.

How did cross-dressed women seafarers manage to go to the toilet in such public conditions? 'Large naval vessels by this time provided wooden latrines rigged in a secluded part of the deck; but on sloops of fifty tons or so such as the pirates still used there was no such refinement. The crew had to urinate and excrete squatting in "the head" – the forechains of the bow.'[28] To avoid detection, transvestite women of the period sometimes devised a false penis: one had a silver tube; another used 'a leather-covered horn through which she urinated and [which she kept] fastened against her nude body.'[29]

The masculine covering for women's urinary devices and secret bodies was plain, practical workwear. Clothes, sometimes so lousy that they could have walked aboard, were washed infrequently – not least because of limited fresh-water supplies. In the navy, clothes were cut out on deck by sailors who made not only trousers and shirts but straw hats and canvas pumps.[30] Pirates – either through theft or because they had money – may have acquired their canvas jackets and loose sailcloth trousers without such effort. The trousers, thickly smeared with pitch, were 'a kind of light armour capable of turning aside dagger thrusts and cutlass swipes'.[31] Certainly some pirates wore lavish costumes, including brocade coats and gold trimmings, not least for attracting women ashore. The crew were up in arms when one pirate captain proposed to borrow his captive's best clothes for a Guinea Coast shore visit '"among the negro ladies" and [they] insisted that the garments be put in the common chest in the care of the quartermaster'.[32] Black Bartholomew wore a crimson damask waistcoat and breeches, feathered hat and heavy jewellery.[33] However, when going into battle, Blackbeard plaited his huge beard and tied it in ribbons. To intimidate the opposition he tucked slow fuses under his hat. Made of hemp and dipped in saltpetre, they gave off alarming black smoke as he lunged to the attack.[34]

Some women working as sailors in the eighteenth century are said only to have donned trousers for convenience in times of battle. As Chapter 11 shows, the two French sea-artists who gave evidence about Mary Read and Ann Bonny testified that 'when we gave chase or attacked they wore men's clothes; at all other times they wore women's clothes.'[35] It is difficult to know how much dressing in trousers was for functional reasons and how much men on the ship did not need or expect to be deceived. Dekker and van de Pol found that disguise was a relative notion and that cross-dressed women's close companions sometimes knew their sexual identity.[36]

The key question is how and why did pirate crews tolerate 'out' women on board? Given that pirate captains' privileges were so circumscribed, what role and what protection did a woman have on a pirate ship by comparison with other vessels where the captain's peccadillos and orders had to be respected?

Seafarers had their own lifestyle with different ways of speaking, acting, dressing and behaving to those of landlubbers. Pirate ships were multicultural places. Reports of hangings for piracy show the ethnic mix of those labouring beneath the Jolly Roger. In 1718, of the 31 pirates hanged, five were from Jamaica, six from London, four from North Carolina, four from South Carolina, five from Scotland, and one each from Antigua, Bristol, Oporto, Holland, Dublin, Guernsey and Newcastle.[37] Pirate vessels appear to have been even more diverse in population than British merchant ships, which were permitted to carry crews of up to three-quarters foreigners.[38] Unlike land-based people of that period, seafarers knew the terrain on which racial conflicts were played out – from slave uprisings in the Caribbean plantations and unrest in colonies to shipboard protests by slaves against cruelty. They could see the injustices and resistances to it, whatever their own racism or attitudes to 'Otherness'.

Because of this diversity, 'the medium of communication could not be the King's English; instead "vehicular languages" were created – creole, pidgin, and "All-American". These drew upon parent languages of north-eastern Europe (English, French, Dutch) and western Africa (Yoruba, Fanti).' Some of the language was 'the specialised vocabulary of the intricate, particular tasks necessary to the technique of sailing. But much of it was not. A "manany" puts off work, a "javel" was a loafer, "scrovy" and "cosier" were names for useless sailors.'[39] And because of the misogyny at sea, women working on pirate ships would use and be used to the hostile terminology which was expressed even at the level of calling a badly made reef knot a 'Granny knot' – which is both ageist and sexist.[40]

The group dynamics on a pirate vessel were better than on a naval vessel, where volatile working-class people brought up in workhouses and as parish outcasts were traditionally 'under-paid and over-lashed'. Some of these people joined pirate ships, on which the lack of an officer hierarchy meant frequent negotiation over status. Johnson shows that the rough-and-ready equality on pirate vessels meant a leader had to be competent and fair or face displacement. Like any co-operative venture, the scope for rivalry and anxieties about being cheated may well have been constant, with mutual trust a rarity. 'Contemporaries who claimed that pirates had "no regular command among them" mistook a different order – different from the order of merchant, naval and privateering vessels – for disorder.'[41] Authority was placed in the collective hands of the crew. Discipline – though large ranges of behaviour were left uncontrolled – depended on a collective sense of transgression.[42]

Leisure activities on ships traditionally include carving, painting (pictures of ships on sea chests, for instance) and knitting. B. R. Burg has suggested that extensive male homosexuality existed[43] and there must also have been masturbation – either solitary or mutual. For the men who were guardians of women captives there was a pay off; they could have sex with them. And when pirates did not share a common tongue, the '. . . international nautical proletariat . . . learned . . . other means of communication, such as the fiddle, the drum, the banjo and dances like jigs and clogging.' [44] Although literacy levels varied, the more educated seafarers read and wrote. Foster, a pirate criticised by Captain Morgan for harshness to prisoners, penned sentimental verse, particularly one work entitled 'Sonneyettes of Love'. [45] Some seafarers were more politicised; a pre-revolutionary consciousness developed through their books and talks. 'Sailors were among the first to study slavery and abolition,' believes Peter Linebaugh. [46]

Unlike merchant and naval vessels, pirate ships' crews distributed any captured goods according to skills and duties. It was agreed in advance that the 'Captain and quartermaster received between one and one-half and two shares; gunners, boatswains, mates, carpenters and doctors, one and one-quarter or one and one-half; all others got one share each.' [47] Privateer crew member Flora Burn was entitled to a one-and-three-quarter share, like all the other sailors. [48] The commander had a two-and-a-half share. Women passing as men obviously received the same pay as men; indeed, that may have been their whole rationale for dressing up as well as a useful compensation for the daily stress of being counterfeit. 'Out' women are likely to have been paid in cash or kind for sexual and other services by the men who used them. Men's sense that women were doing duties that justified their place on the ship may have brought fair shares. However, given the extent to which women's services have traditionally been devalued, this seems unlikely.

When it came to weapons, 'many female soldiers must have been considered boys rather than men, and boys were usually given equipment suited to their physical strength.' [49] Anglo-American pirates of this period fought with the same weapons as other seafarers: musket pistol, sword and boarding axe; [50] Ann Bonny and Mary Read were said to have used weapons as cruelly as men. Cruelty was one of the key words associated with pirates. Aspects of reports of pirates' sadism may be novelists' licence and part of the titillating semi-pornographic mythology written for male readers with penchants for domination and abuse. In reality, few decks were awash with gore and diamonds, while 'walking the plank was never a pirate punishment'.[51] Many merchantmen's crews captured by pirates submitted quietly because it was easier and their cargo was often insured anyway. Efficient pirates needed to get the valuable cargo off intact and could not afford to endanger it through fighting.

Ann Bonny and Mary Read, with their alleged viciousness and scorn of men's cowardice, lived in a brutalised society in which women's ferocity was not as unthinkable as in Victorian Britain. Sociological studies today show that women and men on occasion act the part of a violent person in order to maintain the respect of their peer group; so too would women pirates passing as men or accepted as 'honorary' males. Stories of cross-dressed women seafarers who overdid the swagger on rampages[52] suggest a propensity to overdo the violence too.

Of course, cruelty could be profitable. In situations where speed was crucial, it made a kind of horrible sense to hack off a woman's finger rather than lose time easing off her rings.[53] When information was needed, torture was often the fastest way to obtain it. Violence could also be mistargeted social retaliation. It was not only a case of the oppressed oppressing those still further beneath them: white working-class pirates behaving brutally towards black captives, or towards Caribbean women who laundered for and pleasured them. Class revenge could also be expressed through raping rich men's wives (which happened on land as well as sea) in front of their husbands in order to distress the men into submitting to pirate demands. Marcus Rediker found 'The foremost target of vengeance was the merchant captain.' Pirates questioned the crew of a captured merchant vessel about their captain's behaviour; those masters who had been abusive were whipped, pickled, tortured and executed. Pirate Philip Lyne confessed to having killed 37 captains.[54]

But above all, popular pirate books give lurid accounts of sadistic behaviour towards women as victims of gang rape and terrorisation. These stories have their parallels in accounts today which reflect the deep psychic structures that lead men in patriarchal societies to see women as things to abuse, whether through domestic or workplace sexual abuse or gang rapes perpetuated on women made still more vulnerable by war and displacement, as in 1990s Serbian refugee camps.

'Women and boys were sometimes raped, although in the case of younger women, there was restraint, for the ransom, if any were to be paid, would be higher if no sexual abuse had taken place.'[55] Most volumes include the story about a pirate attack on the Great Moghul, often transforming the (real) elderly woman victim into a young and beautiful princess.[56] Plate 4, 'Horrible abuse of helpless women in cabin', shows the Atlantic capture of the *Morning Star*, an East Indiaman carrying wives and daughters of soldiers and officials coming home on furlough.[57] The women, who later escaped, were luckier than those attacked by Captain Jose Gaspar, 'Gasparilla', who:

> lived in Regal state as king of the pirates on Gasparilla Island. In 1801 he took a big Spanish ship forty miles from Boca Grande, killed the crew, and took a quantity of gold and twelve young ladies. One of these was a Spanish Princess, whom he kept for himself; the eleven Mexican girls he gave to his crew. Gaspar was described as having polished manners and a great love of fashionable clothes . . . but in spite of all these attractive qualities the little Spanish Princess would have none of him and was murdered.[58]

Occasionally, stories of male pirates' gentleness towards captive women are told. Fanny Loviot describes her experiences in the 1850s when captured by Chinese pirates, en route from California to Java:

> 'It was not often that the pirates took any notice of me; but strange to say, whenever they did look at me, it was with an expression of good nature of which I should scarcely have supposed them capable. "They like you" said Than Sing [a fellow passenger] who had been talking with them. "They like you, because your face and eyes are gentle; and they say they no longer wish any evil to happen to you." '[59]

In what is superficially a tale of pirate-as-honourable-gentlemen, but might also be an expression of anti-Spanish racism, pirate captain Henry Johnson rescued Mrs Groves, a passenger captured on the *John and Jane* off Jamaica. The Spanish captain took the stripped Mrs Groves '"to the great cabin and there with horrible oaths insolently assaulted her Chastity." Johnson . . . seeing what was on hand . . .

threatened to blow out the brains of any man who attempted the least violence upon her' and ordered her clothes to be returned to her.[60]

Such stories of eighteenth-century violence under the Jolly Roger betray the turmoil of attitudes towards women. In a time of changing trade and maritime needs, the lives of eighteenth-century women pirates differed in many ways from the privileged existences of Alfhild, Artemisia and Grace O'Malley.

Notes

1. David Cordingly and John Falconer, *Pirates: fact and fiction*, Collins & Brown, 1992, p. 99. See also Philip Gosse, *The Pirates' Who's Who*, Dulau, 1924, p. 245.
2. David Mitchell, *Pirates*, Thames & Hudson, 1976, p. 20.
3. Gosse, *op cit*, p. 328.
4. Cordingly and Falconer, *op cit*, p. 74.
5. *ibid*, p. 110.
6. *ibid*, p. 110.
7. Tonnage initially was a way of measuring ships based on the amount of wine in jar, cask, tun or butt that they could carry. For example, a ship of 50 tons would be capable of carrying 100 butts of wine, because each 4' 6" high butt (containing 126 gallons) weighed half a ton. This does not mean that ships *would* carry such quantities. Pirate ships could not afford to be loaded down so they would carry as little as possible. Remnants from heists – cloves, pepper, equipment – were left behind to rot on shore if sale was not possible.
8. Marcus Rediker, *Between the Devil and the Deep Blue Sea: merchant seamen, pirates and the Anglo-American maritime world 1700-1750*, Cambridge University Press, 1987, p. 279. For seafarers' general conditions, see Christopher Lloyd, *The British Seaman 1200-1860: a social survey*, Paladin, 1970.
9. Rediker, *ibid*, p. 279.
10. *ibid*, p. 279.
11. Cordingly and Falconer, *op cit*, pp. 78-9.
12. Mitchell, *op cit*, p. 84.
13. Rediker, *op cit*, p. 259.
14. Cordingly and Falconer, *op cit*, p. 18. Also Mitchell, *op cit*, p. 82.
15. Peter Linebaugh, *The London Hanged: crime and civil society in the eighteenth century*, Allen Lane, The Penguin Press, 1991, p. 130.

16. *ibid*, p. 130.
17. Una A. Robertson, *Mariners' Mealtimes and other daily details of life on board a sailing warship*, Unicorn Preservation Society, 1979, p. 4.
18. Cordingly and Falconer, *op cit*, p. 114.
19. Seafarers 'needed immunological powers too . . . only half the men sailing with Anson round the world [1740-4] survived . . . Despite Doctor James Lind's discoveries in 1747 of the anti-scorbutic qualities of oranges and lemons, 133,708 sailors died of scurvy (compared with 1,512 killed in action) during the Seven Years War.' Linebaugh, *op cit*, p. 130.
20. Mary Chamberlain, *Old Wives Tales: their history, remedies and spells*, Virago, 1981, pp. 238, 254.
21. Mitchell, *op cit*, p. 23.
22. Rudolf M. Dekker and Lotte C. van de Pol, *The Tradition of Female Transvestism in Early Modern Europe*, MacMillan, 1989, pp. 21-2.
23. Robertson, *op cit*, p. 28.
24. *ibid*, pp. 21, 31.
25. *ibid*, p. 9.
26. *ibid*, p. 37.
27. *ibid*, pp. 9-11.
28. Mitchell, *op cit*, p. 88.
29. Dekker and van de Pol, op cit, pp. 15-16, citing Brigitte Eriksson (ed), 'A Lesbian Execution in Germany, 1721: the trial records', *Journal of Homosexuality*, 6 (1980-81), pp. 27-41.
30. Robertson, *op cit*, p. 8.
31. Mitchell, *op cit*, p. 85.
32. *ibid*, p. 22.
33. Cordingly and Falconer, *op cit*, p. 13.
34. *ibid*, pp. 22, 23.
35. Mitchell, *op cit*, pp. 87-8, citing the sea-artists' testimony.
36. Dekker and van de Pol, *op cit*, p. 19.
37. Linebaugh, *op cit*, pp. 133-4.
38. *ibid*, p. 67.
39. *ibid*, p. 134.
40. For further ideas on the attitudes betrayed and formed by common speech of the period, see Jane Mills, *Womanwords, a vocabulary of culture and patriarchal society*, Virago, 1991.
41. Rediker, *op cit*, p. 261.
42. *ibid*, p. 265.
43. B. R. Burg, *Sodomy and the Pirate Tradition: English sea rovers in the 17th century Caribbean*, New York University Press, 1984.
44. Linebaugh, *op cit*, p. 135.
45. Gosse, *op cit*, p. 129.
46. Linebaugh, *op cit*, p. 136.
47. Rediker, *op cit*, p. 264.

48. John Franklin Jameson, *Privateering and Piracy of the Colonial Period*, MacMillan, 1923, p. 394.

49. Dekker and van de Pol, *op cit*, p. 18.

50. Cordingly and Falconer, *op cit*, p. 70.

51. *ibid*, pp. 11-12.

52. See Julie Wheelwright, *Amazons and Military Maids: women who dressed as men in pursuit of life, liberty and happiness*, Pandora, 1989, especially p. 68.

53. Mitchell, *op cit*, p. 68.

54. Rediker, *op cit*, p. 270.

55. Ralph T. Ward, *Pirates in History*, York Press, 1974, p. 72, referring to the case of earlier Moslem pirates, c. 1000 AD.

56. Mitchell, *op cit*, p. 110.

57. *ibid*, p. 169.

58. Gosse, *op cit*, p. 131.

59. Fanny Loviot, translated by A. B. Edwards, *A Lady's Captivity among Chinese Pirates*, 1858, stored at the British Library under 10057 a19 26. See pp. 15, 16 and 111.

60. Gosse, *op cit*, pp. 173-4.

11 *Tars, tarts and swashbucklers by Julie Wheelwright*

With pitch and tar her hands were hard
Tho' once like velvet soft
She weighed the anchor, heav'd the lead
And boldly went aloft [1]

She stands on the ship's bridge, a froth of lace outlining her blouson. She gazes from behind a curtain of flowing locks and clutches a machete in her right hand. Whether she is Ann Bonny terrifying the men aboard Captain Rackham's ship in Captain Charles Johnson's *A General History of the Robberies and Murders of the most Notorious Pyrates*, Fanny Campbell, the fictional pirate heroine of M. M. Ballou's (aka Lieutenant Murray's) 1856 novel or a swashbuckling supermodel in a fashion spread, the eighteenth-century female pirate figure is an enduring fantasy. She has flung aside domestic constraints, escaped poverty, rejected a husband or arranged marriage to claim the endless expanse of sea as her own. From the eighteenth-century tales of Mary Read and Ann Bonny's adventures with Captain Rackham's crew in the Caribbean, the mythical female pirate has survived as an emblem of women's liberty. As pirate writer Philip Gosse claimed in 1932, 'Nowadays when what used to be called the "tender sex" has invaded almost every profession except the church, it may not seem strange that women should have willingly entered such a rough and manly trade as that of piracy.' Decades later, the female pirate still speaks of an enduring desire for escape.

Generations of women have followed these stories, which belong to the mythology that has grown up around the female tar, but which have remained deeply embedded in a masculine literary tradition. By tracing the female pirate legend from the Jamaican piracy trials of Bonny and Read in 1720 through its reinterpretation by generations of writers to the most contemporary revisions, the nature of the contradictory meanings and popular appeal that surround the female pirate will emerge.

Readers of these pirate stories were – and still are – invited to enter an imaginary world of inverted social expectations. The majority of eighteenth-century pirates were recruited from among captured crews or merchantmen, from Royal Naval sailors or privateersmen who turned volunteer to escape the harsh conditions under which they were forced to serve. Dr Johnson observed that their lives were so marked with disease, meagre rations, sadistic punishment and low wages, 'that being in a ship is being in a jail with the chance of being drowned . . . A man in jail has more room, better food, and commonly better company.'[2] Aboard pirate ships, there was in many cases a rough egalitarianism; men elected their captain and gave him few privileges, even forbidding him a separate cabin or mess. As pirate Francis Kennedy explained, most of these tars, 'having suffered formerly from ill-treatment of their officers, provided carefully against such evil.'[3]

The female pirate, despite her rarity in historical accounts, fits easily into the romance of these anarchic adventurers. The stories even appear to acknowledge that working-class women suffered under similar conditions and would rebel against the authoritarian figure – the captain – responsible for perpetuating an oppressive system. But the pirate legend also reminds readers that the heroine's flight from domestic commitments was a temporary state: the ferocious Ann Bonny doubled as Captain Rackham's mistress and mother of his child; Mary Read offered to give up piracy for 'some honest livelihood', to settle with her common-law husband; Mary Cobham, the prostitute-turned-pirate, sailed with her lover and eventually retired as the respectable lady of a prominent estate in Normandy; Mary Anne Talbot, forced to leave the sea and disabled by her wounds, lived out a precarious existence as a domestic servant. In the chapbooks, ballads and novels based on these cases, the heroine's aberration can be tolerated, even celebrated, because it carried no promise of permanent change. Military conflicts – including pirating on the high seas – provided an appropriately safe container for the woman's inversion. A closure is written into every version of the story: the cross-dressed pirate or tar's disguise is inevitably penetrated; the war ends, the crew is arrested, or a heroine gives up her adventures for love. Read and Bonny's masculine clothes and mythical confidence with the cutlass are consistent with a pirate code that inverted all convention. The female pirate played out her heroism according to rules which she ultimately contradicted: she might behave like a man, but is eventually revealed as a perfectly feminine woman who falls in love, marries, bears children and makes willing sacrifices for her man. The power of male authority is ultimately undisturbed by her presence aboard ship because this presence has no lasting effect. And yet despite the dampening effect of these historical realities and their fictional representations, many contemporary readers still relish the female pirate's defiance of the rules. In this instance, we might read against the text and take from it the significance of the transgression rather than the inevitable denouement.

The mythology is rooted in the scattered documents which chronicle the female pirates' extraordinary lives. In a relative vacuum of factual evidence, however, the legends began to flourish, taking on the shape of those of other martial heroines. The first published accounts of Read and Bonny's adventures coincided with the popularity of a particular heroic archetype in eighteenth-century Anglo-American balladry.[4] With dozens of variations on the theme, the fictional 'female warrior' masquerades as a man and sets off to war to follow a lover, escape a husband or defend her country. She usually makes an excellent warrior but inevitably gives up her Amazonian skills for love and retires from battle covered in glory. Even Johnson's 1724 account of Bonny and Read's trial in *A General History of the Robberies and Murders of the most Notorious Pyrates* suggests that the fictional 'female warrior' overshadowed the facts. Although there were other women who served aboard ships during this period, Read and Bonny were used as the literary standard-bearers of female piracy. The myth's power becomes evident through a close comparison of the trial transcript and the report in Johnson's *History*, which was published and widely circulated four years later. The trial transcript of the High Court of

Admiralty, however, itself reflects the crown's agenda. Charged with trying pirates so that the crown would be assured its share of their booty, the court was designed for efficiency; between 1700 and 1750, more than 2,200 cases were heard. As with Read and Bonny, such a high volume of business often meant that crucial elements of a case went missing.[5] For Bonny and Read, as we shall see, the court transcript tells much, but by no means all, of the story.

At a High Court of Admiralty in St Jago de la Vega, Jamaica, on 28 November 1720, the two women pirates stood accused of having committed 'Piracies, Felonies, and Robberies . . . on the High Sea', in four separate incidents. As part of Captain 'Calico' Jack Rackham's crew, the women 'did feloniously and wickedly . . . rob [and] plunder' several ships, often taking those on board as captives. Both women pleaded 'not guilty' to the charges. The court depositions provide illuminating detail about the pirates' operations, suggesting that their hauls ranged from a few fishing boats with tackle worth £10 in Jamaican pounds to merchant sloops worth £1,000. And although the pirates had not resorted to murder, in each incident the sailors aboard ship claimed they were taken captive 'in Corporal Fear of their Lives'. Read and Bonny were no less aggressive than their male colleagues, according to local witness Dorothy Thomas, who observed that the women instructed the men to kill her if she resisted their attack.

Thomas described how, while sailing on the north Jamaican coast in a canoe stocked with provisions, a sloop approached and Rackham relieved the vessel of 'most things that were in her'. The two women aboard:

> wore Men's Jackets, and long Trouzers, and Handkerchiefs tied about their Heads: and that each of them had a Machet and Pistol in their Hands and cursed and Swore at the Men, to murder [Thomas]; and they should kill her to prevent her coming against them; and [Thomas] further said, That the Reason of her knowing and believing them to be Women then was, by the largeness of their Breasts.[6]

Their presence aboard Rackham's ship was confirmed by Thomas Spenlow, master of a schooner taken on 19 October near Porto-Maria Bay, Jamaica. Two French volunteers, John Bessneck and Peter

Cornelian, probably served aboard the pirate ship; they testified to Read and Bonny's presence during the raid on Spenlow and another the following day near Dry-Harbour Bay. Their account of the women's actions, given through an interpreter, seems to concur with Thomas' claim that Read and Bonny were armed and readily used their weapons. Besneck and Cornelian observed that the women:

> were very active on Board and willing to do any Thing; That Ann Bonny ... handed Gun-Powder to the Men, That when they saw any Vessel, gave Chase or Attacked, they wore Men's Cloaths; and, at other Times, they wore Women's Cloaths; That they did not seem to be kept or detained by Force, but of their own Free-Will and Consent.[7]

This testimony suggests that the women were not disguised on the ship but simply wore male clothes for convenience during raids. The masquerade would have made them relatively anonymous, signalled their role as active crew members, and possibly even afforded them a degree of protection from sexual assault had they been captured. Thomas' testimony implies the women might have commanded the other pirates; their handkerchiefs and trousers – part of the informal pirate uniform – would have been essential to their authority.

The final witness to confirm the women's presence was Thomas Dillon, master of the sloop *Mary and Sarah*, which was lying at anchor in Dry-Harbour Bay when Rackham's crew attacked. When a 'strange sloop came into the Harbour', Dillon and his men raced along the shore to protect themselves and their ship. Once the shots had died away, Dillon hailed the pirate captain and was told, 'they were English pirates and [Dillon and his crew] need not be afraid'. Dillon then went aboard where he noticed that 'Ann Bonny ... had a Gun in her Hand, That [the women] were both very profligate, cursing and swearing much, and very ready and willing to do any Thing on Board.' In this and other descriptions, no exception seems to have been made for the women's presence by the pirate crew or by their captives. They were not marginalised but played a central role in Rackham's raids, as integral members of a tightly knit group.

After hearing the witnesses' testimony, Read and Bonny refused to cross-examine them, offered nothing in their own defence and raised no questions. President Sir Nicholas Lawes and his commissioners then pronounced the women prisoners guilty of the 'Piracies, Robberies and Felonies' against them. For a second time, the women reportedly declined to speak on their own behalf and were sentenced to be executed. Only then did the prisoners 'plead the belly', demanding the court stay their execution as they were both pregnant. The court agreed to suspend their sentences until an inspection to verify their condition could be carried out. While there is no record of whether the inspection was undertaken or what its results revealed, it is certain that neither woman was hanged.

From this evidence, the myth was born. Four years after the Rackham crew's trial, Johnson's history was published with a lengthy chapter devoted to the lives of Bonny and Read. The book, which would later be attributed to Daniel Defoe, rapidly achieved its status as the definitive and most accurate history of eighteenth-century piracy. In 1932, an American scholar of Defoe's work, John Robert Moore, confidently claimed that 'it is hardly too much to say that the author of the *History*, has created the modern conception of pirates.'[8] As late as 1987, pirate scholar Marcus Rediker would still cite *A General History of the Pyrates* as a definitive text: 'Daniel Defoe was the first historian of these pirates. Under the name Charles Johnson, he published an invaluable collection of mostly accurate information'.[9] The attribution to Defoe was later debunked, most convincingly by Peter Furbank and W. R. Owens in *The Canonisation of Daniel Defoe* in which they demonstrate that no external evidence supported Moore's claim that Defoe authored the *History*, aside from similarities to other works. However, the inclusion of Bonny and Read's story in the *History* established the women pirates as a trope with a romantic, literary tradition.

A careful reading of Johnson's version of the trial set against the court transcript reveals subtle alterations on significant points. Johnson divides the chapter on Bonny and Read into two autobiographical sections, describing each woman's early life, her involvement with Rackham's crew and her trial. The author takes full command of poetic licence to flesh out the details of the pirate heroine's histories and characters. But Johnson's moulding bears more than a passing resemblance to other eighteenth-century tales of 'female warriors' and cross-dressers, which suggests the retelling was shaped along conventional lines. Although it is almost impossible to reconstruct the biographical details of Bonny and Read's early life to verify Johnson's account, comparison with the evidence of the trial transcript reveals his addition of several imaginative details. Many of these would form the basis for the legend of the violent, rapacious lady pirates who still appear in women's fashion magazines and on screen today.[10]

Perhaps most significantly, Johnson's biography of Read and Bonny transforms them from accepted members of the pirate crew into exceptional, bloodthirsty Amazons. While the sailors Dillon, Spenlow and Thomas all reported Read and Bonny's aggressive behaviour aboard ship, Johnson adds an important dimension to their testimony. Despite the French sailors' evidence to the contrary, Johnson describes how Read disguised herself as a man aboard ship and was once asked by a captive why this 'young man' risked public execution for the sake of pirating. Read replied:

> that to hanging [if caught] she thought it no great hardship, for were it not for that, every cowardly fellow would turn Pirate and so infest the seas that men of courage must starve; that if it was put to the choice of the Pirates, they would not have the punishment less than death, the fear of which kept some dastardly rogues honest; that many of those who were now cheating the widows and orphans, and oppressing their poor neighbours who have no money to obtain justice, would then rob at sea, and no merchant would venture out; so that the trade in a little time would not be worth following.[11]

The statement reads like a tribute to the imagined Robin Hood values of eighteenth-century piracy: the willingness to endure harsh punishment, even death, in the cause of justice for the poor. Many pirate experts suggest that Johnson (or Defoe) interviewed witnesses after the trial to verify such claims. (Moore speculated that he gathered material from books, unpublished manuscripts and conversations with retired pirates.)[12] Although Johnson may have spoken with someone who had witnessed the trial, Read's statement to the captive does not appear in the court transcript. However, it is frequently quoted in subsequent histories of the female pirates and taken as fact. Philip Gosse uses it in his *History of Piracy*, but claims it was Rackham who asked Read what pleasure she found in a life of constant danger.[13]

Despite the dubious origins of Read's peon to piracy, it has worked to imbue her with male heroics, making her both an extraordinary pirate and woman.

This perception of fantastical female behaviour is reinforced elsewhere in Johnson's *History*: specifically citing 'the evidence against her upon her trial', he quotes the 'forced men who sailed with her' (a reference to Besneck and Cornelian) as stating that during attacks, 'None kept the deck except Mary Read and Anne [sic] Bonny and one more; upon which she, Mary Read, called to those under deck to come up and fight like men; and finding they did not stir, fired her arms down the hold amongst them, killing one and wounding another.'[14] Furthermore, Read allegedly disputed this charge when it was presented in court. The trial transcript contradicts both statements and neither woman is recorded as defending herself. Again, this anecdote about Read's machismo quickly became accepted as fact by virtue of repetition; as early as 1755, it appeared in a London chapbook entitled *The Lives and Adventures of the German Princess, Mary Read, Ann Bonny, Joan Philips, Madam Churchill, Betty Ireland and Ann Hereford*. So from the statements of witnesses who remembered the women as 'being very active' and 'willing to do any Thing', the female pirates became desperadas with superior martial skills and more physical courage than their male crew.

While Read and Bonny embody these most masculine of values, in keeping with the female warrior tradition, Johnson ensures that the women are portrayed as equally feminine by fleshing out stories of their romantic encounters. According to the *History*, a sailor who had been pressed into service in the West Indies from an English ship became Read's closest mess-mate. She then discreetly 'allowed' him to discover her true sex (again, Johnson implies that she was disguised throughout her time aboard Rackham's ship), and they plighted their troth. Although it is absent from the transcript, Johnson claims Read commended the court for acquitting her common-law husband and swore to the court that 'they had both resolved to leave the Pirates the first opportunity, and apply themselves to some honest livelihood.' There were other men tried along with Rackham – George Fetherston, Richard Corner, John Davies, John Howell, Patrick Carty, Thomas Earl and Noah Harwood – but none who was identified as Read's husband. There is another important discrepancy; Johnson suggests that Read's pregnancy was far advanced, her 'great belly' visible by the time she appeared in court. The transcript, however, records only that both Read and Bonny were 'quick with child' – meaning that the defendants were at least 18 weeks pregnant, since it is then that a woman usually begins to feel the foetus moving in her womb, though she may not yet be visibly pregnant. If Johnson's account is to be believed, it seems curious that if Read was in an advanced state of pregnancy, an inspection would be needed to verify her claim.

The impact of Johnson's subtle rewriting is to turn Read from a member of a close-knit pirate crew into a figure who possesses equally exaggerated masculine and feminine virtues. As a pirate, she and Bonny are the bravest men on board, ruthlessly firing into the hold while the rest of the crew cower below during an attack. She epitomises the noble pirate code, supporting the death penalty for pirating as a means to keep weaker men, motivated only by greed, from scouring the seas. Yet she also displays a woman's vulnerability by falling in love, becoming pregnant and finally renouncing piracy to settle into a conventional life with her lover.[15] Johnson even emphasises her pregnancy as a reminder of her womanly, physical presence – that great swollen belly – in the dock.

There is another telling contradiction in Johnson's version of Read's story. According to the *History*, she 'often declared that the life of a Pirate was what she always abhorred, and went into it only upon compulsion . . . intending to quit it whenever a fair opportunity should offer itself'; she first won over her lover 'by talking against the life of a Pirate, which he was altogether averse to'. However, Johnson provides court evidence which confirmed that during attacks, 'no person amongst them was more resolute or ready to board or undertake anything that was hazardous [than Read].'[16] Given that Read had supposedly decided to take advantage of King George's extension of a general Royal Pardon for piracy and quit the trade, why should her statement in court have any validity? By the time Read appeared in the witness box, Johnson tells us that her life had changed dramatically; she was heavily pregnant, deeply in love and her desire for a quiet life appears more believable. Again, an exceptional woman, glorifying masculine values, finally returns to her appropriately self-sacrificial maternal role. According to Johnson, she did not live long enough to fulfil any of her pledges and died of a fever in prison before her child could be delivered.

Of Bonny's sentence, Johnson relates only that she remained in prison until her lying-in, was reprieved and then disappeared. Before Rackham's execution, Bonny was granted permission to see her former lover. Alone in the cell with the condemned prisoner, Bonny is said to have berated him, 'That she was sorry to see him there, but if he had fought like a man, he need not have been hanged like a dog.'[17] The much-repeated, apocryphal statement is impossible to verify; if Rackham died and Bonny disappeared, from whom did Johnson learn about this private conversation? The quote reminds readers, however, that while Read and Bonny were the best warriors on Rackham's ship, they managed to escape death through the most natural of female reasons.

Johnson's *History* was published during a decade which saw a spate of pirate hangings and, as historian Marcus Rediker describes it, 'a burst of propaganda' against their ilk. The result was that the European pirate population went into steep decline, and by 1726 only a handful remained.[18] The dying culture, however, had generated a huge popular interest in the west which Johnson's publication was able to exploit. Aside from the fantasy of the female sailor, her real-life counterparts may have been well known. There are many recorded instances of women who went to sea in a wide range of roles from disguised cabin boys to wives or mistresses, prostitutes, cooks and nurses. The prototype for the pamphlet, entitled the 'Queen Regulations and Admiralty Instructions', first printed in 1731, specifically mentions the presence of women aboard ship. The captain or commander's duties include instructions, 'not to carry any Woman to Sea', which suggests that all-male crews had not always been the norm.[19] The instructions were, of course, frequently ignored by both captains and crew.

The pirate heroines Bonny and Read were both working-class women who had been born illegitimately, without the comfort of wealth or the blessing of social status, and raised as boys for pragmatic reasons. Or so we are told by Johnson. He relates that Read's 'young and airy' mother had been abandoned by her sailor husband like many other cross-dressed heroines of the period. When Mary's brother died a few months after her birth, her mother decided to disguise her baby girl, born out of wedlock, as a boy. Mary's mother then persuaded her wealthy mother-in-law to accept the child as her grandson and provide 'him' with a weekly allowance. When the grandmother died, the mother sent 13-year-old Mary to wait on a French lady as a footboy. The disguise was motivated first by the family's financial straits, as is common in the female warrior story. But 'growing bold and strong' and 'having also a roving mind', Mary quit domestic service to sign aboard a man-o-war. Once she had crossed the English Channel, she left the ship to become a cadet in Flanders during the War of the Spanish Succession (1701-14) and eventually, a foot soldier. She later joined the cavalry where she 'behaved so well in several engagements that she got the esteem of all her officers'.

But the young soldier, typical of English balladry's Polly Oliver, endured the hardships of the rough, male world to remain beside her beloved. 'Neither father or mother shall make me false prove,/I'll list for a soldier and follow my love.'[20] Read soon made the leap from warrior to maiden by allowing her Flemish comrade to discover that his tent-mate was a woman. And, as she was later to distinguish herself aboard Rackham's ship as an equally fearless warrior and perfect wife, she demonstrated her virtue by resisting the Flemish soldier's entreaties and demanding a marriage proposal instead. It was only when the campaign had ended that the couple made their secret public and the celebrated troopers were married. They opened a thriving public house named The Three Horseshoes near Breda (now in the Netherlands), which attracted soldiers and others who had heard of their unusual story.

When the Flemish soldier died and the pub's business began to falter, Read's financial situation forced her to resume wearing trousers. Johnson assumes his readers will accept the logic of such a statement which, however covertly, acknowledges a widow's difficulty in coping alone. Read's escape from the poverty trap led her to join another infantry regiment and then take a ship bound for the Caribbean. *En route*, it was commandeered by English pirates and since Mary was their only compatriot aboard, she was taken captive. They returned to the West Indies after hearing of the general Royal Pardon for any pirate who quit the trade. But peace was short lived once money grew scarce and Read decided to enlist with an outfit of privateers who were cruising against the Spaniards and were fitted out by Captain Woodes Rogers, governor of Providence Island.

The crew soon mutinied against their commanders, however, and turned to plundering any passing vessel for profit. Read was among the mutineers who then joined Captain Rackham's ship, disguised as a young man, according to Johnson, 'for her modesty according to her notions of virtue'. Aside from her lover, Read disclosed her secret only to Ann Bonny, who had at first shown a romantic interest in the 'handsome young fellow'. When Bonny, as a woman, attempted to seduce her, Read, 'knowing what she would be at, and being very sensible of her *incapacity that way*, was forced to come to a right understanding with her' (my italics).[21] Then Bonny unmasked herself, which created an intimacy between the two women and roused Captain Rackham to such a jealous fury that Ann told him the truth about the young sailor's identity.

This delightfully complicated scenario, where the 'female warrior' is seduced by or seduces another, echoes other stories of the period. Hannah Snell, the daughter of a Worcester hosier who disguised herself as James Gray to serve in both the army and navy from 1745 to 1750, had more than one female lover. *The Female Sailor*, her biography which was published the year she retired from sea, recounts that Snell had 'endeavoured to try if she could not act the Lover as well as the Soldier'.[22] After being paid off in Portsmouth, 'James Gray' struck up a romance with a young woman to whom 'he' proposed marriage. 'James' promised that once 'he' had reached London 'he' would send for 'his' fiancée and they would be wed. As befitted the sailor's prerogative with women, however, 'Gray' promptly neglected 'his' promise once 'he' had returned to the capital.

In Hannah Snell's story, the flirtation appears to be part of the sailor's disguise and further confirmation of her masculine habits. Moreover, as with many cross-dressed female tars, Snell's shipmates testified to her courage in 'the most dangerous exploits' and that 'she behaved upon all Occasions with the greatest Bravery and Resolution.'[23] Any suggestion that the woman sailor's amorous relationships with other women are a serious indication of sexual preference and anything more than an elaboration of her male disguise is undermined elsewhere in the text.[24] In Johnson's *History*, once Bonny and Read have exchanged their mutual secrets, Mary promptly falls in love with a (male) fellow sailor. They rapidly become intimate friends and once a mutual trust is established, Read 'suffered the discovery to be made, by carelessly showing her breasts, which were very white'.[25] So profound is Read's passion that she arranges to take her lover's place in a duel to vanquish an enemy she has judged 'too hard for him'. Johnson writes that 'she stood, as it were, betwixt him and death, as if she could not live without him.' The contradiction inherent in Read's superiority with a sword and pistol is resolved because her motives are couched in the language of female devotion and self-sacrifice. Violence was an everyday part of many working women's lives in eighteenth-century Britain and female duellists were common across Europe. Many contemporary French writers noted the famous 'gallant ladies' who regularly challenged each other to duels, 'dressed as men'.[26] So a contemporary reader of Johnson's *History* may have been more impressed by Read's willingness to risk death for her lover's sake than by her skill in handling weapons.

Despite the equally ferocious sentiments Ann Bonny expressed, her bloodlust was balanced – and excused – by her marital devotion. Unlike Read, Bonny first assumed a male disguise to escape a rocky marriage and elope to sea with her lover, Captain Rackham. The illegitimate daughter of a Cork solicitor, Bonny showed early signs of a penchant for adventure and a pugilist's talent. Johnson writes that after her father had emigrated from Ireland to Carolina with his maid – Bonny's mother – and daughter, Ann began to demonstrate her volatile nature. 'She was of a fierce and courageous temper . . . It was certain that she was so robust once, that when a young fellow would have lain against her will, she beat him so that he lay ill of it a considerable time.'[27] Her desire for independence and autonomy was further revealed when she refused her father's choice of husband and married a young sailor who 'was not worth a groat'. Shunned by her family, Bonny and her husband left Carolina for Providence Island. But her marriage was already troubled and Bonny soon left her cowardly sailor for Rackham. She was only a few months at sea with the pirate crew when she fell pregnant with the captain's child. Rackham, following a practice common among sea captains, landed his lover at Cuba, where she gave birth before returning to sea, 'to bear him company'. Johnson ends by stating that although she stayed in a Jamaican prison until she gave birth to her second child, and was then reprieved, she disappeared without trace after her release.

But if Ann Bonny and Mary Read had vanished from public view,

Johnson's *History* ensured their immortality. And the stories about female pirates that followed in their wake bore similar contradictions. Like Read and Bonny, the sailor Mary Anne Talbot was purported to be illegitimate, the daughter of an aristocrat, Lord Talbot, baron of Hensol. Mary Anne's mother died in childbirth after delivering her daughter in 1778 at Lincoln's Inn Fields, London. Mary Anne spent nine years at a provincial boarding school which paid 'careful attention to [her] education and morals', before being enlisted by her guardian, Captain Essex Bowen, as a footboy named John Taylor. In 1792 Bowen set sail with his charge from Falmouth aboard Captain Bishop's *Crown*, bound for the Caribbean. In an autobiography published in *Kirby's Wonderful and Scientific Museum*, in 1804, then again in 1809 and 1820, Talbot suggests that Bowen, of the 82nd Regiment of Foot, grew increasingly abusive towards her. 'I became everything he could desire; and so far aided his purposes, as to become a willing instrument to my future misfortunes.' [28] As an orphan overpowered by an adult, and with no independent income, Talbot had little choice but to follow Bowen's instructions.

Talbot's story is an ironic inversion of those of Bonny and Read, who passed as men to gain financial independence and to follow a lover. Talbot claimed she was forced into a sexual relationship with her guardian, who disguised her as a footboy to retain his control over her. When they arrived in Santa Domingo, Bowen enrolled her in his regiment as a drummer boy for similar reasons. When she objected, he threatened 'to have me conveyed up the country and sold as a slave'.[29] Only after Bowen's death during the Siege of Valenciennes was Talbot free to desert the army and return home. But on 17 September 1793, she signed aboard a French lugger under Captain Le Sage without realising that it was a privateer intent on looting the enemy. The ship cruised uneventfully for four months before it attacked a British vessel, Lord Howe's *Queen Charlotte*. Talbot was carried aboard, and luckily Howe accepted her claim, made during a lengthy interrogation, that she had mistakenly signed aboard a privateer. She was then transferred to Captain John Harvey's *Brunswick*, where she became the captain's principal cabin boy.

Like many 'female warriors' of this period, Talbot describes her masquerade as the least of several evils. But once a male name and identity had been adopted, it proved increasingly difficult for the cross-dresser to revert to her former, gendered state. Despite Talbot's assertion that Captain Bowen first forced her to become 'John Taylor', this masculinity was to become the foundation of her character. After retiring from sea and collecting her naval pay, Talbot was given a room in Mrs Jones' London lodging house where the good landlady had strict instructions 'if possible, to break me of the masculine habit to which I was so much used'. Talbot resumed wearing skirts and blouses but frequently dressed as a tar to join her former mess-mates in the public house, when seeking employment or when making a claim at the naval pay office. The wounds she received during her various naval and military battles continued to plague her and she died at the tragically young age of 30 in February 1808.[30]

Talbot's story appears a more authentic account of an eighteenth-century female sailor than Johnson's version of Read and Bonny's adventures on the high seas. Since Talbot was educated and spoke to Kirby at length, the story he published undoubtedly reflects her experiences more accurately. Talbot resists a romantic interpretation of her cross-dressing, insisting that the disguise protected her from other sailors' attentions, ensured her employment and was credible proof of her naval career. Talbot was a victim of an unscrupulous guardian, not a courageous young wife or lover who sacrificed all to follow her beloved into the male territory of piracy. Most later histories of female pirates, however, follow more closely the tradition established in Johnson's *History*.

An anonymous author calling himself 'a sea captain' includes Maria Cobham's story in his *Lives of the Most Celebrated Pirates*, published at the turn of the eighteenth century. While docked in Plymouth harbour, the infamous pirate captain Cobham goes ashore and meets Maria, a prostitute, whom he persuades to join him aboard ship. She became 'part of Cobham's cabin furniture, and he took her to sea with him'. Despite the tension which arose because of Maria's presence aboard, she managed to win over the crew during a voyage across the Atlantic. As the 'sea captain' describes the crew's reaction to Cobham's indiscretion in bringing a former prostitute to sea:

> Sailors are not fond of seeing their officers indulged in luxuries they cannot themselves enjoy and it would be politic in officers never to create hostile feelings by showing off to the crew that

which must excite in them envious feelings. Where a man is married the case is altered; but where he only keeps a girl, every man says, 'I have as much right to one as he has'.[31]

In her metamorphosis from cabin furniture to pirate, Maria allegedly became increasingly bloodthirsty. Like Read and Bonny, she gained a reputation for her dexterity with a knife and encouraged Cobham's men to execute a ship's crew. When Cobham took a small brig carrying a cargo of broad cloth, the *Lion of Liverpool*, Maria stepped in when its captain refused to surrender. The captive threatened retaliation when the ship reached Liverpool; '"There you shall never come," said Maria and she stabbed him to the heart with a small dirk that she always carried about her; this was a signal for a general massacre, and all the crew were murdered.'[32]

After numerous raids, Maria's ambition grew while Cobham's began to wane. 'He had now quite sufficient to satisfy a moderate man, but Maria was avaricious and spurred him on . . . He was to her a perfect dupe, and did in every thing whatever she bid him.' With Maria's eye on purchasing a large country house in France, Captain Cobham became simply a useful means towards this end. This cast Maria in the darkest annals of female pirate mythology; behind her aggression lay not pragmatism nor romantic love, but pure and simple greed. When Cobham's ship met up with a Flemish brig, *Altona*, Cobham tied up the captain and two mates while Maria shot them. 'For this very barbarous act,' writes the 'sea captain', 'there can be no excuse: they had done her no injury and could do her none.'[33] By the time the ship reached Shedham, Maria's transformation was complete; she now assumed the position of ship's officer and went ashore in uniform. Since Cobham was a wanted man in England, he was ready to retire from piracy into a quiet existence somewhere on the continent. But Maria insisted they make one last voyage to finance her dream home and captured a small East India ship, the *Middleton*. As officer, Maria insisted that as 'security against tell-tales' the *Middleton*'s crew be manacled and thrown overboard. The hapless captain was put in irons and Maria poisoned him during the night.

Cobham sold the ship, paid off the crew and with his own fortune bought an estate from the Duc de Chartes, which ran 20 miles along the French coast near Le Havre. Although retired, he kept a ship in a harbour on the estate's shore and occasionally took ships in the English Channel. But he always returned to the fully retired Maria 'by whom he seems to have been infatuated'. Cobham lived long enough to become a popular citizen and respected magistrate in the area, where he often presided at local courts. But the 'sea captain' reports that when Maria, 'from remorse or some cause unknown, took a dose of laudanum and died', she went unlamented, 'for her temper had nothing feminine in it'.[34]

Maria Cobham's story suggests that a new rendering of the female adventurer had begun by the early nineteenth century. Increasingly stories about exceptional women were imbued with middle-class values which upheld the virtues of passivity, maternal self-sacrifice and domesticity. Unlike Bonny and Read, whose honour could excuse their violent acts, a figure like Maria appears corrupted from the start. A prostitute, she wins over the crew but is later shown to have complete disregard for the pirates' own moral code; she tortures men who cannot defend themselves, resorts to sly methods of disposing of her enemies – by poisoning – rather than fighting a duel, and exploits rather than loves Captain Cobham. After her retirement, she is demonised for her past association with piracy which has unsexed her, while Cobham enjoys a prestigious position. It is not the fact of Maria's violence but her transgression of the rules for which she is shunned.

Further evidence that the pirate heroine was undergoing structural adjustment is apparent from an 1813 version of Mary Read and Ann Bonny's story. The anonymous title *The Daring Exploits of Henry Morgan* borrowed heavily from Johnson but elaborated on the women's renunciation of piracy during their trial. In this edition, Read denies the charges against her and dismisses the witnesses' accounts of the women's 'bold and resolute actions', arguing that 'it was impossible for a woman to be guilty of what they swore against her and that she entered into the service of the privateer purely upon the account of Anne [sic] Bonny, who was her lover.'[35] The accepted script has been altered; Bonny, whose romantic interest has flowered from a passive into an active state, is made responsible for Read's recruitment. But Morgan's use of the word 'lover' is neither explained nor expanded upon, and appears to be a corruption of Johnson's scene where the two women divulge their respective secrets and arouse Rackham's jealousy. However, Morgan's text does leave open the possibility that his audience could read Bonny and Read's relationship as explicitly lesbian, though elsewhere the conventional ideals of feminine modesty and heterosexual purity are clearly valued.

Given the evolution of nineteenth-century ideals of femininity, readers might more readily have accepted that Read would dismiss the evidence against her on the grounds that pirating was unwomanly. Instead, the 1813 account emphasises her sexual virtue – 'she had behaved herself very modestly among the men', and modesty is presented as the paramount reason for her disguise. She first assumed male clothing 'to prevent her being ill used by seamen; and being taken in that disguise, she continued in it for fear of being worse used by the barbarous crew of the pirates.'[36] The women, as this account suggests, were increasingly seen as separate from the pirate crew and with 'art and skill' denied their involvement in the fray. The very fact of their disguise had become more difficult to credit.

Meanwhile, even a cursory search through contemporary periodicals reveals that incidents of female sailors were on the *increase* at this point. Although women aboard British naval ships during the Napoleonic Wars were not paid and therefore do not appear on the ship's muster they are regularly mentioned, often incidentally, in contemporary accounts. *The Annual Register* 1807 recorded without comment Elizabeth Bowden's testimony in a sodomy case aboard a naval ship earlier that year: 'One of the witnesses to this awful and horrible trial was a little female tar, Elizabeth Bowden, who has been on board the *Hazard* these eight months. She appeared in court in a long jacket and blue trousers.'[37] During a period when the press gangs were very active and able-bodied seamen in short supply, such accounts suggest that women's presence aboard may have been tolerated for expediency. Bowden, whose sex was known to the authorities but who was dressed in the tar's outfit of trousers and a jacket, was presumably still employed as a sailor aboard the *Hazard*.

This was not an isolated incident. Two years after the publication of *The Daring Exploits of Henry Morgan*, a London magazine recorded that 'amongst the crew of the *Queen Charlotte*, recently paid off, it is now discovered was a female African, who had served as a seaman in the royal navy for upwards of 11 years.' Disguised as 'William Brown', this woman had served as the captain of the faretop, 'highly to the satisfaction of the officers'. Moreover, the muscular, handsome Brown was praised for exhibiting all the traits of a British tar and comfortably taking grog with 'his' former shipmates.[38] And if women were not disguised and working as sailors, they served aboard ship in a variety of other capacities. Mariner John Nicol, who served in the powder magazine with the gunner aboard *The Goliath* in Lord Nelson's fleet, recorded that while anchored near Syracuse, 'any information [about the war] we got was from the boys and *the women* who carried the powder' (my italics). Nicol also observed that 'the women behaved as well as the men and got a present for their bravery from the Grand Signoir'.[39] Such reports often served as raw material for contemporary ballads such as 'Happy Ned', which was based on the life of Elizabeth Taylor who served aboard a ship during the American Civil War. Immortalised in song, she died at her village near Warrington in 1887:

> My Name was Elizabeth Taylor
> But bless you I've long been a man;
> I served in the fleet as a sailor
> When the war o-secession began;
>
> I fought for the North like a good 'un
> Tho' I wasn't a Yankee myself;
> And why it all ended so sudden
> I'm dashed if I ever could tell! [40]

It was no accident that while the Amazon of fiction was increasingly treated as an exceptional heroine, her real-life counterparts proliferated.[41] Balladeers and novelists worked to shape the female tar into a more acceptably feminine form by couching her story in the melodramatic conventions of contemporary literature.

Such was the case with Lieutenant Murray's (Maturin Murray Ballou's) novel about Fanny Campbell, a New England woman who becomes a sailor and then a pirate captain to rescue her fiancé from a Cuban jail. First published as *The Female Pirate: a tale of the revolution of 1776* and then as *Fanny Campbell: or, the female pirate captain*, in 1845, its frontispiece belies the daring beneath the book's covers. Although depicted as a pirate and sporting both machete and Jolly Roger, Fanny is unmistakably female, with modestly blooming skirts, delicate curls, a shapely figure and soft features. But Murray describes her disguise as

'Mr Channing' in much more convincing terms. She is transformed into:

> a noble-looking sailor ... dressed in blue sailor pants and a short
> pea jacket descending about half-way to the knee, within the
> lining of which a close observer might have seen a brace of pistols
> and a silver hilt of a knife so designed as to cut at both sides while
> it was bent like a Turkish hanger. Altogether you would have
> pronounced him a King's officer in disguise.[42]

'Channing' is such a skilled and intelligent commander that after being appointed third officer aboard *The Constance*, 'he' soon uncovers the captain's plot to turn the American pirate crew over to the royal navy for bounty money. 'Channing' holds the mercenary Captain Brownless captive and takes control of the ship. Set against the background of the American revolution, Campbell's motives for such violations of naval practice are conveniently imbued with patriotic overtones; she is rescuing her lover but also defending her country, both equally noble sentiments.

'Captain Channing' gains the crew's respect for 'his' daring; 'he' commandeers a hostile British ship, *The George*, acquiring an additional crew of 14 seamen and three captives as prisoners of war, and successfully releases William Lowell and another American sailor from a Havana prison. After several days back at sea, 'Channing' summons the escaped prisoner to 'his' quarters, where Fanny finally reveals her true identity to her sweetheart William. He cries in astonishment, 'But I cannot believe that a female, a mere girl of but 20 years, could accomplish what thou hast done Fanny ... Thou hast compassed that which would have done credit to a naval captain.'[43] About her disguise, Lowell comments, 'I never saw you look more interesting.'

While Fanny insists that the lovers must retain their respective positions as captain and crew, she seeks William's permission for her actions first. But William has difficulty in respecting Fanny's authority, and when an English ship appears in sight, he urges her to hide in the hold for her own protection. Fanny stands firm, and when she overcomes 'all her woman's feelings' while interrogating an English prisoner, she imagines herself, 'a man at heart and nothing save stern justice might be expected to come from these lips'. But despite her excellence at the helm and her masculine heart, Fanny marries William when they safely return to their home town of Lynn, Massachusetts, and becomes the mother of two sons. When the Lowells venture out in their ship, *The Constance*, which is renamed *Fanny*, Mrs Lowell has been demoted to second-in-command.

There is intriguing evidence that women readers of the period may have drawn a different conclusion from the tales of female pirates, ignoring the heroine's inevitable restoration to domesticity. Sarah Emma Edmonds, a Canadian woman who cross-dressed to escape from her father's home in New Brunswick and became a soldier during the American Civil War, claimed Fanny Campbell as her inspiration. At the age of 13, Edmonds was given a copy of Ballou's 1856 version of the novel by her mother, and while she scorned Fanny's motive of cross-dressing to rescue a fiancé, she immediately realised the possibility of emulating her heroine's transcendence. She was later to recall feeling that 'all the latent energy of my nature was aroused and each exploit of the heroine thrilled me to my fingertips . . . I was emancipated! and could never again be a *slave*'.[44] Edmonds is very circumspect about her own adventures masquerading as Frank Thompson of the Second Michigan Volunteers in her autobiography, *Nurse and Spy in the Union Army*. First published in 1865, the book coyly disguises the fact that its protagonist was cross-dressed until mid-way through.

Edmond's reticence is revealing of the nineteenth-century ambiguity towards these heroines. Despite the extraordinary prevalence of cross-dressers in contemporary accounts, writers such as Menie Muriel Dowie, who edited an 1893 collection of eighteenth-century female warrior stories, dismisses them as anachronisms. Dowie decided to exclude Bonny and Read from her collection because, 'the account of their lives is freaked with so little genuine romance and smeared with so much coarseness and triviality that I have not thought it worthy to be included with those of other adventurers.' Dowie's introductory remarks consistently distinguish between the 'nobility of mind and character' that contemporary Victorian heroines display and the 'grimy sensuality' of their forebears. 'There is no longer any need for [adventurous women] to put on the garb of men in order to live, to work, to achieve, to breathe the outer air,' she writes, anticipating the sentiments of early twentieth-century pirate writers such as Gosse. Perhaps Murray stumbled upon an important clue when he wrote that

Fanny Campbell's story represented a particular working-class heroism. 'We have designed to show that among the lower classes of society, there is more of the germ of true intellect and courage, nobleness of purpose and strength of will than may be found among the pampered and wealthy children of fortune'.[45] In a period when definitions of class and gender had come more sharply into focus, the crossdresser appeared more threatening than her earlier counterparts. But her swashbuckling momentarily appeared outdated, stripped of interest and reduced to an amusing historical anecdote.

By the turn of the century, suffragettes such as Ellen Clayton were rediscovering the cross-dresser as a potential weapon for their arsenal. Clayton argued in her history of Amazons, *Female Warriors* that women had always been involved in military conflicts, had the potential to fight, and were therefore entitled to be involved in politics. The bawdy adventures of Hannah Snell, Mary Anne Talbot and Ann Bonny stood in sharp contrast to the Victorian feminine ideals of passivity and emotional dependence. Moreover, Clayton cited historical cases of Amazons who had seen action in almost every eighteenth-century European war. In the early decades of the twentieth century, with wellknown English aristocrats such as Radclyffe Hall and Vita SackvilleWest openly sporting trousers, cravats and jackets, female transvestism took on the cachet of modernism. Performer Flora Robson was delighted when playwright James Bridie offered her a part in his play *Mary Read*. The playwright recalled Robson gloomily predicting that her career would soon consist of 'mourning over a procession of tortured spinsters leading to the crack of Doom. She foresaw that she would be expected by London managements to play them all.' When asked if she would consider an alternative, Robson replied, 'Yes, I should like to play a pirate.'[46]

Tyrone Guthrie produced Bridie's play, which opened in London on 21 November 1934. Betty Hardy played Ann Bonny, who describes to Mary Read (Flora Robson) her motives for joining Rackham's crew. 'I had my fill of fine gentlemen in the sugar plantations ... They can't ask a girl for what they want without simpering and playacting. And then along came Calico Jack like a great roaring stallion.' The women form an intimate friendship, bonding over their common desire to rebel against conventional dictates of feminine behaviour. Read and Bonny had once again been rescued from obscurity and imbued with new meaning. Gosse's 1932 publication, *The History of Piracy*, and Professor John Robert Moore's new theories about Daniel Defoe's authorship of *A General History of the Pyrates* had both helped to revive interest in the subject.[47]

What appealed to Bridie's London audience in the 1930s and has kept the female pirates in the public consciousness throughout the western world is their ability to challenge our assumptions about gender. Like their colourful costumes, language and outrageous dexterity with a sword, they are a reminder that sexual difference is largely a masquerade. Though the form has changed – and in the 1960s they turned up in such unexpected places as Pippi Longstocking's South Sea adventures and John Carlova's erotic novel about Ann Bonny, *Mistress of the Seas* – the pirates endure as rebels against narrow precepts of femininity.[48] Even today, the ambiguity the female swashbuckler represents – the best man on the ship and its most tender sweetheart – is highly appropriate for a period in which definitions of sexuality and gender are so fluid. Many recent films, including director Maggie Greenwald's *The Ballad of Little Jo* and screenwriter Callie Khouri's *Thelma & Louise*, have experimented with heroines who make forays on to male territory. But like the outlaws Read and Bonny, America's female celluloid desperadas have nowhere to go once they have broken the rules. The eighteenth-century pirates who died in prison disappeared from public view or settled into domestic bliss share our limited imagination for alternative scenarios. The pirate ship itself, rolling on that endless expanse miles from anywhere that might be called home, is a powerful metaphor for the limbo in which female rebels still exist.

Notes

1. Anon, quoted in Charles Ellms, *The Pirates Own Book, or Authentic Narratives of the Lives, Exploits and Executions of the Most Celebrated Sea Robbers*, Sanborn & Carter, 1837.
2. Quoted in Marcus Rediker, *Between the Devil and the Deep Blue Sea, merchant seamen, pirates and the Anglo-American Maritime world 1700-1750*, Cambridge University Press, 1987, p. 258.
3. *ibid*, p. 262.

4. Dianne Dugaw, *Warrior Women and Popular Balladry, 1650-1850*, Cambridge University Press, 1989.
5. Rediker, *op cit*, p. 312.
6. Trial transcript, PRO CO 137/14/XC18757.
7. All further references to the trial are taken from PRO CO 137/14/XC18757.
8. Quoted in P. N. Furbank and W. R. Owens, *The Canonisation of Daniel Defoe*, Yale University Press, 1988, p. 102.
9. Rediker, *op cit*, p. 255.
10. *Marie Claire*, March 1993, and the forthcoming Columbia Pictures film, *Mistress of the Seas*, are but two recent examples.
11. Captain Charles Johnson, Arthur L. Hayward (ed), *A General History of the Pyrates*, G. Routledge and Son, Ltd, 1926, p. 136.
12. Furbank and Owens, *op cit*, p. 106.
13. Philip Gosse, *The History of Piracy*, Longmans, Green and Co, 1932, p. 205.
14. Johnson, *op cit*, p. 133.
15. Johnson, *ibid*, pp. 134-5.
16. *ibid*, p. 133.
17. *ibid*, p. 141.
18. Rediker, *op cit*, p. 205.
19. 'Women in Action on Board Ships of the Royal Navy', *Notes and Queries*, sixth series, X, 29 November 1884.
20. Quoted in Dugaw, *op cit*, p. 123.
21. Johnson, *op cit*, pp. 133-4.
22. Richard Walker, *The Female Soldier*, (1750) the Augustan Reprint Society, No. 257, 1989, p. 28.
23. *ibid*, p. 29.
24. For a recent discussion about the significance of these passages in Snell's biography, see Emma Donoghue, *Passions Between Women: British lesbian culture, 1668-1801*, Scarlet Press, 1994, p. 94.
25. Johnson, *op cit*, p. 134.
26. Alfred Allison, *The Sword and Womankind*, London, 1900, p. 102.
27. Johnson, *op cit*, p. 140.
28. Kirby, reprinted in Menie Muriel Dowie (ed) *Women Adventurers*, London, 1893, p. 143.
29. *ibid*, p. 147.
30. For further details about Mary Anne Talbot's life, see Julie Wheelwright, *Amazons and Military Maids: women who dressed as men in pursuit of life, liberty and happiness*, Pandora, 1994.
31. 'A sea captain', *Lives of the Most Celebrated Pirates*, Richard Derby printer, no date, p. 295.
32. *ibid*, p. 295.
33. *ibid*, p. 296.

34. *ibid*, p. 297.
35. Anon, *The Daring Exploits of Henry Morgan*, London, 1813, p. 26.
36. *ibid*, p. 27.
37. *The Annual Register, 1807*, W. Otridge et al, London, 1809, p. 496.
38. *Annual Review 1815*, quoted in Charles Dickens, *All the Year Round*, vol. VII, 2 December 1871 – 11 May 1872, Chapman and Hall, p. 452.
39. Gordon Grant, *The Life and Adventures of John Nicol, Mariner*, Cassell, 1937, pp. 193-4.
40. 'Female Sailors', *Notes and Queries*, seventh series, IV, 17 and 31 December 1887.
41. The phenomencn was not confined to Britain and North America. Historians Rudolf Dekker and Lotte C. van de Pol, in *The Tradition of Female Transvestism in Early Modern Europe*, MacMillan, 1989, identify 119 cases of female cross-dressing soldiers, sailors and others, between 1550 and 1839.
42. Lieutenant Murray, *The Female Pirate: a tale of the revolution of 1776*, Cameron and Ferguson, 1845?, pp. 21-2. The US edition is by M. M. Ballou, Murray's real name.
43. *ibid*, p. 46.
44. Frank Schneider, *Post and Tribune*, Detroit, October 1883.
45. Murray, *op cit*, p. 96.
46. James Bridie, *Moral Plays*, Constable, 1936, p. xi.
47. Quoted in Furbank and Owens, *op cit*, p. 102.
48. John Carlova, *Mistress of the Seas*, Arrow Books, 1965.

Section IV:

Chinese women pirates

12 Cheng I Sao in fact and fiction by Dian H. Murray

A sigh sounds and a sough replies,
Mulan must be at the window weaving.
You can't tell the sounds of the loom
From the sighs of the girl.
Ask her whom she's longing for!
Ask her whom she's thinking of!
She's longing for no one at all,
She's thinking of no one special:
'Last night I saw the draft list –
The Kahn's mustering a great army;
The armies' rosters ran many rolls,
Roll after roll held my father's name!
And Father has no grown-up son,
And I've no elder brother!
So I offered to buy a saddle an horse
And campaign from now on for Father.'

In the eastern market she bought a steed,
At the western a saddle and cloth;
In the southern market she bought a bridle,
At the northern a long whip;
At sunrise she bade her parents farewell,
At sunset she camped by the Yellow River;
She couldn't hear her parents calling her,

She heard only the Yellow River's flow surge and splash.

Dawn she took leave of the Yellow River,
Evening she was atop the Black Mountains;
She couldn't hear her parents calling her,
She heard only the Tartar horse on Swallow Mountain
    whinny and blow.

Hastening thousands of miles to decisive battles,
Crossing mountains and passes as if flying!
The northern air carries the sentry's drum,
A wintry sun glints off her coat of mail.

After a hundred battles the generals are dead,
Ten years now, and the brave soldiers are returning!
Returning to audience with the Son of Heaven,
The Son of Heaven, sitting in his Luminous Hall.
Their merits quickly moved them up the ranks,
And rewards, more than a hundred thousand cash!
Then the Khan asked what Mulan desired:
'I have no use for a minister's post,
Just lend me a famous fleet-footed camel
To send me back to my village.'

'When my parents heard I was coming,
They helped each other to the edge of town.
When my big sister heard I was coming,
She stood at the door, putting on her face.
When my little brother heard I was coming,
He ground his knife in a flash and went for a pig and a sheep.

'I opened myself the east chamber door,
And sat myself down on the west chamber bed;
Took off my wartime cloaks,
And draped myself in my robes of old.
At the window I put up my cloudy black tresses,
Before the mirror I powdered my face,
Came out the door to see my camp mates,

My camp mates so shocked at first!
They'd traveled together for many a year
Without knowing Mulan was a girl!'

The hare draws in his feet to sit,
His mate has eyes that gleam,
But when the two run side by side,
How much alike they seem![1]

For an Iowa farm girl, landlocked by flat, verdant fields of corn, the mental voyage to China's coast provided an escape to places of imagined romance where sinister villains lurked in every cove. The power of this and countless other flamboyant visions, conjured up from the realm of the subconscious, probably led me into the world of Sinology in 1970. Chinese history intrigued me because of its challenges. It was a difficult world to enter: I had to understand 3,000 years of history and learn a daunting language well enough to deal with its written legacy. In the end, travelling, living and researching in the country itself caused any lingerings of exoticism to yield before fascinating new chapters in the human struggle to survive. And I chose the topic of piracy for my doctorate in 1975 because I wanted an intrinsically interesting subject that would not be a conversation stopper.[2]

Piracy in China, as in the West, is one of the oldest professions. Records dating back to the fourth century BC suggest a continuous tradition of petty piracy: a small-scale, income-supplementing activity that could be practised out of a neighbourhood cove using the equipment at hand. Its size, intensity, and ebb and flow were often determined by external circumstances, and by the political and social events of the world around the sea.

The piracy of the most famous woman pirate of all, Cheng I Sao (see plate 9) took place during a rebellion in what is now Vietnam. The leaders' need for a privateer force gave employment to Chinese pirates who answered their call. Later, when Vietnamese patronage was no longer an option, leadership from within the pirate ranks enabled an essentially military organisation to be transformed into a big business. The vehicle was a confederation composed of six (and at times seven) well-ordered and regulated fleets consisting of between 40,000 and 70,000 individuals who at their height were under the leadership of Cheng I Sao.

My colleagues and friends, imbued with stereotypes of Confucian China, are always surprised to learn that the leader of this confederation was a woman. Confucian philosophy dictated that throughout their lives women would remain subservient to their fathers, husbands and sons. Confucian politics barred them from public office by prohibiting their participation in what was the world's earliest civil service examination system. Social and economic customs confined them to their homes, limited their public employment possibilities and forced them to hobble about on bound feet. However, the joke among certain scholars has become, 'Whose Confucianism was it anyway?' Were Confucian scholar Chu Hsi and his contemporaries painting a picture of Chinese society as it really operated or were they presenting a vision of how society should operate that accorded more with their own mental dictates than with the ongoing realities of daily life?

While neo-Confucianism may have shaped élite views of properly submissive and chaste women, popular culture was rife with contrasting images of strong-willed, quick-witted individuals who in times of crisis could take charge or engage in diatribe of unforgettable magnitude. Even today, who can fail to admire the inner strength of the women depicted in such recent films as *Raise the Red Lantern*, *Farewell My Concubine*, and the mothers in *The Joy Luck Club*?

For centuries Chinese story-tellers have been in awe of the spiritual prowess of the women of popular fiction. These figures were often regarded as dangerous seductresses in the form of fox fairies or other spirits. In times of stress (such as on the eve of the tri-annual civil service examinations) they were said to beguile vulnerable men and lead them astray. It was this same awe of the unseen powers of women that caused rebels and defenders alike, during the Wang Lun uprising of 1774, to repel their enemies by sending prostitutes up on the city walls to take off their underclothing, loosen their hair, urinate and bleed over the side of the wall to destroy the power of the enemy.[3]

Today, though still in its infancy, the study of women in imperial China is a rapidly expanding field. Although there is much we will never be able to discover about how women of the eighteenth and nineteenth centuries lived and worked, our knowledge is increasing.

As it does, we cannot help but be impressed by the variety of lifestyles and activities that is emerging. Chinese women no longer fit into a single mould.

This is especially true of the South China maritime environment from which the pirates hailed. The coastal provinces of Kwangtung and Fukien boasted a rich mixture of non-Han (non-Chinese) ethnic groups whose social customs were not always in accord with the Han mainstream (Hakka women, for instance, did not bind their feet). Within the maritime world, there were entire communities whose members lived their whole lives on board ship without ever setting foot on land. Moreover, throughout most of South China, the major communication arteries were rivers and much commerce was conducted from the water. Even the brothels, known euphemistically as 'flower boats', were to be found off shore.

In the cramped conditions aboard vessels that housed entire families, women often did as much work as men. Most of the propelling and skulling of the small lighters used for so much of the transport throughout the South China Sea was regarded as women's work, and since most commerce was coastal and did not necessitate long voyages to distant waters, no concept of the maritime world as an exclusively male one developed.

The presence of women aboard pirate ships in China should therefore come as less of a surprise than in the West. Indeed, the evidence suggests that women participated in pirate communities as something other than cooks and bottle-washers; that they sometimes held rank and commanded ships; and that in certain instances they took part in combat (just as, I might add, did their counterparts ashore). What is unusual about the case discussed here is not that it features 'women pirates' *per se*, but rather the extent to which one particular woman, Cheng I Sao, assumed and executed leadership. Also unusual is the way Cheng I Sao, perhaps playing on male fear of her 'mysterious potency', forced government officials to come to terms with her in effecting a settlement. In these instances, she demonstrated skill, cunning and public presence not often associated with Chinese women.

To what extent the episode I describe here is unique, I do not know. Fanny Loviot, a Californian who was captured by Chinese pirates in 1854, reported that: 'The pirates of the Chinese seas make their junks their homes, and carry their wives and children with them on every expedition. The women assist in working the ships, and are chiefly employed in the lading and unlading.'' So it appears that women and children continued to live and work aboard pirate ships well into the nineteenth century. What is unclear is whether Cheng I Sao's level of command was ever attained by any other women. Her closest rival might possibly have been Lai Choi San (Mountain of Wealth), alleged commander of 12 junks in the vicinity of Macao during the 1920s. So far as I am aware, the only account of her activities stems from the American journalist Aleko Lilius and his rather dubious *I Sailed with Chinese Pirates* (London, 1930), which I have not yet been able to corroborate elsewhere (see Chapter 13).

The study of pirates in China, like that of women, is in its infancy. How much farther we can go beyond the mere chronicling of names, events and dates will depend on the availability of sources. Detailed information on women and their lives is difficult to come by under any circumstances, but even more so in the case of pirates and other groups for whom written records were anathema. What pirate, even if she or he were literate, would want to keep written accounts of activities such that if they should fall into government hands, would automatically convict them? This means it may never be possible to fill in the gaps and answer the questions even this brief episode brings to light. The tendency to overwrite on the basis of insufficient evidence has, in my opinion, marred many pirate studies in the West. The subject has been romanticised and glamorised to such an extent that historical fiction has overtaken history, and much of what we think is known is more myth than truth. In China, by contrast, piracy is a subject that has not only not been glamorised, but is virtually unknown. So far as I am aware, no Chinese scholar or historian has attempted to liken Cheng I Sao or any other female pirate to the mythical woman warrior described in the poem at the beginning of this chapter.

Cheng I Sao's story takes place on the South China coast, where piracy was part of a human endeavour to survive. As a gathering point for the flotsam of the earth, the coasts of Kwangtung province attracted those who could make it nowhere else in society. Their only option was to prey on the establishment in any way they could, and in doing so, the line between legal and illegal often became blurred. The gambling parlours, opium dens and floating bordellos that dotted the coast were, in part, the products of their struggle to get by. For individual fishermen, locked into recurring cycles of debt and impoverishment, a quick heist at sea or the temporary recourse to piracy as an activity of the off-season could help them make a living. Once the crisis had passed, those fortunate enough to have escaped arrest would throw off their pirate mantles and slip inconspicuously back into the society from which they had come. One of the leading families was the Chengs, who had been involved with piracy since the late seventeenth century. It was into this family that Cheng I Sao, the woman destined to become the leader of the confederation and China's most famous woman pirate, married in 1801.

Not much is known about this remarkable woman, and the little I believe can be deduced from the sources and stated with certainty is to be found in the first section of this chapter. But lack of 'factual' information seems not to have impeded several generations of twentieth-century pirate scholars from including an obligatory chapter on Cheng I Sao in their general surveys. For the most part, when primary sources were found wanting, these individuals seem to have resorted to 'fictional' details drawn from fertile imaginations. While engaged in research processes of my own, travelling to archives in China, Taiwan, Hong Kong, England and Macao and trying to decipher detailed reports in Chinese, Portuguese, Japanese, Vietnamese and French, I found myself increasingly frustrated, annoyed and finally angered by this genre of imprecise and sloppy history. But despite my dismissal of most of these works as 'rubbish', they have introduced Chinese pirates to western audiences and have coloured the ways many westerners perceive them today. When closely examined, the distortion and 'fiction' that have intruded in these secondary histories are easy to spot because most of the information about the daily lives of Cheng I Sao and the pirates is derived from two English-language primary sources. Both are widely available and they were at least nominally invoked by the three historians on whose accounts I focus here.

The bare facts: what the sources allow us to say

Cheng I Sao (1775-1844) was a Cantonese prostitute who in 1801 married the pirate leader Cheng I and assisted him in the creation of a confederation of pirates. By 1805 this included 400 junks and between 40,000 and 60,000 pirates.[5] She was also known as Shih Hsiang-ku and Shih Yang. Two sons, Cheng Ying-shih (b.1803) and Cheng Hsiung-shih (b. 1807), were born to them.

Sponsorship by Vietnam's Tay-son[6] rulers enabled the scale of Chinese piracy to increase between 1792 and 1802 and associations of several hundred people and several dozen junks to come into being. Tay-son support also provided pirates and privateers with opportunities for communication and co-operation in joint ventures at sea. The Chengs flourished under Tay-son patronage: Cheng I's distant cousin, Cheng Ch'i, was widely recognised as one of the pirates' most able leaders.

The turning point in the Chengs' careers came in July 1802, with the overthrow of the Tay-son and the end of Chinese piracy in Vietnam. Cheng Ch'i was killed in a desperate battle near Hanoi. On 16 July the Nguyen navy reached Son Nam and after defeating the pirates sent them fleeing to China. It was at this point that Cheng I and his wife emerged as the pirates' most important leaders. They re-established their base back across the border in China and later unified the disparate and often quarrelling gangs into a confederation of seven (later six) principal fleets distinguished by a series of coloured banners.

The unexpected death of her husband in November 1807 caused Cheng I Sao to make a well-calculated bid for power that secured her position at the top of the pirate hierarchy. In this capacity, she was responsible for appointing as commander of the most powerful Red Flag fleet her 'adopted' son. Chang Pao was a fisherman's son who had been captured by Cheng I. Cheng I developed a fondness for the young man, adopted him and gave him command of a ship. The death of his mentor brought little change to the fortunes of Chang Pao. He became the paramour and ultimately the husband of Cheng I Sao, with whom he had at least one son.

As the leader of what became a formidable confederation, Cheng I Sao used the creation of Chang Pao's law code to transform the series of personal relationships that existed among the pirates into a more formal power structure. This included penal sanctions as well as elaborate provisions for sharing booty. She also controlled a financial operation that extended far beyond a few sporadic heists at sea. This was achieved by setting up a 'regularised' protection racket that featured the sale of 'safe passage' documents to all coastal fishing workers or shippers, the convoying, for purposes of protection, of the salt fleets to Canton (Guangzhou), and the establishment of financial offices along the coast to serve as fee-collection points.

By 1808, the pirates held the military initiative along the coast of Kwangtung and demonstrated their prowess by killing the provincial commander-in-chief of Chekiang, Li Ch'ang-keng, who had sailed into Kwangtung province on a special assignment. Within the year, the pirates had also destroyed 63 of the Kwangtung area's 135-vessel fleet, and in August 1809 they threatened to attack Canton itself. The strength of Cheng I Sao's confederation forced officials in Canton to enter into a series of negotiations with the British for the short-term use of the vessel *Mercury*, fitted out with 20 cannon and 50 American volunteers. These were followed a few months later by similar negotiations with the Portuguese for the lease of six men-of-war to sail with the imperial navy for several months in late 1809.[7]

These measures failed to bring the pirates to terms, causing the Chinese government to shift its emphasis from 'extermination' to 'pacification' and to offer amnesty to the pirates. Cheng I Sao was quick to understand the advantages such an offer could bring her followers. She took a lead in engineering the pirates' surrender and in obtaining from the government a favourable settlement. After the failure of the pirates' first attempt at surrender, during a conference arranged by Chang Pao and the Liang-kuang governor general on 21 February 1810, Cheng I Sao took the initiative.

In the company of other pirate women and children, she went unarmed to the governor general's *yamen* (headquarters) in Canton on 18 April 1810. Her negotiations succeeded: two days later the surrender took place and the pirates were liberally rewarded. Those who came forward voluntarily were allowed to retain the proceeds of their profession and were granted places in the imperial military bureaucracy. Chang Pao was given the rank of lieutenant, allowed to retain a private fleet of 20 or 30 junks, and paid a large sum of money allegedly to establish his followers onshore.

In November 1810, Cheng I Sao accompanied Chang Pao to Fukien province where he was promoted to the position of lieutenant colonel of the Min-an regiment. There he remained until his death in 1822, after which Cheng I Sao returned to Kwangtung. In 1840, the widow filed charges against the official Wu Yao-nan on the grounds that he had embezzled 28,000 taels of silver allegedly entrusted to him by Chang Pao 30 years earlier for buying an estate. The charge was subsequently dismissed by the Liang-kuang governor general.[8]

After this brush with the authorities, Cheng I Sao spent her last days quietly in Canton, 'leading a peaceful life so far as [was] consistent with the keeping of an infamous gambling house.'[9] She died in 1844 aged 69.[10]

The historical facts and their sources

I found much of the above biographical information in two English-language sources. First, Yuan Yun-lun (Yuen Yung-lun)'s book *Ching hai-fen chi*, which was published in Canton in 1830 and translated into English the following year by Charles Friedrich Neumann as *History of the Pirates Who Infested the China Sea from 1807 to 1810*.[11] This is an unofficial history composed by an employee of the governor general's *yamen* who was acquainted with several Chinese officials killed in combat against the pirates. Grief-stricken, Yuan Yun-lun felt compelled to write an 'objective' account of the pirates and their activities in such a way that the lessons of their ravages and the spirit of those who died at their hands would be preserved for posterity. The book is based on first-hand information relayed to Yuan Yun-lun by people such as Lieutenant Huang Ying-tang, who engaged the pirates directly.[12]

Another account well known in the West is *A Brief Narrative of My Captivity and Treatment Amongst the Ladrones*, written by Richard Glasspoole, who was an officer of the East India Company ship *Marquis of Ely*.[13] (*Ladrone* was the Portuguese term for the pirates.) Glasspoole and seven British seafarers were captured on 21 September 1809 and held by the pirates until 7 December. Glasspoole's diary of this adventure, prepared for the British East India Company, was signed the day after his release. It describes several battles and the movement of the pirates up the various branches of the Pearl and West rivers to 'levy contributions on the towns and villages'.[14]

These two texts corroborate one another and were invaluable in helping me to work out a daily report on the pirates' whereabouts during the most crucial two months of their existence. More important for understanding Cheng I Sao, these two pieces have had a surprisingly wide circulation and have formed the basis for nearly every western account of these pirates I have seen.[15] What is most astonishing about many of these self-proclaimed histories is how far from their sources they stray as a result of the ways their authors have misread, misconstrued or even added to the information contained in these texts. The result has been serious distortion in what western audiences have been told about Chinese pirates of the late eighteenth and early nineteenth centuries.

Even the names of the pirates are problematic, for their spellings differ from account to account. It is difficult to convert Chinese characters into letters like those in the Roman alphabet, and both translations of the key book, *Ching hai-fen chi*, were completed before 'Wade-Giles' became the standard system of transliteration in the late nineteenth century. Sometimes Cheng I Sao's name is written as 'Ching', while her husband, whose name is Romanised in the Wade-Giles system as 'Cheng I', appears in many accounts as 'Ching Yih'. The Wade-Giles Romanisation for the name of his wife, 'Cheng I Sao', simply means 'Wife of Cheng I' and appears in many western texts as 'Ching yih sao'. For the most part problems of Romanisation, though annoying, are fairly straightforward.

The same is not true of translators' attempts to find English equivalents for the meanings, as opposed to the sounds, of the pirates' nicknames. On several occasions Neumann, the translator of our key text, has either misread or mistranslated the names of the major fleet commanders in his endeavour to capture in English the spirit of their *noms de guerre*. For instance, the nickname for Green squadron leader Woo Chetsing (Wu Chih-ch'ing) was 'Tung haepa' (Tung-hai Pa), translated by Neumann as 'Scourge of the Eastern Sea'. 'Eastern Sea' or 'Tung hae' (Tung-hai) was the name of Woo's native village in Kwangtung province. But in this case the character 'pa' means 'uncle', 'elder' or 'earl', so Woo Chetsing's nickname, instead of 'Scourge of the Eastern Sea' would more accurately have been rendered as 'Earl' or 'Uncle from Eastern Sea Village'.

When their origins are understood, the pirates' names lose much of their suggestive exoticism, revealing themselves instead to be in complete accord with the kinds of names widely used throughout South China. Here people tended to address one another with references that denoted their position within the family (Elder Brother, Younger Brother, First Son or Second Son), their place of origin, or something idiosyncratic about the way they looked and acted rather than by their given names.

Fact or fiction: three histories

Three secondary histories, written in English, all draw heavily on the Neumann translation of *Ching hai-fen chi* and on Glasspoole's captivity narrative. These show how, in the hands of certain authors, what began as the pirates' 'history' ended up being more the pirates' 'story'.

Philip Gosse's now classic *History of Piracy*, written in 1932, has provided a point of departure for nearly everyone with a serious interest in piracy. Gosse begins his account of the Chengs by acknowledging that it is not until the early eighteenth century, thanks to the translation of Charles Neumann, that we 'get any very minute account of the activities of Chinese pirates'.[16] He continues by remarking that Neumann's *The History of the Pirates Who Infested the China Sea* 'is chiefly devoted to the exploits of one pirate, and that a woman'.[17] This comment is certainly an exaggeration. Neither the original *Ching hai-fen chi* nor Neumann's translation is chiefly devoted to the exploits of Cheng I Sao. In fact, in the Chinese text of 102 pages, her name appears only 25 times. Instead, the text focuses primarily on the activities of the Red, Black and White flag fleets whose members sailed in the area between Macao and Canton between 1807 and 1810. Cheng I Sao's leadership is mentioned in conjunction with their operations, but the account is by no means 'devoted' to her. Neither is that of Gosse. Despite the interest she has aroused, not very much is known about Cheng I Sao and even Gosse soon moves on to describe the most colourful military encounters between the imperial navy and the pirates.[18]

When it comes to facts, Gosse incorrectly describes Cheng I Sao's husband as the 'admiral of all the pirate fleets' who 'had become such a thorn in the flesh of the government that in 1802 the Emperor appointed him Master of the Royal Stables'. According to Gosse, 'The duties of that exalted post seem to have been only nominal, for shortly Admiral Ching was to be found ravaging the coasts of Annam and Cochin China, until at length the inhabitants rose and after a fierce battle on land routed the pirates and slaughtered the terrible Ching.'[19] Here Gosse has misread Neumann's translation and has also confused Cheng I Sao's husband Ching Yih (Cheng I) with his distant cousin Ching tsih (Cheng Ch'i), one of the pirates' major leaders during the time of their patronage by the Tay-son. It was Cheng Ch'i, not Cheng I, who was appointed 'Master of the Stables' and the appointment was made not by the emperor of China, but by King-sheng,[20] the last Tay-son ruler and child emperor of Vietnam.

The Neumann translation then goes on to describe how King-sheng, with a force of 200 pirate junks, retook the bay of Annam, but how tyranny in its possession caused the inhabitants to turn against him. In the battle which followed, Ching tsih was killed, King-sheng's force was vanquished, and the ruling Tay-son emperors were dethroned.[21] It was only then that Ching Yih (Cheng I), the husband of Cheng I Sao, emerged as the leader of the surviving pirates. Five years after he died (in 1807), Cheng I Sao herself assumed leadership of what had become a formidable pirate confederation. Despite Neumann's explicit descriptions of their relationship, Gosse seems to have missed the fact that two members of the Ching (Cheng) family were important pirate leaders before Cheng I Sao came on the scene and that she was married to the second, Ching Yih (Cheng I), and not the first, Ching tsih (Cheng Ch'i).

Having placed Cheng I Sao in command of the confederation and of its largest squadron, the Red Flag fleet, Gosse takes pains to portray her as 'an excellent business woman', a good military strategist and 'a strict disciplinarian' who 'drew up a code of rules for her crews which somewhat resembled those subscribed to by earlier European pirates.'[22] To keep order on board ship, the pirates seem to have had a 'code of laws' which attracted considerable attention from western authors who mistakenly attributed the invention to Cheng I Sao. The Neumann translation, however, specifically states that this code was not created by Cheng I Sao but was set up by her lieutenant Chang Pao:

Being chief captain, Paou robbed and plundered incessantly, and daily increased his men and his vessels. He made the three following regulations:

First: If any man goes privately on shore, or what is called transgressing the bars, he shall be taken and his ears be perforated in the presence of the whole fleet; repeating the same act, he shall suffer death.

Second: Not the least thing shall be taken privately from the stolen and plundered goods. All shall be registered; and the pirate receive for himself, out of ten parts, only two; eight parts belong to the store-house, called the general fund; taking anything out of this general fund, without permission, shall be death.

Third: No person shall debauch at his pleasure captive women taken in the villages and open places, and brought on board a ship; he must first request the ship's purser for permission, and then go aside in the ship's hold. To use violence against any woman, or to wed her without permission, shall be punished with death.[23]

Though Gosse accurately followed Neumann in introducing the commanders of the various fleets as 'Bird and Stone', 'Scourge of the Eastern Sea', 'Jewel of the Whole Crew' and 'Frog's Meal', in this case his fidelity to his source only served to perpetuate the translator's errors for western audiences.[24] That Gosse should have been more careful in the reading of his sources is clear, but aside from errors in factual reporting, he cannot be accused of fabrication or of wilful distortion of historical evidence.

The same cannot be said of Joseph Gollomb's *Pirates Old and New*, published in 1928. It is a work with fewer scholarly pretensions than Gosse's, but has nevertheless been catalogued as 'history' rather than as 'literature'. Information on Chinese pirates is found in a chapter entitled 'Mrs. Ching Goes A-Pirating'; like Gosse, Gollomb has drawn his account primarily from Neumann's translation of *Ching hai-fen chi* and from Glasspoole's narrative of his captivity.

Gollomb's chapter contains no bibliographic references or notes. On several occasions, however, he mentions the captive Glasspoole, who is incorrectly referred to as 'Homer' instead of 'Richard'. Neither *Ching hai-fen chi*, its author, nor its translator are mentioned by name, but repeated references are made to an unspecified 'historian of China' to whom Gollomb attributes words that were never written.

He 'nominates' the nearest Chinese laundryman to be our guide to the 'far regions in which is set the strangest story in the annals of piracy'. By doing so, Gollomb introduces an ethnic stereotyping totally absent in Gosse. For, according to Gollomb:

> He [the laundryman] is our best guide if we want to see vividly the yellow pirates who will swarm through our story . . . He will help us visualize a people among whom it is womanly to wear trousers and virile to wear skirts; and he may even help bring out the colors of the gorgeous story of Mrs. Ching, chieftain over scores of thousands of Chinese pirates with whom even an emperor had to make terms . . . When in our story we go back only a little over a hundred years the difference between one of Mrs. Ching's pirates and the man you see busy over the laundry ironing board is largely only a matter of clothes.[25]

Gollomb's comments seem typical of widely held popular views about the Chinese in American Chinatowns during the early twentieth century. Recalling the Chinese who lived in the small New Jersey town where he grew up at the turn of the century, author Robert Lawson characterised them as 'foreign', 'outlandish' individuals who 'ran laundries' and wrote 'backwards and upside down, with a brush'. Moreover, 'they kidnapped children; engaged in white slave traffic; were always the villains in movies; strange; dreaded; they might cut you up; sinister, they ate rats; smoked opium.'[26]

A list of American beliefs about the Chinese compiled and published by a Chinese student in the *Literary Digest* of 12 March 1927 contained the following items:

> The favorite delicacies of the Chinese are rats and snakes.
> Chinese men wear skirts and women pants.
> A Chinese is properly a Chinaman and . . . the word 'Chinee' is singular for 'Chinese.'
> They are a mysterious and inscrutable race and . . . they do everything backwards.[27]

Gollomb's effort to account for the rise of piracy within the Chinese water world is every bit as dubious as his characterisation of the pirates themselves. He ignores the ongoing cycles of petty piracy along the South China coast and the influence of the Tay-son Rebellion on the activities of the Cheng family. Instead, he portrays Cheng I as a pirate with a crew of 12 and a leaky rowing boat who, through his own efforts and successful captures, increased his fleet to 1,800 vessels and 70,000 men.[28]

Until recently, Chinese historians frequently placed into their accounts imaginary dialogue which they attributed to their subjects. Their purpose was usually didactic and their goal, moral instruction. These make-believe conversations also provided their authors with opportunities to express their personal feelings about their subjects. Gollomb does not differentiate between the conversations he quotes from Neumann's translation and those he has composed himself. Moreover, he includes physical descriptions of the pirates derived more from fantasy than fact. For instance, on the basis of no discernable evidence, Ching-Yih (Cheng I) is described as a hunchback with a 'huge round face, [and] folds of yellow fat almost hiding his long slant eyes', an old man who 'could plot like the devil himself, fight like a fiend, and live and love as greedily as though his body were fresh and twenty'.[29] Equally fantastic are his description of Cheng I Sao and his reconstruction of her first encounter with Ching-Yih (Cheng I) (thoughout his account, Gollomb refers to Cheng I Sao as 'Hsi-Kai'):

> She was the pick of all the women brought in by the squads of pirates Ching-Yih had sent scouring through the country in search of a fit one for him . . . Brought to him tied hand and foot, she was larger than the women of her race, gloriously formed and, says a Chinese historian, 'before the beauty of her face the eyes of men grew confused.'[30]

The account continues:

> Hers was not the budlike mouth of the Chinese woman, but more the voluptuous mouth of the dancing nautch girls of India. And as she stood looking at the fat old hunchback, her teeth flashed

between carmined lips in one of those splendid rages beautiful to behold, but not agreeable to experience.

In the Orient woman is held as less than man, and Ching-Yih signed to the captors to untie Hsi-Kai that she might kneel before him. Her feet were not deformed by binding as Chinese custom prescribed. The moment her limbs were free she sprang at Ching-Yih and almost succeeded in tearing out his eyes.

The hunchback was delighted. Here was indeed a fit mate for a great pirate chief.[31]

Equally romantic (but also historically unfounded) is Gollomb's reconstruction of how Cheng I Sao assumed leadership of the confederation after her husband died:

A great meeting of the pirate fleet was held to elect a successor to Ching-Yih. Hsi-Kai [Cheng I Sao] arose before the assembled captains. She was dressed in the glittering garb of a male fighting chief; gold embroidered dragons writhed over goreous purples, blues, and reds; gay jade and green, bits of painted ivory, gold and silver shimmered and glittered in the sunlight. In her sash were some of her dead husband's swords and on her head was his familiar war helmet.

'Look at me, captains!' she cried. They looked at her. 'Your departed chief sat in council with me. Your most powerful fleet, the White, under my command, took more prizes than any other. Do you think I will bow to any other chief?'

There she was, in their eyes a goddess of a woman with a record of leadership as proud as any man's. It is not surprising, therefore, that the captains of the fleet should rise as a single man and acclaim her their chief of chiefs.[32]

By contrast, the scene is sparsely depicted by Yuan Yun-lun and his translator Neumann:

It happened, that on the seventeenth day of the tenth moon, in the twentieth year of Kea king (about the end of 1807), Ching yih perished in a heavy gale, and his legitimate wife Shih placed the whole crew under the sway of Paou: but so that she herself should be considered the commander of all the squadrons together, for this reason the division Ching yih was then called Ching yih saou, or the wife of Ching yih.[33]

The final scene Gollomb recreates for his readers is the initial encounter between Cheng I Sao and Chang Paou (Chang Pao), the commander of the Red fleet who became her paramour and ultimately her husband:

> The two fishermen [Chang Paou and his father] were seized and brought before Hsi-Kai for execution . . . The young man crossed powerful bronzed arms over his deep chest, and with a grin of indifference looked the woman in the face . . . He stood head and shoulders taller and broader than any of his captors, and the insolence in his flagrantly handsome face was such that Hsi-Kai could not dismiss it unnoticed . . .
>
> Hsi-Kai, however, who on so many other occasions was indeed the bringer of death, proved on this occasion that she was after all, a woman. From the very core of him to his finger tips he glowed with vitality, with such health as models face and body, into form of beauty and makes of the spirit so robust a thing that even death cannot make it cower.
>
> 'Paou, how well do you know the sea?' she asked.
>
> 'Aside from women there is nothing I know better.'
>
> She turned to her captains. 'Sink their fishing boat,' she said. 'Give the old man new garments and let him eat. And as for Paou, I will attend to him!'
>
> She attended to him with such generosity that soon Paou was wearing the uninform of a captain of Hsi-Kai's fleet . . .
>
> He learned with amazing rapidity . . . And at last he stood at Hsi-Kai's right hand, her chief captain, her prime minister, her lover, and her ablest fighter.[34]

Gollomb's account ignores information presented by Neumann that Chang Pao was originally captured by Cheng I and that it was in his eyes, not those of his wife, that he initially found favour:

> Chang Paou was a native of Sin hwy [Hsin-hui], near the mouth

of the River, and the son of a fisherman. Being fifteen years of age, he went with his father a fishing in the sea, and they were consequently taken prisoners by Ching yih, who roamed about the mouth of the river, ravaging and plundering. Ching yih saw Paou, and liked him so much, that he could not depart from him. Paou was indeed a clever fellow – he managed all business very well; being also a fine young man, he became a favourite of Ching yih and was made head-man or captain.[35]

The only eye-witness description we have of a pirate is Richard Glasspoole's report of an individual he refers to as 'the chief'. Glasspoole was taken to the chief's vessel where he found him 'seated on deck, in a large chair, dressed in purple silk, with a black turban on'. According to Glasspoole, 'he appeared to be about 30 years of age, a stout commanding-looking man.'[36] Elsewhere after his release, Glasspoole added to his description of this individual by stating:

> The chief of the Ladrones, in his person, is a man of dignified person and manners, of sound discretion, temperate habits, and bold and successful in all his enterprises; so that he has acquired an ascendancy over the minds of his followers, which insures to him the most unbounded confidence and obedience.[37]

Nothing in Glasspoole's narrative allows us to identify this figure with certainty as Chang Pao. Yet Gollomb not only assumes this to be the case, but also informs his readers that Glasspoole met both Chang Pao and Cheng I Sao. Gollomb also implies that Glasspoole, 'knew of the personal relation between the pirate captain and Hsi-Kai' and 'realized the delicacy of his own situation' resulting from it. 'It was', according to Gollomb, 'a question of which would prevail, Paou's jealousy of any man whose smile interested Hsi-Kai or his fear of what Hsi-Kai would do should 'some unfortunate accident' happen to Homer (Richard Glasspoole).' Nowhere in the Glasspoole narrative is there any account of a meeting with Cheng I Sao or even any acknowledgement of a woman being in command of the confederation.[38]

Gollomb is equally wrong in his discussion of what happened to the pirates after their surrender to the Chinese government. According to him:

Paou was made mighty commander and by edict became a 'Son of Heaven' and was allowed to wear peacock's feathers with two eyes in sign of his exalted rank. And the unconquerable Hsi-Kai, whose beauty dimmed the eyes of all beholders, went to dwell in a great palace and bore three sons and one daughter to her beloved husband, Paou.[39]

Chang Pao most assuredly did not become a 'Son of Heaven': only emperors were referred to as 'Sons of Heaven', and Chang Pao did not become an emperor. The privilege of wearing double-eyed peacock feathers was granted only to government officials for extraordinary service to the empire. In this instance, it was the governor-general Pai Ling and not Chang Pao who was rewarded with the peacock feathers. Cheng I Sao appears to have had a son as a result of her relationship with Chang Pao, but the claim that she lived in a palace and had three sons and a daughter is unfounded.

In the hands of Joseph Gollomb, historical licence has turned to historical fantasy of the most sexist and racist kind. But equally inexcusable is the way his text has provided the point of departure for the section on Chinese pirates in Linda Grant De Pauw's recent book *Sea Faring Women*.[40] De Pauw begins her account by depicting Cheng I Sao 'as the greatest pirate, male or female, in all history'. Like Gollomb, she attributes the origin of her heroine's piracy to untraceable floods during the spring of 1799, which impoverished China's coastal population to the point of starvation (Gollomb cites a spring flood in 1800). In both accounts, Cheng I Sao appears in male dress wearing her husband's war helmet and bearing his swords:

Madame Ching attended, dressed in the chief's uniform; a robe of purple, blue, and gold, embroidered with gold dragons and bound with a wide sash into which she had thrust several of her deceased husband's swords. She wore his war helmet on her head. The significance of this costume was clear enough: she meant to assume command.[41]

Like Gosse and Gollomb, De Pauw attributes the pirates' code to Cheng I Sao and not to Chang Pao, but unlike her predecessors, she implies that these regulations were written down: 'All of the ships were bound to obey Madame Ching's regulations, which she had posted aboard even the smallest ship of the fleet.'[42] Like Gollomb, she concludes her account by stating that after surrendering, Cheng I Sao 'went to live in the palace provided by the emperor, bore three sons and one daughter, and spent her last years in the less demanding work of a smuggler.'[43]

The carelessness De Pauw exhibits in her use of 'Chinese' sources obtained from Gollomb stands in marked contrast to the careful way she handles Richard Glasspoole's text. Despite not having cited Glasspoole in her bibliography, De Pauw must have had access to either a copy of the 'Narrative' or to more accurate references to it. Unlike Gollomb, she correctly cites Glasspoole's name as 'Richard' and correctly quotes a passage about the pirates having no fixed residence on shore.[44] She also makes no attempt to follow Gollomb in his claims that Glasspoole met either Chang Pao or Cheng I Sao or was privy to any knowledge of their relationship.[45]

What accounts for these disparities? Is there still a double standard which requires greater exactitude when dealing with some (European) materials than with others, such as Asian materials and their translations, for example?

The Chinese historians' view

Distorted and inaccurate though many of the accounts are, Cheng I Sao and her confederation have received more attention in the West than throughout most of China. Until I began working with the memorial collections of the National Palace Museum in Taipei and later in the First Historical Archives in Beijing, China's rich archival sources regarding piracy had lain untouched. Chinese copies of *Ching hai-fen chi* were unavailable in public collections in either Taipei or Hong Kong and were only rediscovered in the British Museum in London in autumn 1976. The other first hand account, an essay, 'Chispu p'ing-k'ou' (Suppressing the Bandits in 1809) by Chu Ch'eng-wen, was inaccessibly buried in the *Nan-hai hsien-chih* (Gazetteer of Nan-hai District), compiled in 1872 and reprinted in Taipei in 1971.[46]

One region where the pirates were somewhat familiar, however, was

Hong Kong. There in the 1950s they became the subject of two historical essays.[47] Apart from greater historical accuracy, what differentiates these Chinese articles most significantly from those in English discussed above is their focus on the male pirate Chang Pao rather than on the female pirate Cheng I Sao, whose name is scarcely mentioned. Chinese historians have simply not found Cheng I Sao very compelling.

A similar situation prevails in the realm of myth, legend and popular culture. Probably the most famous of the Hong Kong region's alleged artifacts is a cave on Cheung Chou (Chang Chou) Island where the pirates were said to have made their headquarters and buried their treasure, clearly labelled on contemporary maps as the 'Cave of Cheung Po Tsai' (Chang Pao-tsai), not of Cheng I Sao. From what little I remember of a Cantonese play *Chang Pao-tsai* by Yao Han-liang that I saw performed in Hong Kong on 28 June 1976, Cheng I Sao and another woman appeared as characters, but the hero was unmistakably the male pirate 'Chang Pao'. Finally, the adventure story *The Cave of Cheung Po Tsai* (Chang Pao-tsai) by F. J. F. Tingay is a classic search for buried treasure that takes place in the vicinity of Chang Pao's cave.[48] Despite the fact that some of the child protagonists are girls, the tale is without mention of a female pirate. Equally curious is the fact that no Chinese author, at least as far as I know, has attempted to portray Cheng I Sao as a woman warrior, in the well-known Chinese literary tradition introduced to modern western audiences by Maxine Hong Kingston in her book *The Woman Warrior: memoirs of a girlhood among ghosts*.[49]

Besides *The Cave of Cheung Po Tsai*, the only other fiction about the pirates available in English with which I am familiar is a short story by Jorge Luis Borges entitled 'The Widow Ching, Lady Pirate'.[50] Like Gosse, Borges presents Cheng I Sao as having been married to a husband who was appointed 'Master of the Royal Stables' by the emperor of China and was succeeded by his widow who later drew up a code of laws. One place where Borges seems to have misread Gosse, however, is revealed in his writing that 'It is a matter of history that the fox [Cheng I Sao] received her pardon and devoted her lingering years to the opium trade. She also left off being the widow, assuming a name which in English means "Lustre of Instruction".'[51] 'Lustre of Instruction' was the way Neumann translates the nickname of Black Flag fleet leader K'uo Po-tai, with whom not even Gosse suggests

Cheng I Sao had the slightest personal relationship.

Borges contributes several additions to the pirate lore, including a fable about a dragon's protection of a fox despite the fox's ingratitude (here, Cheng I Sao is the fox who, despite 13 years of piracy, ultimately receives her pardon from the imperial dragon). In contrast to authors who have imagined Cheng I Sao as a sensual, voluptuous beauty, Borges portrays her as a 'slinking woman, with sleepy eyes and a smile full of decayed teeth', whose 'blackish, oiled hair shone brighter than her eyes'.[52] Like his Chinese counterparts, Borges makes no attempt to link Cheng I Sao to Fan Mu-lan and the woman warrior tradition of the Middle Kingdom. But he does position her within a western sisterhood of female pirates that includes Mary Read and Ann Bonny, though he does not elaborate on what besides gender unites these pirates.

Life on board

Untruths and exaggeration have coloured many accounts of Cheng I Sao and her confederates. But what, if anything, could these historians have said about the quality of women pirates' lives? What information would have been accessible to them? And how might they have been able to tell fact from fiction in the accounts they read and wrote?

These are problems faced by historians every day of their professional lives. The line between 'historical fact' and 'historical fiction' is often difficult to draw with precision. But corroborating information from a variety of sources usually constitutes strong evidence for the determination of 'historical fact'. In this instance, nearly all the information about the pirates' daily lives and their interaction aboard ship is to be found in English-language sources available when each of these historians wrote their accounts.

J. Turner, chief mate of the country ship Tay, was captured by the Red Flag fleet in December 1806. Like Richard Glasspoole, Turner wrote an account of his captivity which was first published in the *Naval Chronicle* of 1808[53] and later in *Further Statement to the Ladrones on the Coast of China; Intended as a Contribution of the Accounts Published by Mr. Dalrymple*.[54] Philip Maughan, first lieutenant of the HC *Bombay*

Marine, arrived in China in May 1806 and was involved in a number of military skirmishes with the pirates. He expended considerable energy talking to local residents in the hope of trying to learn more about them. His essay 'An Account of the Ladrones who infested the Coast of China' was completed in February 1812.[55] A few years after completing his original essay 'A Brief Narrative of My Captivity and Treatment Amongst the Ladrones', Richard Glasspoole added an additional memoir, 'Substance of Mr. Glasspoole's Relation, Upon His Return to England, Respecting the Ladrones'.[56] These accounts provide us with brief glimpses into the ways the pirates lived and conducted themselves aboard ship.

Glasspoole, Maughan and Turner all agree that entire families made their homes on board pirate ships. However, the presence of women on these crafts was strictly regulated. Says Glasspoole, 'The Ladrones have no settled residence on shore, but live constantly in their vessels'[57] which 'are filled with their families, men, women and children'.[58] According to Maughan, the number of women who lived with them was 'surprising';[59] in many instances, according to Glasspoole, 'women command their junks'.[60]

Glasspoole notes that 'with respect to conjugal rights they [the pirates] are religiously strict; no person is allowed to have a woman on board, unless married to her according to their laws.'[61] This observation is supported by Turner, who reports:

> With respect to the women who fall into their hands, the handsomest are reserved by them for wives and concubines . . . having once made choice of a wife, they [the pirates] are obliged to be constant to her, no promiscuous intercourse being allowed amongst them . . . A few are ransomed, and the most homely returned on shore.[62]

According to Glasspoole, on one occasion after about 100 female captives of the pirates were ransomed: 'The remainder were offered for sale amongst the Ladrones for forty dollars each' with the understanding that 'the woman is considered the lawful wife of the purchaser, who would be put to death if he discarded her.'[63] Turner says that captive children were generally retained and brought up as servants.[64]

Of those who were married, the rank and file pirates, according to Turner, typically had no more than one wife. The chiefs and captains frequently had three or more; the greater part of the crew 'were satisfied without women'.[65] Glasspoole's estimate that captains generally had five or six wives is a bit higher.[66]

By all accounts space was at a premium aboard cramped and dirty vessels. Maughan comments that 'Amidst such a herd of villains, it may naturally be supposed cleanliness was but little thought of; consequently their vessels were filthy to an extreme'.[67] 'From the number of souls crowded in so small a space,' reports Glasspoole, 'it must naturally be supposed they are horridly dirty, which is evidently the case, and their vessels swarm with all kinds of vermin.'[68] Once on board ship, every man, according to Glasspoole, was allowed 'a small berth, about four feet square' in which to stow with his wife and family.[69] Maughan adds that 'all those who chose to cohabit with females had generally a small cabin to themselves . . . (where) the number of cabins were considerable in their largest boats.'[70] Turner describes his accommodations on board ship as 'wretched' and relates that: 'At night, the space allowed me to sleep in was never more than about eighteen inches wide, and four feet long; and if at any time I happened to extend my contracted limbs beyond their limits, I was sure to be reminded of my mistake by a blow or kick.'[71]

Ladrones were dressed as lower-class Chinese. Maughan has added that 'a turban, composed of dark-coloured cotton cloth, was usually worn in lieu of a hat.'[72] Food was sparse. Turner describes his fare as having been the same as that of the common Chinese, 'coarse red rice, with a little salt fish'.[73] According to Glasspoole: 'The diet of the Ladrones is rice and fish (the fishermen all paying them tribute), except within they have plundered any village, in which case they get hogs and poultry.'[74] He also notes that certain species of rats were encouraged to breed and consumed as 'great delicacies'. He states there were 'very few creatures' they would not eat; at one point during his captivity, the pirates lived for three weeks on caterpillars boiled with rice.[75]

Glasspoole also describes the pirates as being 'much addicted to gambling', and spending 'all their leisure hours at cards and smoking opium'.[76] On one occasion he watched as members of a fishing boat came aboard the pirate junk. They spent the remainder of the day in the chief's cabin smoking opium and playing cards.[77] On another occasion he reports that:

> whilst the Ladrone fleet was receiving a distant cannonade from the Portuguese and Chinese, the men were playing cards upon deck, and in a group so amusing themselves, one man was killed by a cannon shot; but the rest, after putting the mangled body out of the way, went on with their game, as if nothing of the kind had happened.[78]

These western observers had some overall sense of the confederation and how it operated; according to Turner, 'The whole body of Ladrone vessels that I have seen are under the command of five chiefs, who are independent of each other.'[79] Glasspoole indicates that the admiral of the Red Flag fleet was supreme;[80] Turner provides a description of the confederation's sub-units:

> Each vessel has a captain who directs in a general way all the operations on board, etc. . . . The captain is generally better dressed than the common Ladrones. He also fares somewhat better, and the officers or assistants mentioned above, are some of them partakers of his meals . . . Each division is formed into several squadrons, commanded by an inferior chief by whom the captains of the different vessels are generally appointed and from whom they receive their orders.[81]

Once in motion, the confederation seems to have been a relatively disciplined group whose members fought bravely in combat. Glasspoole reports:

> In their attacks they are intrepid, and in their defence most desperate, yielding in the latter instance to no superiority of numbers; the laws of discipline and civil government are equally enforced on board his [the chief's] junk, and any transgressions from them immediately punished, which, as their vessels are filled with their families, men, women, and children, seems almost incredible. They are taught to be fearless in danger.[82]

Maughan remarks, 'I have witnessed a few instances of intrepidity exhibited by the Ladrones, which, when compared with their general pusillanimous conduct on other occasions, marks them an extraordinary people.'[83]

Women in combat

Women in combat are noted three times by Yuan Yun-lun and his translator Charles Neumann. One engagement occurred in early 1809 near Lao Wan Shan. After describing how the pirate commander advanced 'courageously' and took about 200 prisoners, Yuan Yun-lun remarks:

> There was a pirate's wife in one of the boats, holding so fast by the helm that she could scarcely be taken away. Having two cutlasses, she desperately defended herself, and wounded some soldiers; but on being wounded by a musket-ball, she fell back into the vessel and was taken prisoner.[84]

In the battle between the pirates and villagers of Kan-shih (in Nan-hai district, Kwangtung), Yuan Yun-lun recalls the heroism of a villager's wife. At one point when the villager Chou Wei tang (Chou Wei-teng) was surrounded by pirates, his 'wife fought valiantly by his side' until she, too, was slain with the others.[85] As the foray continued and the pirates made their way into the village, 100 women were hidden in the surrounding paddy fields, but:

> the pirates on hearing a child crying, went to the place and carried them away. Mei ying (Mei Ying), the wife of Ke choo yang was very beautiful, and a pirate being about to seize her by the head, she abused him exceedingly. The pirate bound her to the yard-arm; but on abusing him yet more, the pirate dragged her down and broke two of her teeth, which filled her mouth and jaws with blood. The pirate sprang up again to bind her. Ying allowed him to approach but as soon as he came near her, she laid hold of his garments with her bleeding mouth and threw both him and

herself into the river where they were drowned.[86]

Cruelty was also observed by Glasspoole, who states that the pirates were 'so savage in their resentments and manners, that they frequently take the hearts of their enemies and eat them with rice, considering the repast gives them fortitude and courage'.[87] Turner reports having been told of a similar occurrence:

> At this place a man was put to death, with circumstances (as I was told) of peculiar horror. Being fixed upright, his bowels were cut open, and his heart was taken out, which they afterwards soaked in spirits, and ate. The dead body I saw myself. I am well assured that this shocking treatment is frequently practiced in the case of persons who, having annoyed the Ladrones in any particular manner, fall into their hands.[88]

The plight of some of the pirates' female captives is noted by Glasspoole. He saw the capture of 250 women and several children from a village surrounded by a thick wood on 1 October 1809. The women were:

> sent on board different vessels. They were unable to escape with the men owing to that abominable practice of cramping their feet; several of them were not able to move without assistance, in fact, they might all be said to totter, rather than to walk. Twenty of these poor women were sent on board the vessel I was in; they were hauled on board by the hair and treated in a most savage manner.
>
> When the chief came on board, he questioned them respecting the circumstances of their friends, and demanded ransoms accordingly, from six thousand to six hundred dollars each. He ordered them a berth on deck, at the after part of the vessel, where they had nothing to shelter them from the weather, which at this time was very variable . . .
>
> Here we remained five or six days, during which time about an hundred of the women were ransomed; the remainder were offered for sale amongst the Ladrones for forty dollars each . . . Several of them leaped over-board and drowned themselves,

rather than submit to such infamous degradation.[89]

Occasionally, however, the pirates' cruelty was tempered by compassion. During the heat of battle Glasspoole reports having received special consideration from the chief's wife, who sprinkled him with garlic water which the pirates considered 'an effectual charm against shot'.[90]

A remarkable woman

These brief details of the living conditions, dress, diet and organisation aboard the pirates' ships were etched unforgettably into the memories of the individuals who observed them. Many facts about the pirates' daily routines and personal relationships are probably lost forever, but the accounts of Glasspoole, Turner and Maughan have at least allowed us a glimpse into the existence of women and men who, without the means to tell their own story, might have slipped into oblivion.

Had Gollomb and De Pauw paid serious attention to these reports, they might have found that their own narratives needed no embellishment. For the pirates demonstrated organisational and administrative skills that are amazing in their own right, especially when we consider that they were the products of individuals so denigrated that, as fishing people, they were forbidden from participation in the civil service examinations of the Chinese government. Between 1802 and 1810, with no official patronage or support, they created an organisation strong enough to sustain, both financially and militarily, a force that outnumbered the total participants in the Spanish Armada by two to one. It is an episode so vivid and compelling that it needs little in the way of myth, legend or literature for its enhancement.

Throughout most of the world, piracy has been a male occupation that has tended to exclude women, especially from leadership. In imperial China, Confucian attitudes militated against public roles for women, so we might have expected the presence of Chinese women at sea and their participation in pirate gangs to have been even more restricted. But the phenomenon of Cheng I Sao and her activities is perhaps less surprising in a Chinese context than we might expect. In the world from which these pirates sprang, women participated fully in all aspects of life at sea. Not only did they work and reside alongside their husbands on board ship, they were also responsible for much of the skulling and handling of craft of various types. In this way, their presence on pirate ships was merely an extension of everyday practice. Moreover, by the eighteenth century the precedent for women as leaders of both religious sects and anti-dynastic rebellion had been firmly established.

Finally, Cheng I Sao's ascent was very much in keeping with the tradition of Chinese women rising to power through marriage. Marrying well and then assuming the mantle of power on the death of a husband was the most common avenue of female mobility in nearly every Chinese social circle. Among the élites and the socially well connected, this was the path to power taken by such 'notorious' *femmes fatales* as empresses Wu Tze-hsien and Tzu-hsi, and concubine Yang Kuei-fei.[91] More recently it enabled the rise of Chiang Ch'ing, the fourth wife of Mao Tse-tung.

Nevertheless, Cheng I Sao wielded authority in ways that made her unusual even by Chinese standards, and throughout her career she acted in open defiance of Confucian behavioural norms. As Cheng I's wife she was anything but a docile, submissive homebody. As his widow she not only failed to remain chaste, but even broke the incest taboo when it served her purpose by marrying her adopted son. Despite such conduct, she was able to win the genuine support of her followers to the degree that they openly acclaimed her as the one person capable of holding the confederation together. As its leader, she demonstrated her ability to take command by issuing orders, planning military campaigns and demonstrating that there were profits to be made in piracy. When the time came to dismantle the confederation, it was her negotiating skills above all that allowed her followers to cross the bridge from outlawry to officialdom. And all this was done by a woman so common that her personal identity is virtually unknown.

Yet despite her success, Cheng I Sao did not create an institutional structure capable of surviving without her. With no tradition of either bureaucratic or ideological continuity to bolster them from generation to generation, such informal personal creations of power are usually dependent on the charisma of their founders. This makes them difficult to preserve for more than a generation. Consequently, when Cheng I's wife decided to retire, no individual, either female or male, could step into the organisation and operate the structures through which she had exercised power.

In looking at the themes of fact and fiction that have been discussed in this chapter, I have noted with irony that there seems to have been greater concern for 'truth' and accuracy from non-historians than from historians. For instance, Yuan Yun-lun, the employee in the governor-general's office whose *Ching hai-fen chi* was translated into English by Charles Neumann, felt compelled for the purposes of moral instruction to write an 'objective' account of the pirates and their activities. He elaborates at some length on this goal in the preface of his book, taking pains to point out that he is providing a 'true account' whose every detail has been checked for accuracy. Similarly, Lieutenant Maughan's concern for the integrity of his account emerges early in his essay when he apologises for the quality of the information available to him: 'In giving my opinion of the Ladrones, I trust every allowance will be made for the imperfect means I had of procuring information, being chiefly through the fishermen and lower classes of Chinese.'[92] Such concern on the part of serious, well-intentioned amateurs deserves our sincere commendation.

As a historian, I cannot but end this chapter humbled once again by the challenges of my own profession and the responsibility of recreating, often from very fragmentary evidence, the lives and times of those who have gone before us. These are lives whose reconstruction, it seems to me, must be undertaken with the deepest respect and care, regardless of their settings.

Notes

1. The source of Fan Mu-lan and the woman warrior tradition of China may be this anonymous poem from sometime between the third century BC and the sixth century AD. It has been translated into English as 'The Ballad of Mulan' by William Nienhauser and appears in *Sunflower Splendor Three Thousand Years of Chinese Poetry*, edited by Wu-chi Liu and Irving Lo, Indiana University Press, 1975, pp. 77-80.
2. Scattered paragraphs in the notes and conclusion of this chapter have

been reprinted from my book *Pirates of the South China Coast 1790-1810*, copyright 1987, by the Board of Trustees of the Leland Stanford Junior University. All material used here and taken from the book is reproduced by permission of Stanford University Press.

3. Susan Naquin, *Shantung Rebellion: the Wang Lun uprising of 1774*, Yale University Press, 1981, pp. 100,101.

4. Fanny Loviot, translated by A. B. Edwards, *A Lady's Captivity Among Chinese Pirates*, 1858, but stored at the British Library under 10057 al9 26, p. 78.

5. Studies of Chinese prostitution are in their infancy, but those with further interest in the topic are advised to pursue Gail Hershatter's article 'The Hierarchy of Shanghai Prostitution, 1870-1949' in *Modern China*, vol. 15, No. 4 (October 1989), pp. 463-98.

6. In 1771 the Tay-son Rebellion broke out in what was the southern Vietnamese or Annamese province of Binh Dinh. Its leaders were three brothers, Nguyen Van Nhac, Nguyen Van Lu and Nguyen Van Hue, merchants engaged in the betel commerce with the hill peoples of the province. The name 'Tay-son', meaning 'Western Mountain', derived from their native village. By 1773 this band of leaders and their followers had managed to seize the provincial capital at Qui Nhon. From there the movement spread and the rebellion, climaxing more than a century of revolt and social unrest, became a massive upheaval that constitutes one of the major episodes of eighteenth-century South-east Asian history. Until their defeat by a scion of the Nguyen rulers from Hue, the Tay-son were continually challenged, and it was in that context, finding themselves in need of manpower and resources, that they made their appeal to the pirates along the coast of China, who in 1792 were recruited into their service. (Charles Maybon, *Histoire moderne du pays d'Annam, 1592-1820*, Plon-Nourrit, 1919, pp. 289-347; Le Thanh Khoi, *Le Viet-nam, historie et civilisation*, Les Editions de Minuit, 1955, pp. 296-322. This paragraph is based on information in Dian Murray, *Pirates of the South China Coast, 1790-1810*, Stanford University Press, 1987, pp. 32-40.)

7. For more information see Murray, *ibid*, pp. 133-6.

8. The two provinces of Kwangsi and Kwangtung are referred to as the Liang-kuang (the two kuangs) and thus the Liang-kuang governor general was the chief administrative official of these two provinces.

9. 'Chinese Pirates: Ching Chelung; His Son Cheng Ching-kung; Combination of Gangs in 1806; Narratives of J. Turner and Mr. Glasspoole; Chinese and Portuguese Join Their Forces Against the Pirates: Divisions Among Them, and Their Submission to the Government', *Chinese Repository* 3: 62-83 (June 1834), p. 82.

10. The sources for this biographical account of Cheng's life are: *Nan-hai hsien-chih* (Gazetteer of Nan-hai District), comp. by Cheng Meng-yu, 26 *chuan* (1872), reprint edition, Taipei, 1971, 14:20b and 25:20b; Yuan Yun-

lun, *Ching-hai fen-chi*; 2 *chuan*, Canton, 1830, 1:5a-b; *Kuang-tung hai-fang hui-lan* (Essentials of sea defence in Kuang-tung), comp. Lu K'un and Ch'eng Hung-ch'ih, 42 *chuan*, n.d., 42:26b, 32b; 'Canton Consultations. Consultations and Transactions of the Select Committee of Resident Supercargoes Appointed by the Honourable Court of Directors of the United East India Company to Manage Their Affairs in China Together with the Letters Written and Occurrences', Factory Records G/12/100-G/12/174, March 1791 to January 1811; 'Memorial of Lin Tse-hsu', TK20/5/15 reproduced in Yeh Lin-feng, *Chang Pao-tsai ti ch'uan-shuo ho chen-hsieng* (Chang Pao-tsai in fiction and fact), Hong Kong, 1970, p. 69; 'Chinese pirates . . .', *Chinese Repository*, 3, *ibid*; 'Hsi-Ying-P'an yu Chang Pao-tsai huo-luan chih p'ing-ting' (Sai Ying Pun (West Camp) and the end of the ravages of the pirate Chang Pao-tsai) by Hu Chih-yu (Woo Kit-yu), in *I-pa-ssu-erh nien i-ch'ien chih Hsiang-kang chi ch'i-tui wai-chiao-t'ung* (Hong Kong and its external communication before 1842), 1959, pp. 151-70. This account of Cheng's life is similar to one prepared for the *Biographical Dictionary of Chinese Women* which is currently being edited by Clara Wing-chung Lau, Hong Kong Baptist College.

11. Karl Friederich Neumann (Charles Fried) trans., *The History of the Pirates Who Infested the China Sea from 1807 to 1810*, written by Yuan Yun-lun, Chiang hai-fen chi. London, 1831. A second, less accessible translation of *Ching hai-fen chi* was made by John Slade under the title 'A Record of the Pacification of the Seas' which appeared serially in the *Canton Register* beginning 20 February 1838 with vol. 11, no. 8.

12. This information appears on p. 9a of Yuan Yun-lun's *Ching hai-fen chi* and p. 21 of Neumann's translation.

13. This account was first published in *Sketches of Chinese Customs and Manners in 1811-12 Taken During a Voyage to the Cape, etc. With Some Account of the Ladrones, in a Series of Letters to a Friend* by George Wilkinson, esq., Bath, 1814. It was also published separately under the title *Mr. Glasspoole and the Chinese Pirates: Being the Narrative of Mr. Richard Glasspoole of the Ship Marquis of Ely: Describing His Captivity of Eleven Weeks and Three Days Whilst Held for Ransom by the Villainous Ladrones of the China Sea in 1809; Together with Extracts From the China Records and the Log of the Marquis of Ely; and Some Remarks on Chinese Pirates, Ancient and Modern*, by Owen Rutter, Golden Cockerel Press, 1935. The version cited here is appended to the Neumann translation of *Ching hai-fen chi* and occasionally bears his editorial comments.

14. Glasspoole, 'Narrative', p. 107.

15. These accounts include: Henri Musnik, *Les Femmes pirates: adventures et legendes de la mer*, Le Masque, Paris, 1934; Joseph Gollomb, *Pirates Old and New*, New York, 1928; 'Chinese pirates', *Chinese Repository* 3, *op cit*, Charles Ellms, *The Pirates Own Book or Authentic Narratives of the Lives*,

Exploits and Executions of the Most Celebrated Sea Robbers, Salem, 1924; Charles Hill, 'Pirates of the China Seas', *Asia*, 1924, pp. 306-10+; and Linda Grant De Pauw, *Sea Faring Women*, Houghton Mifflin Co, 1982.

16. Philip Gosse, *The History of Piracy*, Tudor Publishing Co., NY, 1946, p. 271.

17. *ibid*, p. 271.

18. Like Gosse's version of the story, my own endeavour to write a sustained account of Cheng I Sao also contains substantial portions of material about other topics. See 'One Woman's Rise to Power: Cheng I's Wife and the Pirates' in *Women in China: Current Directions in Historical Scholarship*, Richard W. Guisso and Stanley Johannesen (eds), Philo Press, 1981, pp. 147-62.

19. Gosse, *op cit*, p. 271.

20. King sheng, whose name reads as Ching-sheng in accord with Wade-Giles Romanisation, was the Quang-toan emperor of Vietnam.

21. Neumann, *op cit*, p. 5.

22. Gosse, *op cit*, pp. 272-3.

23. Neumann, *op cit*, pp. 13-14.

24. Gosse, *op cit*, p. 272.

25. Gollomb, *op cit*, pp. 272-3.

26. Robert Lawson, *At That Time*, New York, 1947, pp. 43-5.

27. These items are quoted by Harold Isaacs, *Scratches on our Minds: American Views of China and India*, M. E. Sharpe, Inc, 1980 (originally published John Ed. Day Co, 1958) pp. 118-19.

28. Gollomb, *op cit*, p. 277.

29. *ibid*, p. 275.

30. *ibid*, p. 277.

31. *ibid*, p. 278. The source of Gollomb's speculation may have been an anecdote recounted in the Neumann translation of how upon being captured and tied to the yard-arm, a villager named Mei Ying grabbed hold of a pirate and threw them both overboard upon her release.

32. *ibid*, pp. 279-80. Nowhere (except perhaps Gollomb) have the pirates ever been described as wearing war helmets and so far as we know their only headgear was cotton turbans. Philip Maughan, 'An Account of the Ladrones who infested the Coast of China' in *Further Statement of the Ladrones on the Coast of China; Intended as a Contribution to the Accounts Published by Mr. Dalrymple*, Land, Darling, and Co, 1812, p. 26.

33. Neumann, *op cit*, pp. 12-13.

34. Gollomb, *op cit*, pp. 282-3.

35. Neumann, *op cit*, p. 12.

36. Glasspoole, 'Narrative', *op cit*, p. 103.

37. Richard Glasspoole, 'Substance of Mr. Glasspoole's Relation, Upon His Return to England, Respecting the Ladrones' in *Further Statement of the Ladrones on the Coast of China*, op cit, p. 44.

38. Gollomb, *op cit*, p. 280. Glasspoole's overall grasp of the pirates' organisational structure appears to be weak, and his references in the 'Narrative' to a 'head admiral' give no indication that he knew this person was a woman. My guess is that during his captivity, he probably heard vague references to a 'head admiral' whom he never met and assumed to be a man. However, at some point, perhaps even after his release, Glasspoole seems to have learned of a woman and in his subsequent writings makes one brief reference to her: 'The chiefs of the divisions are related, and a woman is at the head of this confederacy, whose son was the principal, a very intelligent and humane man, not torturing his prisoners, as the other chiefs are greatly disposed to do. The Ladrones look up to this chief with uncommon reverence, calling him a god.' ('Substance of Mr. Glasspoole's Relation . . .') *op cit*, p. 40. Even at this point Glasspoole seems to manifest confusion about the relationship between the principal male and female leaders of the pirates, believing them to be mother and son.

39. Gollomb, *ibid*, pp. 308-9.

40. Linda Grant De Pauw is a professor of history at George Washington University. *Sea Faring Women* was published in 1982 by Houghton Mifflin Co.

41. De Pauw, *op cit*, p. 49.

42. De Pauw, *ibid*, p. 50.

43. See Gollomb, *op cit*, pp. 308-9 and De Pauw, *ibid*, p. 52.

44. Although De Pauw gives no citation for this quotation, the passage is from p. 127 of my edition of Glasspoole's 'Narrative'.

45. De Pauw, *op cit*, pp. 51-2.

46. The essay is found 14:19b-23a. Like *Ching hai-fen chi*, 'Chi-ssu p'ing-k'ou' was written by a man who had witnessed the pirates' depredations first hand. Chu Ch'eng-wen was a teacher in Kan-shih township who upon hearing of the impending arrival of Chang Pao and his forces successfully led his community in local defence measures.

47. The first 'Chang Pao-tsai shih-chi kao' (Examination of the affairs of Chang Pao-tsai) by Yeh Lin-feng was published serially in the *Hsiang-kang hsing-tao jih-pao* (Hong Kong Islands Daily), beginning 7 August 1953. The second 'Hsi-Ying-P'an yu Chang Pao-tsai huo-luan chih p'ing-ting', *op cit*, was published in 1959.

48. F. J. F. Tingay, *The Cave of Cheung Po Tsai*, Oxford University Press, Kuala Lumpur, 1960.

49. Maxine Hong Kingston, *The Woman Warrior: memoirs of a girlhood among ghosts*, Alfred Knopf, Inc, 1975.

50. Borges' story was translated from the Portuguese by Norman Thomas Di Giovanni and appears in *A Universal History of Infamy*, Dutton, 1970, 1979.

51. *ibid*, p. 48.

52. *ibid*, p. 43.

53. The account titled 'Account of the Captivity of J. Turner, Chief Mate of the Ship Tay, amongst the Ladrones; accompanied by some Observations respecting those Pirates' appears in *Naval Chronicle*, 1808, vol. 20, pp. 456-72. Turner was released from captivity in May 1807.

54. *Further Statement of the Ladrones* . . .op cit, pp. 46-73. This is the account of Turner's captivity cited here.

55. *ibid*, pp. 7-32.

56. *ibid*, pp. 40-5.

57. Glasspoole, 'Narrative', *op cit*, p. 127.

58. Glasspoole, 'Substance', *op cit*, p. 44.

59. Maughan, *op cit*, p. 26.

60. Glasspoole, 'Narrative', *op cit*, p. 41.

61. *ibid*, p. 127.

62. Turner, *op cit*, p. 71.

63. Glasspoole, 'Narrative', *op cit*, p. 113.

64. Turner, *op cit*, p. 71.

65. *ibid*, p. 71. Turner's comment is corroborated by archival sources, for 22 palace memorials submitted by the governors and governors general of Kwangtung between 1796 and 1800 cite 50 instances of homosexual activity among the pirates (these documents are now in the National Palace Museum, Taipei). My endeavour to understand what meaning these actions had for the pirates has been published under the title 'The Practice of Homosexuality Among the Pirates of Late 18th and Early 19th Century China' in *International Journal of Maritime History*, vol. IV, no. 1 (June 1992), pp. 121-30.

66. Glasspoole, 'Narrative', *op cit*, p. 127.

67. Maughan, *op cit*, p. 26.

68. Glasspoole, 'Narrative', *op cit*, p. 128.

69. *ibid*, p. 128.

70. Maughan, *op cit*, p. 26.

71. Turner, *op cit*, p. 61.

72. Maughan, *op cit*, p. 26.

73. Turner, *op cit*, p. 61.

74. Glasspoole, 'Substance', *op cit*, p. 43.

75. Glasspoole, 'Narrative', *op cit*, pp. 104-5.

76. *ibid*, p. 128.

77. *ibid*, p. 105.

78. Glasspoole, 'Substance', *op cit*, p. 44.

79. Turner, *op cit*, p. 66.

80. Glasspoole, 'Substance', *op cit*, p. 42.

81. Turner, *op cit*, p. 68.

82. Glasspoole, 'Substance', *op cit*, pp. 44-5.

83. Maughan, *op cit*, p. 15.

84. Neumann, *op cit*, p. 24.

85. *ibid*, pp. 46-7.
86. Neumann, *op cit*, p. 48.
87. Glasspoole, 'Substance', *op cit*, p. 40.
88. Turner, *op cit*, p. 56.
89. Glasspoole, 'Narrative', *op cit*. p. 113.
90. *ibid*, p. 123.
91. John K. Fairbank et al, *East Asia: tradition and transformation*, Harvard University, 1978, pp. 98, 120, 480.
92. Maughan, *op cit*, p. 23.

13 *Between warrior junk and A Doll's House?*

Our women's world is sunk so deep, who can help us?
Jewellery sold to pay this trip across the seas,
Cut off from my family I leave my native land.
Unbinding my feet I clean out a thousand years of poison[1]

Chinese women pirates in the twentieth century were operating in a very changed world from that of Cheng I Sao. In 1904, the country's most famed revolutionary feminist Jiu Jin wrote the above poem as she was sailing off to Japan for two years of radical studies, leaving behind husband and children in Beijing. Men were cutting off their pigtails, women were refusing to bind their feet, warlords were deposed and Manchu rule was identified as oppressive and challenged.

A ferment of uprisings brought the Revolutionary Alliance of Sun Yat-Sen to power in 1911 and the collapse of the Manchu dynasty. Women were deeply involved in this struggle, as fighters, couriers, nurses and arms smugglers.[2] From 1906 to 1908, women could buy their own daily newspaper on the Beijing streets and read about the militant British suffragists, who were one of their inspiring forces.

But the 1911 revolution did not bring women the changes they wanted. They protested, and a cultural renaissance began after 1916[3] including the May 4 movement of 1919. Birth-control pioneer Margaret Sanger visited from the US; Ibsen's *A Doll's House* (translated 1918) was highly influential, with Chinese Noras identifying with the tale of female confinement in a meaningless marriage and restricting home. Women had become part of the low-waged workforce and in 1922 up to 60,000 silk-mill workers downed tools in the first major women's strike, demanding a day of rest every two weeks, a ten-hour day and increased wages. By 1921 there were women's associations in all the major cities. For urban and elite women, this challenging period brought a great sense of what freedom might mean.[4] By the late 1920s, women's conditions in some of the areas liberated from the power of regional warlords, especially Hankou, had improved, with the granting of divorce rights and a reduction in working hours.

Two Chinese women pirates are recorded in the second and third decades of the twentieth century. While Lo Hon-cho and Lai Choi San are described in western literature as feisty women, there is no evidence to suggest that their bravery and independence were a product of feminist unrest, or that their pillaging was brought on by an overdose of Mrs Pankhurst and Alexandra Kollontai. Since radical political movements had less significance for underprivileged women in rural and coastal areas, it is more likely that family business traditions and economic need led the two women to the work. Like Cheng I Sao, both Lo Hon-cho and Lai Choi San gained their power as pirate leaders through men in their families. What evidence we have about their piracy suggests that it conformed to traditional patterns, although Chinese piracy itself was changing.

The invention of steam-powered vessels meant that piracy tactics differed significantly from those used in Cheng I Sao's time. European and American traders now had iron-hulled steam frigates like the East India Company's *Nemesis*, with 120 horsepower and two 32-pound guns. The *Nemesis* 'could outfight and outmanouvre junks of all sizes. Using rockets and cannon, these iron steamers . . . could devastate a fleet of Oriental ships' – and did so, in 1841.[5] Sail-powered pirates could no longer give chase to faster western ships, though they could still attack Chinese vessels as the Chinese were slow to modernise and the first steamship company was not set up in China until 1872.[6]

By the time the first known twentieth-century woman pirate was operating, piracy was focused on Macao and Hong Kong to the southeast of China. Between 1921 and 1929 at least 29 incidents of piracy were recorded in the main Bias Bay area, 65 miles east of Hong Kong, and there were others on the West River and along the coast between Bias Bay and Shanghai. Ships with names such as *Jade*, *Seang Bee*, *Irene* and *Delhi Maru* were attacked for gold bars, opium, silk, bar silver (or in one more mundane case, wool serge). Passengers' jewellery, money and clothing were also taken. Crew and passengers were seldom shot, though there were some woundings.[7]

Rather than pirates attacking a laden merchant vessel from their own craft, the new technique involved more of a take-over from within. 'The Chinese pirates have adapted themselves to modern conditions. They work from a safe base ashore, they have an elaborate intelligence system, and they combine subtlety with force of arms.'[8] Aleko E. Lilius, an American journalist more interested in ripping yarns than in veracity, reported that usually between 10 and 60 pirates would board the target ship at a dock, as passengers. The leaders travelled first class, sometimes wearing 'European clothes and tortoise-shell-rimmed spectacles',[9] and the pirate mob third class. They smuggled guns aboard with the help of people working in the docks: 'stevedores who, though not on the ships' articles, are invariably allowed to travel on these ships and have permission to sell goods ie fruit, cigarettes, cakes, teas, and act as hawkers to the passengers.'[10] Before the ship sailed the pirates would investigate its movements and place themselves strategically in various locations aboard ready to hijack it when it was well out to sea. The signal was a whistle or 'a hellish beating of the gongs'[11] after which the crew of the passenger or cargo ship would be attacked:

one group storms the bridge, another attacks the engine room, and a third keeps the passengers at bay. The piracy invariably occurs near Bias Bay, where the ship is brought and the cargo loaded in to waiting sampans and junks. The rich passengers, both white and Chinese, are taken ashore to be held for ransom.[13]

Lilius does not report any women in these gangs, but that does not prove they were not there. However, the two twentieth-century women pirates on record operated somewhat differently.

Lo Hon-Cho

I know about 1920s pirate Lo Hon-cho only from a brief press report quoted apparently verbatim in A. Hyatt Verrill's *The Real Story of the Pirates*, a compilation of adventure yarns written in 1923 (Philip Gosse also summarises it in his 1935 *The History of Piracy*). Verrill says the following despatch came from Hong Kong in October 1922:

> Mrs Lo Hon-cho, China's woman pirate chief, who for a year has been terrorizing the countryside about Pakhoi, is reported to have been captured.
>
> When her husband, who was a noted pirate, was killed in 1921, Mrs Lo Hon-cho took command of his ship and crew and succeeded so well that her pirate fleet soon grew to sixty ocean-going pirate junks.
>
> Youthful, and said to be pretty, the female pirate gained a record and a reputation as the most murderous and ruthless of all China's assortment of banditti. During the revolution, Mrs Lo Hon-cho joined forces with the Sun leader, General Wong Min-Tong, and received the rank of Colonel.
>
> Together the General and the lady Colonel gathered forty thousand dollars from the city of Pakhoi as ransom to prevent it being looted.
>
> After the General returned to Canton, she resumed her piracies, preying upon fishing fleets, villages and farmers. In her attacks on villages, she usually took fifty or sixty girls prisoners, later selling them into slavery.
>
> On her return from one of these forays, this woman pirate stopped at a village on the coast and while feasting was surprised by a Chinese warship. In the battle that followed, forty of the junks were destroyed. Mrs Lo Hon-cho escaped, but soon after was betrayed by one of her followers in return for a promise of pardon from the military commander of Pakhoi.[13]

The brevity of this report, and the apparent absence of any other information, means that we do not know whether Lo Hon-cho was motivated by money or politics, what her day-to-day life was like, or

244 | Bold in Her Breeches

what happened to her after she was betrayed. It seems likely that she was at least in her mid-20s. If she was from a noble background, her feet might have been bound (photographs prove that women with bound feet could be mobile; for example they worked in the fields in the 1920s and 1930s).[14] Although she was married (it was still a time of arranged marriages), there are no references to children. We can only speculate as to how she learned her seafaring skills and how she felt about the life she led.

Significantly, Lo Hon-cho is presented for western consumption as physically attractive to men – 'pretty' and 'youthful' – and as in other dominatrice fantasies she is reported as being not only tough and successful, but 'the most murderous and ruthless of all'. No one seems to have researched this woman using Chinese-language sources, so everything about her, including her very existence, awaits further investigation.

Lai Choi San

Lai Choi San lived and worked in and around the Macao area of southeast China in the 1920s. Portuguese until 1999, Macao is made up of Macao town and a group of small islands, Taipa and Coloane, and is a port province with an important fishing industry. The town is 40 miles west of Hong Kong, cut off from it by the estuary of the Pearl River in which Lai Choi San operated. In the 50 years before her career started, the town had declined rapidly as Hong Kong boomed.

Our only source for Lai Choi San's story is Aleko E. Lilius, a journalist hired by American and European newspapers to gather informaiton about 'the most infamous gang of high sea pirates that infest the South China coast'.[15] His book, the enticingly titled *I Sailed with Chinese Pirates*, published in 1930, is presented as non-fiction, but reads more like fiction. The cover blurb on the 1991 paperback reprint claims that this 'rip-roaring tale of adventure on the high seas [is] verified by the author's own photographs'. The many images in that edition (see plate 10) certainly verify that Lilius acquired some photographs of a Chinese ship with women on board, one of whom is armed. But there is no 'proof' that this is a pirate vessel or that a woman *commanded* it.

Lilius calls Lai Choi San 'Queen of the Pirates' – a title also bestowed on Grace O'Malley and Cheng I Sao by western writers. The title suggests dynastic power over a large area but hardly seems appropriate to a woman running a seafaring business for pragmatic purposes. Lilius came across Lai Choi San when he visited Hong Kong, where he frequented a brothel run by a toothless European 'Madame Pompadour' and staffed by 'La Belle Marie', and was guided by someone he calls the 'Earless One'. Through these go-betweens he sought ways on to pirate ships to interview pirates. He was not specifically looking for a woman pirate, but was introduced to Lai Choi San as someone who might allow him aboard.

Like western stories of Cheng I Sao, Lilius' description of Lai Choi San tries to make her attractive to (male) European readers by downplaying her Chinese appearance, highlighting her beauty and focusing on her ruthlessness:

> What a woman she was! Rather slender and short, her hair jet black, with jade pins gleaming in the knot at the neck, her earrings and bracelets of the same precious apple-green stone. She was exquisitely dressed in a white satin robe fastened with green jade buttons, and green silk slippers. She wore a few plain gold rings on her left hand; her right hand was unadorned. Her face and dark eyes were intelligent – not too Chinese, although purely Mongolian, of course – and rather hard. She was probably not yet forty. Every move she made and every word she spoke told plainly that she expected to be obeyed, and as I had occasion to learn later, she *was* obeyed. What a character she must be! What a wealth of material for a novelist or journalist! Merely to write her biography would be to produce a tale of adventure such as few people dream of.[16]

An unnamed American who had sailed the Macao waters for 15 years told Lilius:

> So many stories centre about her that it is impossible to tell where truth ends and legend begins. As a matter of fact, she might be described as a female Chinese version of Robin Hood. They have much in common. Undoubtedly she is the Queen of

the Macao pirates . . . I have almost doubted her existence . . .

. . . she is said to be both ruthless and cruel. When her ships are merely doing patrol duty she does not bother to accompany them, but when she goes out on 'business' she attends to it personally. When she climbs aboard any of her ships there is an ill-wind blowing for somebody.[17]

Like Cheng I Sao and Lo Hon-cho, her power is seen as coming from a patriarchal source; she is not a pirate in her own right. Lilius says that through an interpreter Lai Choi San told him:

Her father had had four sons, but they were all dead. She had been his only daughter and being a frail and delicate child had not been expected to live. Her father used to take her with him on his trips along the coast, regarding her more as servant than a child of his own. And now she loved the sea.

The old man had started his life penniless, as a mere coolie . . . He had been a brave lad, and probably ruthless. He got into the good graces of a brigand chief, whose haunts were somewhere along the West River. This chieftain made him his Number One man, and when a few years later the old bandit 'died unexpectedly' the Number One man proclaimed himself chief. And so he took possession of a few junks and went on the warpath against the neighbouring pirates, who he drove out of their strongholds. Thus he became respected and feared among the seafaring merchantmen along the South China coast, made a goodly amount of money, and collected junks as one collects stamps or Chinese porcelain . . . When he died . . . he left Lai Choi San seven ships, the strongest and largest on the waters of the West and Pearl Rivers. She also attested that she had 'acquired' a few more and that today she actually owns twelve large armoured junks.[18]

She appears to have managed the business – an extortion racket, protecting fishing junks from harassment by other pirates – very competently. Lilius' unnamed American source, who sounds like the kind of drinking-den gossip-monger any ethical journalist would mistrust, also told him about Lai Choi San's father:

the authorities had given him some sort of refuge here in Macao, with the secret understanding that he and his gang should protect the colony's enormous fishing fleets and do general police duty on the high seas. He even obtained the title of *Inspector* from somebody in authority, and that, of course, placed him morally far above the other pirate gangs.

You may ask why I call them pirates, since their job is only to 'guard' the numerous fishing craft. However, the other gangs want the same privileges as the present 'inspectors' have, therefore they harass and plunder any ship or village they can lay hands upon . . . it is up to the protectors to undo the work of these others and to avenge any wrongs done them . . . This avenging business is where the piratical characteristics of the 'protectors' come in. There is frequent and profitable avenging going on wherever the various gangs meet. Lai Choi San is supposed to be the worst of them all.[19]

The scene conjured up is one of hundreds of junks on the seas; Lai Choi San's armoured junk raises its brown sails against the orange dawn sky, cannons camouflaged on either side; bare-chested men in wide-brimmed hats, some with scarlet 'kerchiefs round their necks, man the decks. 'On a nearby junk a Taoist priest in demon-red robes kowtowed and burned firecrackers to his special deity in order to drive away the evil spirits – all this for a few cents silver.'[20] On ship, like the heroines of most pirate stories, Lai Choi San wore sensible clothing, including trousers which appear to be of sailcloth or heavy poplin:

What a different Lai Choi San . . . Now she wore a jacket-like blouse and black trousers made of the strong glossy material commonly used by coolies for garments. Her two *amahs* were dressed in similar fashion. As soon as she stepped on board she kicked off her slippers, and for the rest of the voyage padded about barefooted.[21]

Admiringly, Lilius tells us 'she is rich, probably rich beyond comprehension. She owns a house in Macao which she occupies occasionally. But her home is in one of the villages on the West River.' Her name, he says, means 'Mountain of Wealth':

Not exactly a feminine name. Still, her career was not very feminine either. Had she no ambitions to settle down to a peaceful
life, I asked . . . she replied with a shrug. She probably could not
think of an answer. But I think I know it. The trade of buccaneering in one form or another, is actually in the blood of the
South China coast people.[22]

Lilius claims to have witnessed her ruthlessness when she was negotiating with two other pirate leaders. Her 'negotiation' in fact consisted
of capturing them – and Lilius' book includes a hilarious photograph
of two bound men lying on deck 'to prove it'. But she is also portrayed
as a good mother and a sexually available woman of some finesse. She
is said to have had many lovers, but when asked her views on 'the
eternal question of Love . . . would not answer . . . And then, for the
first time, I read sadness in her eyes.'[23]

According to Lilius, Lai Choi San had two children. Her 20-year-
old son had been engaged since early childhood to the only daughter
of the richest man in Shekki, a neighbouring town of Macao.

There would be a wonderful wedding with a dragon procession,
and all the presents would be carried on lacquered trays along the
streets of the city . . . She wanted him to be a rich rice merchant
and go to Mei Kwo, which is Chinese for America . . . She wanted
him to go there, sell rice to the foreign people and get himself a
[fantastically tall] building like those she had seen in the paper. But
she did not want him to sail up and down rivers looking for loot.[24]

Her other child, a brave five-year-old son, sailed on one of her other
vessels, smoked and was learning the trade. 'She did not want him to
sail with *her* on her ship; it was better that he should stay away from his
mother. But whenever the junks were in harbour at any of the islands
she always had him brought over.'[25] Although Lai Choi San is accompanied all the time by two women, they do not fight or take part in
sailing the ship; the term Lilius uses for them, *amahs*, usually means a
nurse or wet-nurse, which seems strange since their principal role on
ship, as he describes it, is to carry messages. Lilius does not record how
Lai Choi San's career ended, nor whether her younger son took over
the family business.

A feminist version of the classic piracy yarn might have the two women's great-grand-daughters in Beijing creating a 'woman's roots' exhibition complete with their foremothers' ship's instruments, an old libel writ against Lilius, a pair of trousers damaged in a demonstration and a sea-stained copy of *A Doll's House*. But it is far more likely that Nora never made it on to any junk, and that if she had, Lai Choi San and her *amahs* would have been far too busy extorting dues and conning journalists to attend to women's rights ashore.

Notes

1. Jiu Jin (1875–1907), cited in Jonathan D. Spence, *The Gate of Heavenly Peace: the Chinese and their revolution 1895–1980*, Faber & Faber, 1982, p. 52.
2. Kumari Jayawardena, *Feminism and Nationalism in the Third World*, Zed Press, 1986, p. 182.
3. *ibid*, p. 183, using Delia Davin, *Woman-Work, woman and the party in revolutionary China*, Oxford, 1979 and Jean Chesneaux, Marie-Claire Bergère and Françoise le Barbier, *China from the 1911 Revolution to Liberation*, The Harvester Press, 1977.
4. Jayawardena, *ibid*, pp. 183–9. For more details of women's lives in China see Margery Wolf and Roxane Witke (eds), *Women in Chinese Society*, Stanford University Press, 1975; Elizabeth Croll, *Feminism and Socialism in China*, Routledge 1979.
5. Ralph T. Ward, *Pirates in History*, York Press, 1974, p. 171.
6. *ibid*, p. 171. See also Grace Fox, *British Admirals and Chinese Pirates 1832–1869*, Kegan Paul, 1940, for full and clear details of the period.
7. Aleko E. Lilius, *I Sailed with Chinese Pirates*, The Mellifont Press, nd but c. 1930, pp. 8–14.
8. (Introduction to) Richard Glasspoole, *Mr. Glasspoole and the Chinese Pirates*, Golden Cockerel Press, 1935, p. 5.
9. *ibid*, p. 5.
10. Lilius, *op cit*, p. 14, citing a 1926 confidential report of piracy on the S.S. *Sunning*.
11. *ibid*, p. 17.
12. *ibid*, p. 16.
13. A. Hyatt Verrill, *The Real Story of the Pirates*, Appleton and Co, 1923, p. 373.
14. I am grateful to Dian Murray for drawing this to my attention.
15. Lilius, *op cit*, p. 7.

16. *ibid*, pp. 30–1.
17. *ibid*, pp. 31–2, citing an American who had sailed those waters.
18. *ibid*, pp. 44–5.
19. *ibid*, pp. 31–2, citing the same anonymous American.
20. *ibid*, p. 32.
21. *ibid*, p. 34.
22. *ibid*, pp. 45–6.
23. *ibid*, p. 48.
24. *ibid*, pp. 47–8.
25. *ibid*, pp. 47–8.

Section V:

Women and piracy today

14 *With fax and fast outboards*

Heisting watches by e-mail,
my make-up mirror records your deals.
And I
fax hotels and fake identities
while mama trawls the tideline,
discarding plastic kindling.

iracy in the late twentieth century is far removed from fictions of eighteenth-century swashbuckling. Today, piracy takes two main forms: highly organised and wholesale theft of cargoes and ships, and maritime mugging. Like all business fraud, from bugging rival computer companies to creative accounting or straightforward theft, piracy is a major irritant to capitalism. It is a cause for concern for navies and shipping agents, shipowners and traders, seafarers' unions, Interpol, marine underwriters and United Nations diplomats. The shipping industry loses an estimated $300 million a year from it.[1] 'Pirates are no laughing matter. The reality today is that pirates carry carbines instead of cutlasses. Whether women or men, they present a growing threat to the lives of seafarers and the safety of shipping in some of the world's busiest shipping lanes,' says Brian Orrell, the General Secretary of British seafaring officers' union NUMAST.[2] Piracy curtails people's freedom of movement and attacks their right to travel and work without fear of injury or death. In tones

of justified outrage – reminiscent of the feelings expressed in 1980s
'Women Reclaim the Night' protests – the 1993 British Trades Union
Congress condemned piracy and called for more effective action
against it. 'Imagine the outcry there would . . . [be] if airlines . . . [were]
attacked at the same rate or trains ransacked on an average of twice a
week!' [3]

On the whole, piracy in the late twentieth century involves different
methods, vessels, weapons and types of people than those described in
the rest of this book, though one ship was recently robbed of $40,000
in the Natunas Islands by a boat flying a skull and crossbones,[4] and
today's 'maritime mafia' work for the most part on the same beautiful
and notoriously lawless waters – the South China seas – on which
pirates have preyed for centuries. Other piracy 'risk areas' include
West African ports from Senegal to Angola; Colombian, Venezuelan
and Brazilian ports such as Rio de Janeiro and Santos; and Vietnamese
waters.[5] As the sea is such a large and unsupervised site on which many
valuable items in transit are exposed and vulnerable, so maritime crime
is an important activity in both the trade and crime worlds. Piracy has
strong connections with smuggling, protection rackets and international terrorism (including state terrorism). In some cases it could be
seen as an extension of the workplace pilfering that often takes place
when impoverished people have access to goods – whether on the scale
of ripping open wharfside pallets of chocolate bars[6] or seizing
containers of arms to sell to mercenaries.

Little hard evidence exists to prove that women are involved in 'the
squalid, sordid and shocking reality of piracy today',[7] but pointers
suggest that they are the supporters in the background, a role consistent with the patterns described in Chapter 8, where coastal women
were seen to service men, providing food and shelter, producing new
generations who might follow the same trade, and hawking the products of men's work. Research into women's roles in less-developed
countries indicates that they are unlikely to play an active part in what
is still a man's world – the world of mobility, power and big-time crime.
Men own and drive boats; women stay at home on land or are involved
below decks and behind the scenes. As office cleaners and clerical
workers, they may well discreetly photocopy and pass on the information – by fax, hand or phone – that enables men to establish the movements of the ships they terrorise and to heist the best cargoes. Piracy

experts believe that property-owning Hong Kong-based Chinese women may have a role in the secret and most audacious big business realms of piracy, especially those linked to the Triads. As members of a culture with access to power and privilege, these women succeed through their connections with powerful men and an assertiveness that comes from their social status.

Women are also, as in the days of kidnappings on the Spanish Main, survivors of pirate aggression – as passengers, crew and owners of attacked vessels. Today's victims range from the seven-month-old daughter of the master of the *Valiant Carrier* tanker, who was injured by pirates near the Indonesian coast in April 1992, to yachtswoman Lydia Tyngvald, who in 1979 was killed by pirates after firing a warning shot at them.[8] The UN High Commissioner for Refugees calculated that between 1980 and 1985 2,283 women were raped and 592 kidnapped during pirate attacks on Vietnamese boat people in the Gulf of Thailand.[9] Around 60 per cent of the boat women between the ages of 10 and 59 were estimated to have been sexually assaulted by pirates.[10]

Defining piracy

Piracy is defined variously today. The 1958 Geneva Convention's definition is one of the standard ones used:

Piracy consists of any of the following acts:
1. Any illegal acts of violence, detention, or any act of depredation, committed for private ends by the crew or passengers of a private ship or a private aircraft, and directed:
A. On the high seas, against another ship or aircraft, or against persons or property on board such ship or aircraft;
B. Against a ship, aircraft, persons or property in a place outside the jurisdiction of any State.[11]

Miles of computer paper and scores of international conferences are devoted to discussion about whether piracy should be an international concern and how best to control it. Currently at least 80 per cent of attacks take place on waters which are the responsibility of individual states and countries (boundaries range from between 12 and 200 miles offshore) with the remainder committed on the high seas, where the deterrence or capture of pirates is the responsibility of all nations.[12] Piracy today is a predictable by-product of inequalities between countries in different stages of economic growth, carried out for the most part by people from countries that are being rapidly developed and have a tradition of raiding and smuggling.[13] Pirates from poorer countries rob the travelling stores of wealthier nations, for survival. In the case of maritime mugging, highspeed motorboats have replaced the galleons topped with billowing sails; the booty is no longer spices and gold but the less glamorous and more easily disposed of goods that are seized in any land-based heist – from hairdryers to dollar bills.

In the case of the wholesale theft of ships or their cargoes, highly organised international networks with connections with corrupt judiciary and sophisticated equipment have created a business of a scale and type that make Artemisia's tactics look benign. Merchant vessels randomly boarded and seized by gangs of yo-ho-ho scallywags who add the ship to their pirate convoy. Today, such ships are hijacked in an organised way with all appearances of respectability, including uniformed officers, as part of an operation run through faxes, accommodation addresses, computers and long-distance strategic planning rather than *ad hoc* thuggery.

But the motivation of pirates in the 1990s is much the same as that of sea-robbers of earlier days: money. For people who have lived off the water for hundreds of years, the sea is a logical place to look for gains. Their income is not just a product of stolen goods: the Badjaos (sea gypsies) of the Sulu Islands may get some of their livelihood from smuggling, but they also collect sea cucumbers to sell to Chinese epicures. Others work as underwater farmers growing agar-agar seaweed, extracts of which are used by westerners 'in everything from cosmetics to ice-cream'.[14] Hard-pressed Chinese fishing people, whose local waters supply vegetables, fish and saleable goods, recently demanded a ransom for the damage done to sea kale by a Russian ship sheltering from a storm in their area.[15]

The more organic kind of piracy, undertaken by unemployed people in impoverished coastal communities whose feet seldom touch pavements, is perhaps understandable in a world of rocketing prices, miserly incomes, media pressure to consume and little integrity or prospect of equality,[16] especially when piracy and the violence that accompanies it as an integral part of local culture. In some cases pirates are outlawed by regimes wishing to disown crime and distance themselves from accusations of corruption; other pirates have close connections with their countries' ruling structure and a far from *picaresque* reputation. Increasing use of the sea for operations such as oil-extraction has brought increased opportunities for complex strategies such as attacks on installations and eco-terrorism.

Finding out about modern-day piracy

The lack of evidence about women's involvement in piracy in all the periods covered in this book is even more acute when it comes to female pirates operating today. The gate keepers, the people who know about piracy, are men. And men often do not notice women, or else they discount the roles that women have, as 'not really' piracy. At first this had the effect of making me, as a feminist historian, more tenacious, but as I repeatedly drew blanks in my search for late-twentieth-century female pirates I began to wonder if in fact there are none, and my research into modern piracy would have to be about discovering and understanding why women are excluded. As part of my research I travelled to South-East Asia, the area where most piracy is carried out. In communities where seafaring is still a major part of everyday life, I found it easier to understand how piracy takes place and how it is viewed.

In the tiny Indonesian paradise island of Penyengat, poet R. M. Yamin, whose grandfather was headman, showed me a cluster of wooden stilt houses lapped by the Sulu sea. This lush and car-less place is the former capital of the Riau kingdom. Yamin told me a family tale of how in the 1940s five or six fishing families turned to piracy because of diminishing catches. This made the others miserable, and the pirates were asked to stop, but were not reported to the authorities. In Indonesia, 'it is accepted by most people that there will be piracy, because corruption is a way of life here. Corruption enables piracy to continue without restriction – except perhaps the pressure to give bigger kickbacks to the authorities.'[17]

It is also easy to see why women are not pirates; they are largely excluded from power and mobility. Throughout South-East Asia, it is mainly men who drive – especially public vehicles such as buses, taxis and jeepneys. In some countries, women riding pillion on mopeds sit side-saddle. On water, beneath the burning sun, women paddle old canoes on small rivers, selling food from jetty to jetty for tiny sums, while men own sea-going motorboats hired by tourists requiring fast access to distant sites and earn several hundred times the money a woman might earn from domestic sales of starfruit and tamarind, rice and coconut.

My research involved conversations with people from Singapore to the Philippines – on oceans, at ultra-modern container terminals, in shipping offices, on ancient and busy docksides and by the sides of busy but barely patrolled channels. Yachties in cocktail bars told stories of how their Caribbean holidays were marred by the threat of drug-trafficking pirates who yacht-jack at gunpoint. Progressives attacked pirates as entrepreneurs seeking individual and violent solutions to structural and systematic problems of inequality that require well-planned collective international solutions. Women's Studies lecturers toyed with the thrilling idea that women might be involved in this stereotype-defying work but expressed reservations about its lethal practice. The result of these discussions was the acquisition of many stories about the limited role women may play in modern-day piracy together with a lot of intelligent hypotheses. But no one could be definite about what is anyway a fairly unknown world, piracy. To penetrate the field would require years of subterfuge, as well as bribes for informants and bodyguards for interviewers and even a permanent safe haven for interviewees.

It may be that there are no significant present-day women pirates. Jan Euden, a director researching modern piracy in South-East Asia for a television documentary series, points out that if television crews who spend several months and thousands of dollars in pirate locations do not unearth any of these media desirables, then perhaps there are none.[18] When Captain Charles Johnson was looking for information about Ann Bonny and Mary Read in the eighteenth century, he used handwritten parchment letters from merchants that may have taken years to cross oceans. Today's researchers have international faxes and e-mail but the same problem: reports come from the people who are attempting to stamp out piracy or from its victims, rather than from the pirates themselves.

Why would a pirate talk about piracy? To get money and perhaps out of vanity or for the thrill. The risk of arrest and possibly trial and execution means the reward would have to be worth it. Western television crews in search of rent-a-quote pirates can be a rich bonus in a desperately impoverished environment. According to rumours in Manila, interviews with pirates cost anything from $500 upwards. Jan Euden explains:

> In certain parts of the world – particularly the Philippines – you can be put in touch with people who might be called pirate-brokers. Some are motivated by a sympathy with nationalistic groups who use piracy as a fund-raising resource, but there are others who have become almost pirate junkies, the way some war correspondents got high on the Vietnam War.
>
> Some people working for the western media think they can phone up and get a pirate on demand. But in reality, finding a pirate is a complicated and time-consuming process which involves going to remote places, paying money for information and access, and for protection when you get there. Getting hold of anyone to do anything in the Philippines is difficult, if only because of telecommunications problems and the massive power cuts that frequently bring life to a standstill. When I did finally make contact with someone whom I had been told could lead me to pirates, we met in a shady bar in the red-light district of Manila, with a sign advising patrons to leave their guns at the door. I waited rather nervously for this stranger; I didn't even know what he would look like, but he assured me I'd know him when he arrived, and I did. Over rather a lot of beers, we discussed what I wanted and what he thought he could provide. The deal was some expenses up front, no guarantee of results and no price to be fixed until the 'research' had been done. He promised to keep in touch and the waiting began. Eventually there were some results and negotiations began on a price.[19]

One *South China Morning Post* journalist was told in his meeting with 'Rene's' gang: 'The ground rules are no real names and no explicit photographs. Under no circumstance should their story appear in the Philippines press.'[20]

But how can a modern researcher know that the person they are talking to really is a pirate, rather than someone with plausible accessories and a convincing interpreter? In making her decision Jan Euden took into account the danger of kidnap and loss of expensive camera equipment as well as the likelihood of inauthenticity.

> After a long and heavy discussion with our pirate-broker and his sidekick, the film crew and I debated the risks. It had to be a joint decision, especially as I'd been told that – as a woman – I couldn't go. So I could hardly expect them to go where I couldn't. We were uncertain as to what protection we could really get, and in the end decided against taking the risk. We also had doubts about whether we would be meeting genuine pirates, since a balaclava and a gun are two of the easiest props to acquire in the Philippines.[21]

Feminist researchers are less likely than male television crews to have the resources or desire to spend years in the tough criminal world of pirates in search of what might be slender information. In Northern Luzon, Philippines, a local woman activist helps feminist researchers to link up with local women – for instance to study methods of abortion, which is illegal. She knew of many women smugglers in the area, who bring PX goods in and said, 'You could certainly meet them. But you'd really need to be here for at least six months, so that they could get to know you and see if they could trust you.'[22] Pirates would be similarly cautious.

Most information on modern piracy comes from the government and semi-official agencies charged with stopping maritime crime – whether illegal dumping of toxic waste, fraud, piracy, or the terrorist seizure of whole ships (as with the *Achille Lauro* in 1985). Coastguards, police, navies, commercial organisations and shipowners use the information collected and disseminated by the International Maritime Bureau (IMB). Based in Barking, East London, with a regional office in Kuala Lumpur, the IMB monitors reported piracy worldwide. Set up in 1981, it is part of the International Chamber of Commerce, an indication of how important the containment and eradication of piracy is to the flourishing of capitalism.

But despite modern communications networks and computer systems, information about late-twentieth-century piracy is slight and often unreliable. Collation of evidence is not systematic, partly because it is 'victim driven'. Joanne Long, who used to work for the IMB in Kuala Lumpur, believes that only two out of every three incidents are reported.[23] Sometimes this is because of inconvenience and because victims do not expect effective action to be taken; in other cases shipowners may keep quiet about attacks for fear of increasing their insurance premiums. 'If you report an incident, the ship has to stay in port and it costs £20,000 a day for that ship to be kept in. Therefore they [ships' masters'] just don't report them.'[24] Crew might have to be flown back to give court evidence; the captain's reputation might be damaged. Others say nothing because they have been threatened or paid to keep their mouths shut or because reporting seems irrelevant: nothing will be done.

Observers are waiting to see whether a new system to enable easier reporting will have any effect. Ships with computer terminals can now enter details of a piracy attack into ASAM (Anti-Shipping Alert Messenger) by satellite or high-frequency radio. This links into the DMA (Defense Mapping Agency) file that records incidents of piracy, terrorism and other violence at sea.[25]

How much piracy is there?

In late 1993 piracy is in a quiet phase, perhaps as a result of a blitz of publicity and a number of high-profile preventative measures. The IMB identifies four main conditions as necessary for piracy: 'need or greed; target opportunities; marine capability; lack of effective law enforcement. The first three conditions still exist, but at the moment the fourth does not.'[26] The volatile cocktail is temporarily unmixed. In 1992, 115 pirate attacks were reported worldwide. South-East Asia accounted for all the 107 cases recorded in 1991 and 73 of the 115 reported in 1992. By contrast, on the West Africa Coast in 1981 there were 12 reported attacks in a single day. In the Singapore area, particularly in the Singapore Straits, the narrow waterway that links the Malacca Straits and the South China Sea, 150 attacks were made between 1980 and 1984. Hong Kong 'official documents say the incidents in the area have increased while pirate attacks on the previously badly-infested Malacca Straits between Malaysia and Indonesia have dropped dramatically after the two countries agreed to cooperate on anti-piracy patrols' in 1992.[27]

Like bandits of old, operating on profitably busy highways, so too do seaborne highway robbers utter their Dick Turpin equivalent of 'Stand and deliver' at the bottlenecks in the world's most active seaways. Singapore is the second-busiest port in the world, with Hong Kong and Rotterdam first. The 965-kilometre-long Singapore Straits are the main route from the eastern hemisphere to the west and the busiest seaways in the world, after the Panama and Suez canals. The only way to avoid this choke point is to lose four or five costly days sailing south of Sumatra.

The Singapore Straits are an increasingly important link between Japan, the effective 'capital' of a developing worldwide business empire, and the Middle East oil fields,[28] with some 200 ships a day passing through a channel less than a mile wide. They have to go very slowly (between 10 and 12 sea miles per hour) to avoid reefs and shoals, and since loaded tankers have low freeboards (the 10- to 15-foot distance between deck and waves) and small crews, they are as easily targeted as a lone pedlar on a lame pony rounding a mountain pass. The area, especially around the Phillip Channel (the east-bound channel of the Singapore Straits), is full of small islets and mangrove swamps where fast boats can easily lurk. Because the straits belong not only to Singapore but are also under the jurisdiction of Malaysia and Indonesia, catching pirates is a matter for international diplomacy. East of Singapore, nests of pirates are known to exist in the Natunas Islands and the Chinese-contested Spratly Island in the South China sea; in the Sulu Sea between Borneo and the Philippines; and in the Gulf of Thailand, between Cambodia and Thailand.[29] Piracy around the southern-most island in the Philippines, Mindanao, and the Sulu archipelago is connected with Muslim separatism.

Maritime mugging

I have found only one recent account of women as maritime muggers: on 4 October 1983 a Panamanian-registered ship, the *Amazona*, was raided at Bonny, West Africa at 4.30 a.m. by women pirates who plundered the laundry.[30] No further details are available, but given that a ship's laundry usually contains only one or two sturdy automatic washing machines, the most easily removed goods would have been items such as shirts and sheets, an iron, detergent and perhaps a washing basket – an indication of women's lack of confidence and means of profitably disposing of more valuable booty.

In 1974 a woman was involved in taking over a ketch, the *Seawind*, in the Pacific. The owners, Mr and Mrs Graham, a retired couple from Fort Lauderdale, Florida, failed to make pre-arranged radio contact with a ham in Hawaii. A search was mounted and the coastguard and FBI discovered a yacht that answered to the *Seawind*'s description and tried to board her. As they did so, convicted drug-runner Stephanie Sterns rowed away and was caught off Honolulu. Her companion, Buck Duane Walker, an escaped federal prisoner, bank-robber and drug-trafficker, tried to swim ashore. Both were convicted of grand theft, and Walker of murder too. After Mrs Graham's bones had been washed ashore, Walker 'boasted that he had shot the couple after making Mr Graham walk the plank.'[31]

Today, different styles of pirate raids take place in different areas. Reports received by the IMB indicate that pirates most commonly attack between 10 p.m. and 6 a.m. (the time when most women with children are at home babysitting, not out at sea). The booty is seized at sea, either when the ship is at anchor – usually waiting to unload in the docks – or when it is under way. Pirates try not to alert the whole crew: generally only four or five members of a crew of between 15 and 20 might be awake. There are no scenic sword-battles: a more typical scenario would be of one or two men creeping on to a ship unnoticed, slugging the captain or knifing the crew member who holds the safe keys, then disembarking within ten minutes with the petty-cash box and videocassette recorder. 'I've seen so many reports that include stealing the chief engineer's gold chain from round his neck,' says Ken Luck of the IMB.[32]

Often a gang of young people speed up to a vessel under way, climb aboard up the hawsepipe or using nylon rope and grapnels, steal whatever is easily available – for instance from open containers on deck – and then vanish. If a ship is very low in the water, they may push themselves aboard using bamboo poles. Ships are not supposed to keep their deck lights on when under way in case other ships assume they are at anchor, so a ship's deck can be a dark place unless safety-conscious owners have fitted wide-beam floodlights to the stern. Often crews of big vessels do not realise what has happened until minutes or hours later. At other times the intruders rape, maim and kill. Only 2 per cent of pirate attacks are successfully repelled.

Target ships range from inadequately guarded luxury yachts moored in the moonlight of Lesser Antilles coves to fishing skiffs, from ferries to huge tankers struggling past the Indonesian mangrove swamps in the Phillip Channel. They are caught unawares because low-profile pirate craft often cannot be picked up on the target ship's radar unless it has yacht radar fitted too. Not all crews are trained in anti-attack techniques, including surveillance, paying attention to radar blind spots, response and alarm procedures.

Maritime muggers today are usually tiny groups of between three and eight men in their 20s or 30s in small fast boats, often rigid inflatables with Yamaha motors. They can travel at up to 40 knots, whereas a merchant ship might do 18 knots and the converted Second World War lighthouse-tenders used by some Philippines coastguards cannot do as much as 10.[33] West African pirates have used canoes made of a single hollowed-out treetrunk, sailed by one person with nets, ostensibly fishing, while in the Bahamas 16-foot skiffs have been reported. The sophistication of some boats is seen as proof that the Indonesian military are involved. 'Look, how else would people in a poor country get access to a fast boat? If you buy an outboard motor here, then everyone knows about it. And we're talking about 100-horsepower motors here, huge ones. Who is going to get access to that, other than men in the armed forces?' says a Singapore-based informant.[34]

The most likely route by which a woman could gain access to a life of piracy would be through working within a pirate gang. When the Blackbeard of modern piracy, Emile Changco, and his gang were arrested in 1993, a woman, Susan Frani, who may also have been a pirate, was with them.[35] A maritime mugging is a high-tension situation in which each member of the small team has to be useful. Some male pirates pick up their skills from fathers and brothers; others learn from vocational training from which women are culturally excluded (Changco was an outstanding student at nautical college, and gained his ocean-going master's certificate at the early age of 29).[36] If women are barred from learning seafaring, knifing, shooting and thieving skills, from being part of the armed forces, how could they participate in pirate raids?

In Muslim Mindanao, a few women have been known to fight on land alongside men in the Moro Liberation Front. They have been pictured in national newspapers taking part in violent outdoor activities – in a society where transport is by boat and guns are as common as watches – wearing bandanas and machine guns, not veils. This has led some South-East Asian political observers to speculate that if women can be guerrillas in the rain forests and coconut groves, perhaps they can also be fighters at sea. They believe the most likely role for such women would be as couriers carrying information, food and arms. (women in the Huk Guerrilla movement did this kind of work 40 years earlier though working for revolutionary not private ends).

But Mazlan Abdul-Samad the regional manager of the IMB office in Kuala Lumpur and a slightly built man with a friendly persona points out:

> In South-East Asia, it is unlikely that women become pirates. This is because of the culture. Piracy is a man's game. Based on the reports we have had, there has never been any narration at all about women being in the party or boarding the ships. It is unlikely that women would be pirates because of their physique which means they are not likely to be able to project the necessary impression, to instil fear. For example, I may have a gun but I may not be able to instil fear into the crew of the ship on board because I may not look like a fearless pirate.[37]

Pirates' weapons include AK47 automatic rifles, bottles, bolt-cutters for removing padlocks, staves, sharpened screwdrivers, arrows dipped in excretia or poison, jemmies and revolvers,[38] though the most common instruments of terror are speed and intimidating body language. Some use local materials such as jungle bolos, two-foot-long machetes, home-made bombs or Double Happiness Chinese crackers. In Jurong, Singapore, a group tied up their victims' hands with raffia.[39] One Philippines pirate 'conceded some of their arsenal was taken from supplies at the Clark Air Base in Angeles City'[40] while there is also the possibility of:

> much collusion between terrorist groups and indeed, perhaps, Government troops and Government armies in certain parts of the world where they do not get paid properly by their own authorities. They are practising a bit of free enterprise with weapons probably supplied by this country [Britain] on crews sailing on ships out to their part of their world.[41]

Far from being dressed in picturesque brocade jackets and feathered tricorn hats, male pirates today are reported as wearing anything from loincloths to ragged jogging suits, black bandanas, US Army surplus combat uniforms, and trainers or plastic flip-flops. Pirates who robbed the Danish *Arktis Sun* in the Persian Gulf in February 1990 wore black robes and red Arab scarves.[42] Emile Changco was pictured (in prison) wearing mirrored sunglasses, new jeans and a neatly pressed white T-shirt. He leaned on an inlaid malacaca cane which he said he used because he was dying of cancer.[43]

Some of the items reported stolen reveal the extent of pirates' poverty and desperation: Ovaltine, clothes, the side window of a Bedford lorry, a pocket full of ship's cutlery, a few fathoms of polypropylene rope. Others choose resaleable goods such as drugs, electrical ware, cigarettes, pharmaceuticals, food, computers or gas lighters. Reports of losses range from cocoa butter in the Canary Islands and Chloroquine tablets in Monrovia to cement in Apapa and handbags in Lome.[44] Some of the stolen goods are taken from the ship as travelling warehouse, but others are taken from the ship as home, and as small floating office. Pirates often steal the crew's personal property – videotapes and credit cards, televisions and binoculars. The best booty is cash: heists have been as high as $1,000, twice the average annual income of a waged Indonesian. Many pirates know that captains keep the safe keys in desk drawers or on the bookshelf (often behind the dictionary, or in one case under an old radio). The captain's cabin can also yield malt whisky, his Seiko watch and wallet.[45]

Often a pirate attack is the result of a tip-off by a coastguard contact or of visits by contract cleaners. One port operator claims, 'They not only know the whereabouts of the ship's safe. They know its contents and even its combination. That suggests this is where women working in offices could have had a hand.'[46] Some plunderers have inside information from the cargo manifests, which list the goods and their value; in one case, pirates climbed aboard saying 'We've come for the perfume.'[47] If ships are known to be carrying Filipino crew, then the odds are that they will have thousands of US dollars on board to pay the wages in cash. Sometimes pirates bribe the increasingly common ship's security guards as part of widespread corruption networks.

Women's involvement may be more common in passing on information and hawking, including smuggling.[48] In societies overseen by men, women tend to go unnoticed by official surveillance and are seldom expected to be conveyors of contraband or intelligence reports. A former port manager, looking out over Manila Harbour, pointed out:

> The only women a coastguard pirate patrol sees on water today are prostitutes, not pirates. They get ferried out to the bigger ships waiting to come into the docks to load or unload. The people on the radio in port say 'do you want some fun?' And fun means sex. So they send the women out. And they get a cut of the women's profits. The man who ferries the women out is probably their pimp, so he is in on it anyway. The women stand up in the boat to be looked at and the sailors lean over the rails of their ship and point to the ones they want. All very humilitating. The only connection with piracy is possibly that the women notice whether there is anything worth stealing, say from the man they are with, and pass that information on. Then pirates might come aboard later and steal the seaman's gold watch and videos or whatever. The women would get a small percentage of that, because they are part of that underworld network.[49]

Women in the sex industry may well have pirate customers too, as well as tourists and US servicemen. Others may willingly or unwillingly turn a blind eye to what their menfolk get up to. 'Rene', an urban pirate from Manila and 33-year-old father of three, tells his wife that the money he gives her is 'borrowed from friends'.[50] In more rural areas, wives, mothers and daughters may nurture pirate families. As in the days of old, some might be in shacks on beaches, near the sight of operation. The more prosperous would be clustered around a battery-operated colour television in a concrete bungalow further away from the high water mark. Work would include cooking for pirates preparing to raid – using calor-gas stoves on bigger ships or driftwood fires on shores. It would mean looking after pirates when they got home – from washing their fake Levi 501s to soothing their bruises with Savlon or Tiger Balm.

In a few exceptional cases, piracy is a way of life for women. Frances Guillain, a French-Tahitian mother who spends much of her time sailing the South China seas with her five children, was one day invited to dock in a small cove. The family who lived here, including the mother, Linda, gave Frances and her family a wonderful evening of food and dancing. It was only when they got up to leave that they realized this gathering was of a family of notorious pirates who terrorised the Philippines coast, robbing and murdering. 'So it seems piracy still survives as a family trade. Linda is both pirate and mother. By day she ambushes ships and perhaps even makes use of their machine gun, and by night she cooks her children rice and fish,' conclude German writers on women's piracy, Ulrike Klausmann and Marion Meinzerin.[51] This last sentence may be a little fanciful, since piracy is usually conducted at night, but it does indicate the knowledgeable and sometimes active role women in coastal communities may play, whether their business is piracy or fishing.

More sophisticated piracy

The IMB has found that the high-level and sophisticated pirates operating in the Philippines, who carry out meticulously planned and executed large-scale heists, are mainly overseas Chinese from Hong Kong, Taiwan, Singapore, Malaysia and Indonesia. Such pirates often have a background in trade and business, can transfer millions of dollars in cash in a matter of hours, are highly knowledgeable about the movements of shipping and law-enforcement patrols and also run gambling and prostitution operations.[52] They are reputed to design their heists from luxurious suites in distant five-star hotels. The IMB head told a recent press conference "'Throughout the Far East, well-organized gangs are stealing whole cargoes and whole ships" . . . Some of the stolen ships . . . have been used to take immigrants to the US at $15,000-$25,000 a head.'[53] Between 1990 and 1992, 21 ships were stolen to order by criminal gangs.

Increasing numbers of crime syndicates, especially in parts of West Africa, carry out shrewdly and strategically planned operations. Some specialise in wholesale theft of cargoes,

> ranging from livestock feed to motorcycles [which] have been sold and the ships re-registered, or sold or operated clandestinely. Some of these cases appear to be simply one part of a complicated customs and insurance fraud, perhaps involving organized crime.[54]

Other syndicates run phantom ships with fake names. They hear about shipping agents who want some cargo transported, arrange to ship it, load it up on a vessel owned by a non-existent company which they use as a cover, then disappear. The ship is repainted, renamed, and the cargo sold. In the case of the Cyprus-flagged *Martha*, pirates even brought stencils with them to paint a new ship's name on the funnel once out at sea.[55]

Women with power in South-East Asian society usually belong to the wealthy elite from which Cory Aquino and Imelda Marcos came. They are often of ancient Chinese stock. If women pirates exist, researchers believe that they might pirate on a high level, especially in Hong Kong, where the triads are based and where it is not so unusual for wealthy women to own ships.

Journalist Stephen Vine, writing about modern piracy in the magazine *GQ*, found a woman co-owner of a ship, Doris Ho, who tried to beat the pirates. Several years ago she took part in an expensive operation to get back her hijacked ship, the *Isla Luzon*. It vanished and its $5 million cargo turned up months later in Jakarta, Indonesia's tough capital. A year later the ship itself reappeared in the South Korean port of Pusan. It took a further six months' battle to get it back from its new 'owners' Asia Maritime Express, a company registered at a non-existent address in the Philippines. Ho reports that she 'helped convene a meeting with fellow shipowners to discuss ways of combating piracy . . . Coastguard officials . . . told the shipping magnates that while they had some 8,000 men at their disposal, that amounted to only one man for every island in the Philippines. "We came up with a blank" Ho ruefully recalls.'[56]

These modern stories suggest that the women now involved in piracy are still of two sorts, as they were of old. On the one hand, there are those working-class women whose labour – paid or unpaid – brings them into proximity with pirates, be it at remote tropical jetties or in high-tech harbour offices. Because most piracy takes place in a part of the world where machismo – and Catholicism – are part of the culture, so these women's role is a quiet, secondary one. As shipping-agency VDU operators and sex-industry workers, they inform and assist seaborne thieves in their heists; as mothers and partners, they succour men when they come home to have their clothes washed and their wounds salved. Susan Frani might be compared to Ann Bonny or Maria Cobham, in that she may have been the sole woman in a pirate gang, or there by virtue of her sexual attachment to the leader. On the other hand, the wealthy women whose families take part in high-level business fraud have the same power to wield, and the same habit of commanding and daring, as Artemisia, Granuaile and the idea of Alfhild.

The trade may have lost its romance for outsiders today, but for women in less-developed countries who still have limited access to opportunities for gain, and still rely on payment for sexual services as their main route to riches, theft on sea or land offers useful possibilities.

Notes

1. P. G. McEwan of NUMAST, the National Union of Marine, Aviation and Shipping Transport Officers, supporting a motion calling for action on piracy, *TUC Handbook 1994*, TUC, 1994, p. 408.
2. Quote given by telephone, 8 February 1994.
3. McEwan, *op cit*, pp. 408–9.
4. Eric Ellen (ed), *Piracy at Sea*, ICC Publishing SA/International Maritime

Bureau, 1989, Appendix 1, p. 247. *The Ikan Mas*, a Malaysian-flagged vessel, was attacked in January 1982 and pirates stole $40,000 in cash and property.

5. Department of Transport Merchant Shipping notice M1517 (1993).
6. Roger Villar, *Piracy Today*, Conway Maritime Press, 1985, p. 94.
7. McEwan, *op cit*, p. 408.
8. I. R. Hyslop, 'Contemporary Piracy' in *Piracy at Sea, op cit*, p. 33. Lydia Tyngvald was sailing on the *Artemis de de Pythgas* in 1979 when she was shot through the head.
9. P. W. Birnie, 'Piracy Past Present and Future' in *Piracy at Sea, ibid*, p. 143.
10. Estimates quoted by Hyslop in *Piracy at Sea, ibid*, p. 35.
11. *ibid*, Appendix 14, p. 312.
12. For discussions on this issue see B. Harlow, 'Rethinking Piracy Control in a Modern Maritime Context' in *Piracy at Sea, op cit*, p. 201; Birnie, *op cit*; and McEwan, *op cit*, p. 408.
13. See Jon Vagg, 'Rough Seas: contemporary piracy in South-East Asia', paper to the International Congress of Asian and North African Studies, Hong Kong, 1993; and 'Piracy: South-East Asia in the 1990s', paper to the British Criminology Conference, July 1993.
14. Nicholas Woodsworth, 'A life of piracy and pillage on the ocean wave', *Financial Times*, 6 February 1994.
15. The *Sibirskiy 2114* was a chartered vessel carrying motorbikes. Moscow Radio, 2 June 1993.
16. See Vagg, 'Rough Seas', *op cit*.
17. Interview with anonymous Singapore maritime expert, December 1993.
18. Interview with Jan Euden, November 1993.
19. *ibid*.
20. 'I don't like the job but I need to feed my family', *South China Morning Post*, 2 May 1993.
21. Euden, *op cit*.
22. Interview with anonymous woman informant, Manila, January 1994.
23. Stephen Vine, 'Troubled Waters', *GQ*, April 1993.
24. McEwan, *op cit*, p. 408.
25. Frank Pentil, 'The MARAD View of Maritime Piracy' in *Piracy at Sea, op cit*, p. 208.
26. Telephone conversation with Ken Luck of the IMB, October 1993.
27. Yojana Sharma, 'Hong Kong: Anger over failure to report Chinese piracy', *Inter Press Service*, 27 May 1992.
28. See 'Plan to make vessel reporting mandatory in the Malacca Strait', agency article by Agence France Presse, 2 July 1993.
29. Villar, *op cit*, p. 31.
30. *Piracy at Sea, op cit*, Appendix 1, p. 257.
31. Samuel P. Menefee, 'The US and Post-War Piracy' in *Piracy at Sea, op cit*, p. 68.

32. Conversation with Ken Luck at IMB, October 1993.
33. Malcolm Macalister Hall, 'Pirates back in bloody business', *Telegraph Magazine*, 24 April 1993.
34. Information from anonymous informant, December 1993. See also Vagg, 'Piracy: South East Asia in the 1990s', *op cit*, for discussion of the Indonesian military's suspected involvement.
35. Dea Birkett, 'A wife on the ocean wave', *Guardian*, 7 May 1992.
36. Macalister Hall, *op cit*.
37. Interview by JS, October 1993.
38. Hyslop, *op cit*, p. 9 and Vagg, 'Rough Seas', *op cit*, p. 6.
39. Villar, *op cit*, p. 27.
40. 'I don't like the job but I need to feed my family', *op cit*.
41. P. E. McGregor of NUMAST, *op cit*, p. 409.
42. Reuter feature on Dutch pirates, 6 December 1992.
43. Macalister Hall, *op cit*.
44. Villar, *op cit*, p. 16, and *Piracy at Sea*, *op cit*, p. 264.
45. Interviews with maritime experts including IMB, Singapore and New Zealand officials, November 1993–January 1994.
46. *ibid*.
47. Reuter feature on pirates, *op cit*.
48. Describing a voyage on the *Lady Ruth* tramp, in the Sulu seas: 'The pair of middle-aged women sleeping to one side of me looked like two dears on a shopping spree and, in a way, they were. They were professional smugglers, they proudly told me. They were going to Sitangkai, the last port in the Sulu Chain; from there it was just a four-hour ride by speed-boat to Sabah, in Borneo, where they would buy gold to bring back and sell. Were they not afraid of being caught, I asked. "Not at all," one smiled comfortingly. "Naval and customs patrols are all paid off." What about pirates? "Yes, they *are* a little more trouble" said the other. It was as if we were discussing nothing more sinister than avoiding bores at cocktail parties. "You just have to choose a boat fast enough to out-run them."' Woodsworth, *op cit*.
49. Interview with anonymous man (TP), Manila, January 1994.
50. 'I don't like the job but I need to feed my family', *op cit*.
51. Ulrike Klausmann and Marion Meinzerin, *Piratinnen*, Verlag Frauenoffensive, Munich 1991, translated for this book by Karen Holden.
52. Ray Moseley, '90s pirates take aim at Pacific ships', *Chicago Tribune*, 3 October 1992.
53. *ibid*, citing Eric Ellen of the IMB and ICC-IMB Special Report, *Organised Maritime Crime in the Far East*, p. 19.
54. Vagg, 'Rough Seas', *op cit*.
55. Reuter feature on Dutch pirates, *op cit*.
56. Vine, *op cit*.

Endnote

Today's eyes on their old breeches

In late-twentieth-century Britain, those interested in women reclaiming power have increasingly seen women pirates as heroic, strong, free, often lesbian figures. What images have enabled us to hold this view and what tales of tough women on ships are we creating ourselves to celebrate our pirate foremothers?

In 1927, the year before all British women won the right to vote, Fryniwyd Tennyson Jesse published what may be the first novel about piracy by a woman: *Moonraker*. Although the narrator is male, the most startling figure is Captain Lovel, a seafarer of 20 years standing. Love of a man leads Sophy Lovel to reveal her sex, exposing her bosom 'white as foam, small and delicate as that of a young girl' to prove her well-disguised feminity. The crew mutinies not so much because of the discovery that their beloved captain is a woman as because of her new soft-heartedness. 'One of them called out: "Us don't want to get rid of 'ee, Cap'n, if you'd be as you used, and bring us to good loot. It's your packet o' sissies us can't abide. Get rid of them and we'll turn to again."' Sophy curses them to the ground but finally blows up the ship (and herself with it), apparently unable to deal with the life that faces her – a woman with a man but no ship. The book was reissued in the 1980s by feminist publishing house Virago with a young woman who looks like a pirate on the cover rather than an image of the main (male) narrator.[1]

Throughout the 1930s, 1940s and 1950s, Arthur Ransome's *Swallows and Amazons* novels offered young women the rare opportunity to see themselves as sailors capable of handling their own boats. Nancy and Peggy Blackett, who flew the Jolly Roger over their 14-foot dinghy, gave generations of progressively educated girls a role model. Ransome also published a novel about a Chinese woman pirate, *Missee Lee* (1941).[2] Lee, educated at Newnham College, Cambridge, was seen as 'at once a funny, sinister, touching and by the end, curiously impressive figure . . . [with] many comic contradictions' ('She gripped her Horace as if the book were a pistol holster and she were about to pull a pistol from it.'[3] Ransome's unpublished notes show her writing in Chinese characters beneath a photograph of her hockey team 'Breakers of hearts and shins'[4] betraying a pleasure in hurting men romantically and in playing a fast game aggressively, and an equation of the two. In the end, Missee Lee obeys the call of Confucious not Horace, for her father's sake. But 'Miss Lee's attitude of cheerful disdain towards these men [whose hearts her hockey team broke] closely resembles that of Madame Sun to the leaders of the Kuomintang, writes Ransome's biographer, and indeed Madame Sun Yat Sen was the model for her character.[5]

Playwright Steve Gooch, in the programme notes for his play *The Women Pirates: Ann Bonney and Mary Read*, performed by the Royal Shakespeare Company in 1978, quotes a contemporary lesbian view of the two pirate heroines, contending that Ann was certain to have known Mary's sex before she made advances to her.[6] Knowledge of the two female pirates was so well-established by this point that Ann Bonny's life history appeared in a tiny biographical booklet for children which was distributed inside Shredded Wheat packets. This is how Gooch was inspired to write his play.[7] But male reviewers' responses suggest that whatever the author's feminist intention, the spectacle of wild dominating women aroused a combination of fear and sexual interest. The *Guardian*'s Michael Billington complained that Gooch turned 'the two heroines into eighteenth century women's libbers.'[8]

Today, women pirates have been reclaimed by feminists, lesbians, bisexuals and women interested in sado masochism; the spotlight is fixed on their sexual activities. In Joanna Russ' *The Adventures of Alyx*, the dashing Alyx fancies Blackbeard's damp black beard and uses him as a lover, though she thinks him a bit limited intellectually.[9] And Erica Jong's passionate protagonist in *Fanny* has a bisexual orgy on a ship visited by Ann Bonny. To her great joy, Fanny found:

> Annie was the Alpha and Omega of our pleasure . . . did she
> devour me! O what a clever Tongue our Annie had! Words she
> fumbl'd with but Flesh flow'd for her . . . the key of her tongue
> unlockt places in my lock of Love that had ne're been unlockt
> before! O, O, O, I blush to think how Annie quite undid me . . . It
> almost seem'd Annie had workt in a brothel breaking young
> Country wenches to the Trade, for she so excited my blood with
> her expert touch.[10]

In the 1977 West German lesbian cult film *Madame X, an absolute ruler*,
made by Ulrike Ottinger, tigress/captain Madame X (Tabea
Blumenschein) sends out a telegram inviting women to give up their
safe, boring existences. '*Chinese Orlando* – stop – to all women – stop –
offer world – stop – full of gold – love – stop – adventure at sea – stop –
call *Chinese Orlando* – stop!'[11] They come and the ship sails off with
Madame X at the prow controlling with her 'castrated' arm in a huge
black leather studded glove (see plate 14). Within the film, a letter
from Karla Freud Goldman describes the shipboard dynamics: 'habits
of passivity and dependence in their [the crew's] character structure
made them docile tools in the hands of Madame X, a charismatic
personality consumed with narcissism and whose lust for power grew
with the quasi-masochistic submission of women beyond all bounds.'[12]
This version of piracy suggests it is an activity in which women can
explore other kinds of power. A different lesbian interpretation of
pirate life is given in Fiona Cooper's novel *The Empress of the Seven
Oceans*, in which a group of seventeeth-century women cast off their
hard lives ashore and set sail for the southern seas where they swash-
buckle, lead a hedonistic lesbian life and commit a plethora of vengeful
acts against witchfinders and dockside scum. There is little critique of
violence here and much celebration of women's wonderfulness.[13]

In Diana Norman's *The Pirate Queen*, one of a new breed of women-
authored (heterosexual) historical romances with indomitable semi-
feminist heroines, Granuaile's long-lost pickpocket granddaughter
Barbary Clampett holds the key to her family's treasure.[14] And as
part of a feminist-inspired trend of providing strong female characters
in children's literature, from proud Maid Marions to stroppy

Cinderellas, Central TV in 1991 screened a six-part series called *Tales from the Poop Deck*. Husband-and-wife screenwriters Lenny Barker and Vicki Stepney's central character is described as the 'most ruthless scoundrel of all, a fearsome tyrant whose name strikes dread in the stoutest heart.'[15] The female Captain Blackheart is never beaten psychologically or physically but seems to be heading for normalcy when she marries an idiotic English naval officer. Upending gender stereotypes, the crew of vicious (male) rascals become misty-eyed as she kisses her dolt, and the huge heavyweight mate designs apricot-coloured frocks for the (pirate) bridesmaids. However, unable to bear the prospect of boredom as a wife in Worthing, Captain Blackheart hoiks up her bridal skirts, leaps over the wedding table and escapes to her ship. Her future mother-in-law, 'Long Joan Silver', follows her and joins the crew for a life of apparently enduring comradeship, roving and power.

While today's ways of thinking in more developed countries apparently permit a wide acceptance by women and men of the idea of sparky desperadas wielding cutlasses, the more complex reality on most ships is that authoritative women are still struggling to win respected status – or even gain a toehold. The lost history of working women seafarers has surfaced in the last few years, marking an important stage in both women's and maritime history. Reviewing what has been written and why, analysing what has been omitted and how this can be retrieved, 1990s historians can reach for a deeper way of understanding pirates of both sexes. These non-fiction approaches will enable refreshing views of real pirates to emerge, set against a background of imperialism and the political management of unruly human behaviour.

And fictional versions of woman pirates today offer exciting insights into women's potential to be free from metaphorical corsets and petticoats; to be bold – in breeches or in whatever clothes we choose.

Notes

1. F. Tennyson Jesse, *Moonraker*, 1927, reprinted by Virago in 1981 with a detail from *Charlie is My Darling* by Sir John Everett Millais on the cover, p. 149.
2. Arthur Ransome, *Missee Lee*, Cape, 1941 and Puffin, 1986. I am grateful to Richard Purver for drawing this information to my attention.
3. Hugh Brogan, *The Life of Arthur Ransome*, Hamish Hamilton, 1985, p. 381.
4. Christina Hardyment, *Arthur Ransome and Captain Flint's Trunk*, Cape, 1985, p. 172.
5. Brogan, *op cit*, p. 382.
6. Susan Baker, 'Ann Bonny and Mary Read, Lesbian Pirates', from a pamphlet, *Womem Remembered*, 1976, quoted in the RSC programme notes for the 1978 production of *The Women Pirates*.
7. Steve Gooch, *The Women Pirates: Ann Bonney and Mary Read*, Pluto Press, 1978, p. ii.
8. *RSC Year Book 1978*, edited by Simon Tussler and jointly published by the RSC and TQ Publications, p. 62.
9. Joanna Russ, *The Adventures of Alyx*, The Women's Press, 1985.
10. Erica Jong, *Fanny*, Granada, 1980, pp. 495–6.
11. Quoted in Andrea Weiss, *Vampires and Violets: lesbians in the cinema*, Cape, 1992, p. 129.
12. *ibid*, p. 131.
13. Fiona Cooper, *The Empress of the Seven Oceans*, Black Swan, 1993.
14. Diana Norman, *The Pirate Queen*, Headline, 1991.
15. Central TV press release, 1991, p. 1.

Further reading

Piracy and banditry in general

Burg, B. R., *Sodomy and the Pirate Tradition: English sea rovers in the 17th century Caribbean*, New York University Press, 1984.

Cordingly, David and Falconer, John, *Pirates: fact and fiction*, Collins & Brown, 1992.

Ellms, Charles, *The Pirates Own Book, or Authentic Narratives of the Lives, Exploits and Executions of the Most Celebrated Sea Robbers*, Sanborn & Carter, 1837, 1844.

Exquemelin, A. O., *The Buccaneers of America*, (1678), The Folio Society, 1969.

Hobsbawm, Eric, *Bandits*, Pelican, 1972.

Johnson, Captain Charles, *A general History of the Robberies and Murders of the Most Notorious Pyrates*, (1724), published as Daniel Defoe, *A General History of the Pyrates*, Manuel Schonhorn (ed), Dent, 1972.

Mitchell, David, *Pirates*, Thames & Hudson, 1976.

Rediker, Marcus, *Between the Devil and the Deep Blue Sea: Merchant seamen, pirates and the Anglo-American maritime world 1700–1750*, Cambridge University Press, 1987.

Verrill, A. Hyatt, *Love Stories of the Pirates*, Collins, 1924.

Ward, Ralph T., *Pirates in History*, York Press, 1974.

Cross-dressing women in history

Dekker, Rudolf M. and van de Pol, Lotte C., *The Tradition of Female Transvestism in Early Modern Europe*, MacMillan, 1989.

Dugaw, Dianne, '"Rambling Female Sailors": *the rise and fall of the seafaring heroine*', *International Journal of Maritime History*, IV, no. 1, June 1992.

Wheelwright, Julie, *Amazons and Military Maids: women who dressed as men in pursuit of life, liberty and happiness*, Pandora, 1989 and 1994.

Individual pirates

Chambers, Anne, *Granuaile, the life and times of Grace O'Malley, 1530–1603*, Wolfhound Press, 1991.

Glasspoole, Richard, *Mr. Glasspoole and the Chinese Pirates*, Golden Cockerel Press, 1935.

Lilius, Aleko E., *I Sailed with Chinese Pirates*, The Mellifont Press, nd but c.1930, and Oxford University Press, 1991.

Index

Alf 81–5, 87

Alfhild 24, 37, 43, 52, 78, 80–90, 173, 270

Amazon/s 10, 63, 72–3, 79, 89, 94, 182, 194, 197

Amazonian 72, 68, 177

Appleby, John 114, 123–4

Artemisia 17, 33, 52, 53, 64–74, 78, 256, 270

Austen, Jane 28, 126

Barbary Coast 26–7

Bingham, Sir Richard 95, 104–6

Blackbeard 31, 117, 144, 149, 166, 168, 264, 274

Bonny, Ann 6, 10, 19, 31, 36–40, 43, 53, 55–8, 139, 141, 143, 149, 154–7, 168, 170–71, 176–8, 180–93, 196–8, 225, 258, 270, 274, 275

Borges, Jorge Luis 224–5

Bouboulina Lascarina, Admiral 74–5

buccaneer/s 4, 23, 27, 53, 149, 165–6

Burg, B.R. 41, 144–5, 170

Burn, Flora 28, 40, 143, 170

Campbell, Fanny 194–7

Cardingly, David 25, 30, 164

Chambers, Anne 28, 118

Chang Pao 210–12, 215, 220–24

Cheng I Sao 33, 37, 39, 58, 203–25, 231–2, 240–41, 245–6

Cobham, Maria 32–3, 36–9, 56, 127, 139, 143, 172, 177, 190–92, 270

Cooper, Fiona 15, 274

cross-dressed 39–42, 43, 53–4, 80, 140, 142–4, 149, 152, 153, 164, 166–7, 186–7, 196

cross-dresser/s 140, 149, 190, 196–7

cross dressing 45–6, 141, 190, 196

Dampier, William 27, 53, 149

Damsholt, Nanna 79, 80, 83, 88
Defoe, Daniel 115, 181–2
Dekker, Rudolf 40, 141, 143, 151
168
Drake, Sir Francis 20, 29–30, 65,
100, 142, 165

Elizabeth I 29, 30, 68, 95, 104–6,
119, 149
Ellms, Charles 4, 54, 80–81,
114–15, 127, 135
Euden, Jan 259–60
Exqemelin, Alexander 27, 48, 53,
114, 132

Falconer, John (*see* Cordingly,
David)
'female warrior' 178, 186–7, 189,
196
femme fatale/s 6, 9, 232
Frani, Susan 264, 270

Gallowglass 97, 104
Glasspoole, Richard 212, 214,
216, 221, 223, 226–8, 230–31
Gollomb, Joseph 54, 216–23, 231
Gooch, Steve 3, 274
Gosse, Philip 3, 13, 21, 54, 58,
114, 126–7, 134, 145–6, 151,
176, 182, 194, 197, 214–17,
222, 224
Granuaile 22, 33, 37–8, 42, 52,
93–107, 270, 274

Herodotus 65–6, 68–72
Hobsbawm, Eric 13, 15, 20, 124
homosexual 41
homosexuality 170

Hyatt Verril, A. 54, 243

International Maritime Bureau
(IMB) 260–61, 263, 265, 268–9

Johnson, Captain Charles 39, 53,
57, 113, 116, 121, 122, 126,
129–31, 147, 169, 176, 178,
181–90, 192, 258
Jolly Roger, the 121, 154, 162–4,
169, 173, 194, 274
Jong, Erica 15, 274

Kidd, Captain 148–50, 155, 157
Killigrew, Lady 118

Ladgerda 89
Ladrone/s 221, 226, 228, 230, 233
Lai Choi San 33, 37, 44, 58, 208,
241, 244–9
Lon Hon-cho 33, 37, 241, 243–4,
246
Lee, Tanith 7, 8
lesbian 15, 155, 193, 273–5
lesbians 40, 139, 145–6, 274
lesbianism 41, 155
'Letters of Marque' 28–9
Linebaugh, Peter 55–6, 170
Lilius, Aleko E. 208, 242, 244–9
Loviat, Fanny 19, 172, 207

Maughan, Philip 225–8, 233

Neumann, Charles Friederich
212–16, 218–20, 224, 229, 233

O'Flaherty, Murrough 99, 104,
106

O'Malley, Grace 28, 63, 93–4, 101, 114, 173, 245 (*see also* Granuaile)

Pauw, Linda Grant de 222–3, 231
Peterson, M.J. 22, 26, 32
phallic woman 8, 9, 81
picaresque 56–8, 256
picaro 55–6
Pol, Lotte van de (*see* Dekker, Rudolf)
privateers 23, 26, 27, 29, 37, 115, 145–6, 153, 186, 192, 210
prostitution 33, 140, 152, 155, 192, 209, 268
prostitute/s 43, 129, 133, 140, 147, 155–7, 177, 185, 190, 209, 267

Rackham, Captain 53, 57, 163, 176–7, 179–83, 185–8, 192, 197
Read, Mary 3, 6, 10, 19, 30–31, 36–9, 40–41, 43–4, 52–3, 55–8, 139, 141, 143, 145–8, 151–7, 168, 170, 171, 176–93, 196–8, 225, 258, 274
Rediker, Marcus 115, 144, 149, 156, 171, 181, 185
Russ, Joanna 18, 274

Saxo Grammaticus 79–81, 83–5, 87–90
Sigrid the Superb 24, 88–90
Snell, Hannah 54, 187, 197
Spufford, Margaret 54–5, 57

Talbot, Mary Anne 177, 189–90, 197
Tibbott-ne-Long 100, 104–7
transvestism 141, 144, 148, 197
transvestite 37, 167
Turner, J. 225–8, 231

Xerxes 66–70

Zipes, Jack 58